Just Talk

STUDIES IN MELANESIAN ANTHROPOLOGY

General Editors

Donald F. Tuzin
Gilbert H. Herdt
Rena Lederman

Just Talk

Gossip, Meetings, and Power
in a Papua New Guinea Village

Karen J. Brison

UNIVERSITY OF CALIFORNIA PRESS

Berkeley / Los Angeles / Oxford

We wish to thank the University of Pittsburgh Press for permission to use material from the following article:

"All Talk and No Action? Saying and Doing in Kwanga Meetings," *Ethnology* 28(1989):97–115.

University of California Press
Berkeley and Los Angeles, California

University of California Press
Oxford, England

Library of Congress Catatoging-in-Publication Data
Brison, Karen J.
    Just Talk: gossip, meetings, and power in a Papua New
Guinea village / Karen J. Brison.
        p.   cm.—(Studies in Melanesian anthropology; 11)
    Includes bibliographical references and index.
    ISBN 0-520-07700-8   ·
    1. Kwanga (Papua New Guinea people)—Politics and
government.   2. Kwanga (Papua New Guinea people)—Social
life and customs.   3. Big man (Melanesia)—Papua New Guinea—
Inakor.   4. Oral communication—Papua New Guinea—Inakor.
5. Language and culture—Papua New Guinea—Inakor.
6. Social structure—Papua New Guinea—Inakor.
7. Inakor (Papua New Guinea)—Politics and government.
8. Inakor (Papua New Guinea)—Social life and customs.   I. Title.
II. Series.
DU740.42.B75   1992
995.3—dc20   91-34511
                                                                      CIP

Printed in the United States of America

1   2   3   4   5   6   7   8   9

To my parents

Contents

Maps and Figures

Plates

Preface

The Melanesian big-man is best known to the outside world as a rugged individualist who makes his name by building complex networks of debt and clientage which allow him to call up pigs and shell valuables from his followers at the right moment to vanquish his rivals with impressive prestations. But to many Melanesians big-men are primarily "men of talk" who keep their communities in order and protect them from enemies by "talking hard" in public meetings and by keeping their fingers on the pulse of gossip networks to gather information about impending raids, possible "roads" to cargo, or threats of supernatural attack through sorcery. The close association between leaders and talk is part of a more general preoccupation with the power of words, which are believed to make and break reputations and to destroy and restore relationships.

It is this "talking" side of Melanesian politics that this book addresses. My entry to the world of political talk was through public community meetings. I set out to study meetings in a Papua New Guinea group and discovered that, largely by chance, I had hit upon an ideal group for such a project in choosing to live among the Kwanga of the East Sepik Province. The residents of the village of Inakor, where I lived for just over two years from August 1984 to October 1986, held community meetings almost every week (barring excessive rain) to discuss matters of common concern such as disputes, proposed marriages, rumors of sorcery and adultery, and bad weather. The villagers also met for at least two afternoons following most deaths to determine the cause, generally assumed to be sorcery.

Speakers in Kwanga meetings used both Neo-Melanesian and Kwanga. I never attained a sufficient level of fluency in Kwanga to follow long speeches. I could carry out simple conversations in Kwanga after about ten months and could often understand enough to have a sense of what was being talked about but public speeches were too rapid and full of figures of speech and allusions to matters of which I had no knowledge for me to be able to follow them without the help of a local interpreter. For several months I relied on neighbors and friends to summarize what was going on in meetings when I was unable to follow discussions. Relying on impromptu translations, however, proved to be frustrating since people were usually intent on listening to speakers and were unwilling to deal with a troublesome ethnographer. Gradually, I began tape-recording selected meetings and going over them later with an informant. Most often, I relied upon my neighbor, Lekutombwai, and sometimes her husband, Wulawula, to help me translate the tapes but I also recruited two men, Pita Sambunumbo and Wa'aluku, from the neighboring village of Asanakor to help when discussions concerned their village. I thank all of these people for devoting hours of their time to this tedious task.

At first I asked informants just to translate Kwanga sections into Neo-Melanesian. But I quickly became aware that the Neo-Melanesian speeches in the meetings generally contained so much innuendo and so many allusions to past events that I could not understand them—even when I had thought I had followed the discussion perfectly. Consequently, I began to ask my informants to comment on the Neo-Melanesian speeches as well and to explain the background of the events discussed and give their interpretation of the speaker's meaning. I played a minute or two of the meeting tape to my translator, recorded his or her translation of the section into Neo-Melanesian on a second tape, as well as his or her responses to my various questions about the speakers and the issues under discussion. The quotes in the text are taken from the translations of the speeches into Neo-Melanesian.

Because quotes have often gone through two translations (from Kwanga to Neo-Melanesian and then again to English) much subtle linguistic information has been lost. This method also, of course, introduced some distortion on the part of the translator. I tried to control for such distortion by asking questions, based on my limited ability to follow Kwanga speeches, about things which I thought translators had missed. These methods suggested to me that translators most often erred on the side of omission. All translators were impatient with repetition on the part of speakers (which was frequent) and had to be pressed to include repetition so it is likely that they often left this out of their translations. It is also probable that translators sometimes missed subtle allusions in speeches. Indeed, they sometimes suspected that the speaker's words carried a deeper meaning but were not sure what it was and mentioned this. I believe that translations do, however, accurately reflect the subject matter of the original speech, the kinds of figures of speech and allusions which were used (which I told my translators I was particularly interested in and which translators often spontaneously commented on since they shared my interest in the form as well as the content of speech), and the tone of remarks (e.g., sarcastic, humorous, etc.), and, I believe, provide good illustrations of the ways in which Kwanga speakers try to influence others by commenting on current events, if not of all the linguistic devices they use to give their words authority. I have avoided making subtle analyses of rhetorical devices, believing that my transcripts do not warrant such analyses, and have commented instead on the concerns expressed by speakers in meetings, and the reaction to their words in the meeting and afterwards.

After going over the tape recording of a meeting with a translator I followed up on what I had learned by seeking out those involved in the discussions and asking them about the case. The follow-up helped me to get some sense of what kind of range of interpretations there was among members of the community about what had gone on in meetings.

Translators' comments proved to be an invaluable source of information on the local attitudes toward "talk." Although my position as an outsider who did not possess the normal stock of information about past events and personalities made it particularly difficult for me to understand speeches, I gradually began to realize, after many frustrating efforts to get my various informants to agree on what had been said and done in a meeting, that many statements were meant to be ambiguous and that speakers were not entirely dismayed when their remarks generated more confusion than they eliminated. In fact, the local people, were (like many Melanesians) preoccupied with the "hidden underside" of talk: they suspected that speakers often concealed more than they revealed and that they preferred to make veiled allusions to important information. I was at first amused by the fact that speakers seemed to spend as much time "talking about talk"—or complaining about the way discussions tended to confuse rather than illuminate issues—but came, in the end, to realize that this preoccupation with rules of debate revealed something fundamental about the system: in Kwanga villages few things are ever resolved once and for all. Instead, over the years, meetings and private discussions about conflict and other matters of common concern generate layers upon layers of stories, none of which have ever been judged conclusively true or false. I became fascinated by this accumulation of stories and by the ways in which accounts that the whole community seemed to regard as plausible but unprovable "just so stories" could have an insidious effect on relationships and reputations. In fact, telling such stories was the principle means of building reputations and influencing people, as my informants themselves realized when they adopted the English word "politics" to refer to interminable discussions that never seemed to lead anywhere.

Translating and transcribing meetings also made me aware that by the time any incident was discussed in public meetings there had already been a great deal of discussion about it in private contexts. Ambitious men were devoted gossips who made special trips to visit distant relatives in other villages to hear the latest rumors and who strategically spread rumors themselves in order to build reputations as powerful men who controlled sorcerers. This underworld of gossip was considered to be so important that much of the time in meetings was spent trying to establish which of the rumors were true and which were false. Furthermore, I soon realized that discussion was by no means ended by public debates: people continued to gossip about events for months and sometimes even years to come and to revise their views in light of subsequent occurrences that seemed to shed new light on things. Although many ethnographers have commented on the importance of oratory in establishing political reputations in Melanesia (see especially Harrison 1990; Lederman 1984; Read 1959), observing the Kwanga convinced me that public debates were but the most visible moment in a continual process of interpreting events and building reputations. To understand leadership, then, one had to look at gossip and rumor as well as the more accessible public speeches. I began to turn an avid ear to the casual conversations of my friends and neighbors, jotting down what they were gossiping about and asking them about the latest rumors. Eventually I was delighted to find, if only occasionally, my determined efforts to keep up with the gossip meant that I, too, had heard all the requisite stories necessary to interpret a public discussion, though, even in the final months of my stay in Inakor, my sense of a good and plausible story seemed to differ enough from that of my friends and neighbors that I could seldom anticipate what they were going to say about a current crisis with much accuracy.

I am greatly indebted to many people who helped me during the process of researching and writing this book. I benefited during both processes from having two unusually supportive families, my adoptive family in Inakor and my real family in North America. Lekutombwai Teimba, Wulawula Makuto, and the children of their household—Atiruwa, Kiliwapi, Nainala, Huandar, and Nelafuku—made me feel welcome in their home and helped me in more ways than I could possibly mention. In particular, Lekutombwai voluntarily devoted hours of her time (even after spending long days in her garden) to helping me translate tapes and understand disputes with long and complex histories. This book could not have been written were it not for her goodwill, generosity, patience, and intelligence. Wulawula also spent many hours helping me with my work and made my stay in Inakor much easier by organizing the building of my house and by recruiting others to help me with my work. I also thank Atiruwa and Kiliwapi for looking after me and keeping me company. Other residents of Inakor and Asanakor also went out of their way to help me and make me feel welcome. I spent many pleasant and productive hours chatting with Sumbwendungwa, Naitete, Nika, Jimmy, Induwamwa, Aika, Tuliki, Wobisumbwai, John Hokwerka, Porumbwai, Sinjihe, Wobenuku, Ainala, Ukunduwepi, Eron, Elisabet, Humwaembi, Masarowa, Marakwambu, Makicha, Nububwai, Maria, Tuchali, Kely, A'oi, Kokoroki, Tungwala, Mwalanipi, Wasenjeri, Mwanchinbuli, Makret, Hokini'ai, Awesubwa, Gahainuku, Namieruku, Hoponumbwai, Pita, Wa'aluku, Wa'alamini, Mattyu, Mak, and Waifuku. As well, I thank all of the other residents of Inakor and Asanakor for their hospitality.

I also owe a great deal to my North American family for their support while I was in Papua New Guinea and afterwards. My sister, Sue Brison; my aunt, Mary Britting; and my grandmother, Ruth Britting, were particularly diligent letter writers and senders of care packages. My father, David Brison, and his wife, Susan, visited me in Inakor and contributed a great deal to my thinking about the Kwanga. My brother, Jeffrey Brison, spent many hours helping me work out my thoughts about the Kwanga. Finally, my mother, Jane Badour, as always, did everything she could to make my life more pleasant (including writing to me at least once a week for my entire two-year stay in Inakor!).

I have also benefited greatly from support from several organizations and individual members of the academic community. I wrote this book as a postdoctoral fellow in Asian and Pacific Area Studies at the Institute of Culture and Communication, East-West Center, and also as a Rockefeller Humanities Fellow at the Center for Pacific Islands Studies, University of Hawaii at Manoa. I thank the Institute of Culture and Communication, the Rockefeller Foundation, and the Center for Pacific Islands Studies for their generous support. Donald Tuzin suggested I study the Kwanga and then made this research possible by funding it (under a National Science Foundation grant) as part of a comparative study of three adjacent language groups in the East Sepik Province (including the Bumbita Arapesh studied by Stephen Leavitt, and the Ilahita Arapesh studied by Tuzin and his family). He also improved my research immeasurably by making many helpful suggestions in monthly meetings during the year that he and his family were in Ilahita. Later, Tuzin greatly improved this book in his capacity as an editor of this series of Melanesian ethnographies. Any stylistic virtues of this book are due to the efforts of F. G. Bailey who pointed out the worst "sins" of my writing, and even rewrote particularly awkward and important passages. He showed great patience in going over not one, but several, drafts of several chapters with his ruthless red pen. The remaining awkwardness of the prose is, of course, my own doing. Fitz Poole also read and commented on the manuscript and, before that, introduced me to the literature on Melanesia and helped me to formulate a research question. I also thank Geoffrey White, Gilbert Herdt, and two anonymous reviewers for the University of California Press for reading and commenting on sections of the manuscript. I thank Stephen Eyre, as well, for sharing his ideas about the Kwanga and surrounding groups with me. Theodore Schwartz and other participants in the University of California, San Diego, Melanesian seminar listened to oral presentations based on two chapters and made many useful comments.

Last but not least, Stephen Leavitt, first as a colleague and friend, and later as my husband, helped me in innumerable ways. He held my hand through many difficult moments in Papua New Guinea and contributed much to my understanding of the Kwanga by sharing his insights with me. Later, he read and commented on several sections of the manuscript and endured my many bad moods during the writing process with infinite patience. Finally, he devoted many hours to creating the maps and some of the genealogies that appear in this book, and he contributed the photographs reproduced as Plates 3, 6, and 7.

CHAPTER ONE

Gossip and Politics

Most American children learn the adage "Sticks and stones will break my bones but names will never hurt me"—meaning, of course, that they should turn the other cheek when someone calls them names or spreads nasty rumors behind their back because mere words can have no serious impact on their well-being. "Reality"—in this case their good character—will be there for all to see no matter what people say about them.

People in many parts of the world, however, would not agree with these ideas. Young (1971: 135) reports that the residents of Goodenough Island in Papua New Guinea, for instance, view malicious gossip as being almost as dangerous as sorcery. In other areas, people call public meetings just to deny slanderous rumors.[1] Indeed, the Kwanga of the East Sepik Province of Papua New Guinea devote much of their time in weekly community meetings to looking into recent rumors of things like adultery and sorcery. Evidently, these people believe that the truth will not necessarily shine through a lie unless they do something to bring it to everyone's attention.

In the following pages, I will argue that this concern with rumors reflects a situation in which unsubstantiated stories can have far-reaching political and social consequences. In Kwanga villages, and in small relatively egalitarian communities everywhere, no one can automatically command respect or obedience, and autocratic attitudes tend to arouse resentment. Consequently, people try to prompt others toward certain conclusions and courses of action without seeming to do

1

so by casting interpretations of recent events in public meetings or in private conversations. They suggest that their rivals are lazy and ignorant, or that they are involved in nefarious secret plots. At the same time, speakers usually take the opportunity to at least imply that they themselves are much more knowledgeable, moral, and worthy characters. In this way, individuals try to influence others but avoid the appearance of ordering them around. Speakers usually even take care not to make potentially unpopular suggestions; they just tell stories about what might have happened without spelling out their charges so that, if challenged, they can always say that their words have been misconstrued.

This sort of "talk" is of particular importance to the constitution of power in those Melanesian communities where leaders gain prominence through the control of specialized magical, ritual, and secular knowledge. It has been clear since Malinowski's work on the Trobriand Islands (1926) that there is a close link between sorcery, magic, and leadership in many areas of lowland and insular Melanesia. Leaders are either believed to be sorcerers or to have a close relationship with sorcerers; in either case, people obey leaders because they think that sorcerers punish those who are insubordinate. I will show that it is through hinting that they have knowledge of the activities of sorcerers that Kwanga leaders gain reputations as powerful people whose words should be heeded. Whether or not magic is actually practiced,[2] it is everywhere so secretive an activity that its social impact is felt only through such attributions. But speakers always leave their remarks ambiguous enough so that they can later deny any knowledge of sorcerers. All the hints and rumors convince the audience both that there is a close relationship between leaders and sorcerers and that these powerful men can never be challenged since no one can ever be sure of who did what when.

There is another reason why rumors and other kinds of stories about recent events are of concern in Kwanga villages and other communities like them: rumors can easily take on a life of their own in small villages and have consequences that no one anticipated or desired. Communities where everyone shares a common circle of acquaintances whom they can then gossip about tend to generate rumors (Merry 1984). Gossip circulates rapidly through dense social networks, and when people hear the same rumor from several different sources they often forget whatever doubts they initially had and think that the story must be true. Moreover, in Inakor, a Kwanga village in the East Sepik Province, rumors are distorted in certain systematic ways as they travel through community: people are inclined to have a suspicious attitude toward their neighbors and are prepared to believe the worst of them. Consequently, rumors become increasingly alarmist as they spread, and thus they can easily aggravate situations, escalate conflict, and have harmful repercussions for individuals. In fact, the very leaders who gossip and hint to build reputations for power and wisdom often find themselves the victim of malicious rumors that can eventually destroy their standing in the community. Leaders become social outcasts and many do everything they can to divest themselves of their powers in order to get out of the public eye and stop the backbiting. Thus, gossip and rumor are essential both to constituting, and, ultimately, to destroying the position of leaders; Kwanga villagers have good reason to think that "names" might really "hurt them."

These reflections on gossip, innuendo, oratory, and power in Kwanga (and Melanesian) politics speak to a broader concern with the role of "verbalizations" (Pocock 1984) and "first order interpretations" of experience (Bruner 1986) in constituting society and culture. Scholars have suggested that individuals are not born into unalterable social and cultural worlds. Instead, social relations and cultural beliefs emerge from a continual process of social negotiation. When people talk about recent events they "pose and counterpose" (White and Watson-Gegeo 1990: 3) interpretations of these incidents which are carefully crafted to suit their own psychological and political purposes. As Pocock (1984: 28) says, such verbalizations "act upon people—and so constitute acts of power—in at least two ways: either by informing them and so modifying their perceptions or by defining them and so modifying the ways in which they are perceived by others." What we hear, in other words, influences what we think and do. Moreover, the mere act of voicing an opinion in a public meeting contributes to reproducing relations of authority by displaying the right of the speaker (and those of his or her age, gender, or other social category) to comment on communal problems. Thus, the authority and power of groups of people like Kwanga leaders is at least in part created and maintained through a process of discussion and, conversely, can be challenged in the same contexts. Similarly, cultural beliefs that underpin relations of authority are either reinforced or challenged through discussion. When speakers in Kwanga meetings, for instance, suggest that sorcerers killed someone who showed disrespect for community leaders, that account reproduces the general belief in the close relationship between sorcerers and leaders.

When others argue, as sometimes occurs, that God has the ultimate power to decide who lives and dies, they challenge the belief system that supports community leaders. Beliefs and social relations, then, can either be reproduced or altered in a process of social interaction, and so we should not reify concepts like "culture" and "society" but should show how general ideas and relations of power and authority are continually re-created and reshaped in interaction. Taking such a performance-centered view will allow us to study the ways in which cultural beliefs and social relations can be changed and modified.

In investigating gossip, innuendo, and oratory in Inakor and Asanakor, I will try to show that people do construct their social and cultural worlds when they talk about them. But they do not do so just as they choose. Speakers hint and cast strategic interpretations of events in meetings and in private conversations, but to fully appreciate the impact of these verbalizations on social relations and beliefs, one must follow these stories as they are retold by others in different circumstances and are altered in the process. Some interpretations voiced in meetings or in gossip seem to "ring true" to people and they are retold many times and are re-invoked when people try to understand present crises by looking to the past for clues as to sources of tension in the community. Such stories eventually comprise a sort of oral history and come to constitute the "map" of events, relationships, and personalities to which people refer when deciding what to do or when trying to understand new puzzles. Accounts like these, then, are very influential in shaping and altering social relations in the community. But they only come to be taken for granted as truth in this fashion after they have circulated through the community and have been retold by many people in many contexts, and the accounts are systematically distorted in this process of retelling. In fact, as I have suggested above, the consensus about events and personalities which eventually emerges is often quite the opposite of what the original speaker intended; for instance, leaders who hint knowledge of the activities of sorcerers in many cases come to be considered evil and malicious individuals. Consequently, when we study the ways in which people "constitute" social worlds by talking about them we must move beyond the original speech—and guessing at the motives of the speaker—to examine the ways in which consensus is shaped by many voices as accounts circulate through a community. For that reason, it is important to study gossip and rumor.

Gossip and Reputation in an Inakor Meeting

It is Monday morning in Inakor. It is early, and the air is still cool. Families sit around small fires in front of their houses. Occasionally someone reaches out to turn one of the yams that are roasting for the morning meal. A slit gong sounds. Slit gongs are used to send messages from one part of the village to another. This particular beat signals a meeting. But no one moves.

Later, the sun is higher in the sky, and the air is warmer. The yams have been pulled from the fire and their charred outer skins removed with dull knives. Small children clutch them in grimy hands. People begin to wander to Namingawa, the central meeting plaza of the village. Namingawa is a hamlet like the other thirteen hamlets in Inakor, but centrally located and with a slightly larger clearing. Thatched huts ring a large open space scraped bare of grass to leave a packed earth surface. People take shelter from the hot morning sun on the verandas of houses. Men from different parts of the village, who see little of each other during the week, sit in groups joking and chewing betel nut. There never seems to be enough betel, and the men make a game of hiding it or stealing it. Nearby, women cluster around two or three new mothers, vying for the pleasure of holding the babies and pinching their faces and limbs admiringly. Pigs, dogs, and chickens wander through the plaza looking for food.

About a half hour after the first arrivals, when most of the village has gathered, the "Kaunsil" (a Neo-Melanesian term that is best translated as "Councillor"; I will use this English version), a tall man in his mid-fifties wearing shorts and a khaki shirt (much worn, spotted, and faded but bearing prominently his badge of office), rises and goes to the middle of the plaza where he stands quietly waiting for the others to notice and pay attention. Councillors are elected by each village to sit on the Local Government Council, which comprises members from all the villages in a district. It meets monthly, and Councillors are expected to report the proceedings to their constituents. They are also responsible for assigning community labor (such as maintaining roads, schools, and medical aid posts) on the compulsory government labor day, Monday. This is the ostensible purpose of today's meeting, but there are other matters to be seen to first.

All around the edges of the plaza people tell each other to be quiet and listen. The Councillor speaks softly and rapidly and is inaudible to much of his audience. As he begins, his three-year-old daughter runs out to where he stands, and he picks her up and continues. He speaks of the problem of rain. There has been a great deal of rain for the past few weeks, and people are concerned because they cannot dry coffee beans in the sun, a necessary step in processing them for sale. This is of particular concern because the price of coffee is unusually high (a little over one kina[3] per kilogram), and people are eager to sell before the price drops. In addition, some people are late making their new gardens, a process that entails cutting and burning the underbrush and tree branches. This too requires dry sunny weather. The Councillor introduces the problem:[4]

We are going to talk about the rain now. You guys always blame the rain on me. You always say: "When we are still harvesting our yams, he is cutting his new garden. He cuts away the underbrush and cuts the tree branches to make a new garden plot and then burns it all away. And then when he is finished with this he goes to Hapandi and Wanjeri [the rain magicians of the village] and asks them to make rain to wash the ashes away and to make the ground soft so that he can plant his yams." You say that and you put all the blame on me. So now I will open this topic up, and you will all talk about it and find out the cause of this rain.

The Councillor is evidently concerned about a rumor that he has commissioned rain. The implication is that the Councillor is noted as a hard worker and is well ahead of less industrious gardeners in the village. Although others are still harvesting their last season's crops, he is already planting his next year's crop. Since the cutting and burning of new garden plots requires clear sunny weather whereas planting and growing yams requires rain, the Councillor maintains that others have been spreading slanderous rumors to the effect that he has been selfishly making rain to suit his own purposes. He continues, complaining about a rumored insult from his rival Bwalaka, a man well-known for his contentiousness, who has apparently said something about the Councillor's lack of interest in "business," a term used to refer to money-making activities, principally coffee growing:

Bwalaka has said: "The Councillor is not a man of business. He is just a man who plants yams. He never thinks of business. He thinks only of yams, so he is always going and asking the rain magicians to make rain." I heard this and I was angry. If I don't have a large coffee garden that is because I don't want to. If I wanted to have a large business I would just go to my people [i.e., moiety], and they would give me a piece of land to do it. But I myself don't want to, so I don't ask. But you, Bwalaka, I see that you use only this small piece of land for your coffee garden. They gave this to you and you planted it. When you try to get more land they rebuff you and tell you you can't have any more. So I wouldn't make too much of this point of my small business if I were you. If I wanted to have a big business, all the men in my moiety would give me the land. They wouldn't rebuff me or talk against me. So this insult you have made about me, it's like this: each man has his own strength. This talk you have made about me, I think you are just bragging. I will just close my mouth and work and you will see. I will beat you. You have just this small coffee garden but you are always shooting off your mouth. You'll lose. I don't act like that. I don't go and make a small coffee garden and then come and brag: "Oh man, I've got a huge coffee garden.". . . Me, I am a man who acts like a woman. I'll just work away quietly, and you'll see. I'll beat you in the end.

Bwalaka has evidently accused the Councillor of causing the rain because he has more interest in his yams than in coffee, an attitude considered backward and "bushy." The Councillor responds here by implying that Bwalaka has no land and does not have the support of his group—grave challenges in this area where a man's access to land is one of the most important criteria for evaluating his worth—and by insinuating that Bwalaka is a braggart who exaggerates the size of his coffee gardens whereas the Councillor is "like a woman"—that is, quiet and unassuming but hardworking—and has impressive harvests. This remark is very sarcastic since it throws back at Bwalaka one of his frequent complaints, that the Councillor is an ineffectual community leader because he is quiet and soft-spoken "like a woman" and does not speak forcefully "like a man."

When the Councillor is finished, Ambwambuli, a small man of about sixty years, stands to give his opinion about the cause of the rain. He says, "I see it like this: I noticed that when all the Christians went down to [a neighboring village] for the big Easter meeting there, we didn't have any rain in Inakor. Whatever grudge he has, he makes all of us suffer for it. It wasn't us who did anything to him; it was them. This is Hapandi's rain. I know it." Ambwambuli blames one of the two rain-makers, Hapandi, for the current bad weather, reasoning that since there was no rain when Hapandi, a Christian, was out of town attending an Easter celebration, this proves he must be behind the rain. Ambwambuli implies that "they," the Christians, have done something to provoke Hapandi and complains that it is not right that everyone, Christian and non-Christian alike, should be punished with rain.

After a brief digression, others take up the topic of the Easter celebration in Yubanakor. Apparently, on the way to Yubanakor, a rumor spread among the Christians that Hapandi was carrying a sorcery implement. Hapandi had converted to Christianity during a big revival meeting almost a year before and had claimed at that time to have seen the error of his ways and given up sorcery. But neither the Christians nor the non-Christians had much faith in this claim, and they went on accusing him of killing people. Allegedly the rumors on Easter weekend prompted some Christian women to make a covert search of Hapandi's string bag. The non-Christians now say that the rain is Hapandi's response to that incident. Indeed, the Councillor and Ambwambuli say that the Christians' continual abuse of Hapandi provokes him to kill people, a remark that is particularly pointed since the Christians frequently accuse the non-Christians of doing exactly the same thing.

Hapandi has been sitting quietly listening. He is a small thin man in his mid-sixties who seldom has much to say in meetings and speaks with a distinct stutter, particularly when he is agitated, which is often. Now he says that he knows nothing about a search for a sorcery implement and has been nowhere near the water hole whose spirits he sometimes calls upon to make rain. Everyone ignores him, and several non-Christians repeat that it was the Christians who provoked Hapandi. Some Christian women respond that the only search of Hapandi's bag was for food, and that they know nothing of a rumor about Hapandi carrying a sorcery tool. An attempt is now made to trace this rumor, and someone suggests that it started when a young man was bitten by a centipede while walking to Yubanakor. He did not see the insect and thought he had been attacked by a sorcerer. But the Christian women say that they were not walking with this man and heard none of the talk so, by implication, they could not have suspected sorcery and could not have searched Hapandi's bag for that reason. Someone else suggests that the rumors started when Mary, a Christian woman alleged to have prophetic powers, predicted that someone would die during the Easter celebration. But Mary claims that all she said was that she could feel that the village was full of "sin" so someone would probably die soon.[5]

The accusations between Christians and non-Christians fly back and forth until Hapandi, in a state of great agitation, rises again and says, "When I am up in my hamlet, no one comes to visit me! The only people who come to visit me are people who come with hatchets [to kill me]! Now I am finished with Christianity. You guys are crazy!" He continues with bitter sarcasm, "I am not a Christian; I am not a Christian! I was not baptized; it was only the rest of you who were baptized. I am not a Christian; I was not baptized; I do not have a new name! I am a heathen[6] man and you always lie about me and mess me up so now I am finished with Christianity!"

Hapandi is, in effect, protesting that he became Christian (and was baptized and given a new Christian name in front of a large crowd) in order to prove to the village that he had given up sorcery. But no one believes him. He is treated as if he were not a Christian, that is, as if he were still practicing sorcery, so he now refuses to continue going to church.

The exchange of insults between Christians and non-Christians continues, punctuated with warnings that Hapandi is angry and will surely ensorcel someone now. Finally, Techambu interrupts, "You Christians and non-Christians, listen to me, we are not talking about sorcery. We are talking about rain!" And everyone agrees, "Yes, yes, we are talking about the rain—it rains all the time and we can't get our gardens planted, so let's talk about the rain. If we don't get our gardens planted soon we will have a poor harvest."

The discussion continues with little resolution until the Councillor intervenes and announces the next item on his agenda.

There follow discussions of an upcoming meeting with the village to the north to dispute the ownership of a piece of land that the two villages have been fighting over for several generations; the fact that the orderly who runs the public medical aid post in a neighboring village will soon be leaving because a local man has seduced his wife; and the statement by a local European missionary that people should not build houses with corrugated iron roofs under coconut palms (most houses have sago thatch roofing but iron roofs are universally coveted) because debris from the palms will clog the gutters. It is afternoon when the Councillor finally gets to the official purpose of the meeting, the assigning of community work. Today, women will cut the grass in the village cemetery and around the aid post; the men will build a new toilet for the courthouse. People gradually disperse, the women and children leaving first and the older men a little later. After a leisurely couple of hours of community work, they go off to their own gardens to collect greens, yams, bananas, and firewood. Such is a typical Monday in Inakor.

Gossip, Reputation, and Politics in Inakor

On most Mondays the residents of Inakor, a village with a population of less than four hundred and few ventures of communal concern, meet in Namingawa for several hours, starting at around nine in the morning and often continuing well into the afternoon. The meeting just described illustrates some of the typical features of community discussions. At first glance, it seems that the participants are trying to find out who is causing the rain and how they can stop him. But a closer examination reveals that many of the speakers are more concerned with addressing rumors about themselves. The Councillor, for instance, introduces the topic because he is concerned about his reputation. He suspects that people think he has commissioned the rain and wants to convince them that this is not so. He also wants to prove that he is not backward and bushy, as his rival, Bwalaka, has implied. According to the Councillor, when Bwalaka suggested that the Councillor was behind the rain he also made several pointed remarks about the Councillor's lack of interest in cash cropping. When the Councillor defends himself in the meeting he takes the opportunity to imply that Bwalaka is "all talk and no action" when it comes to coffee growing. Both men seem more interested in slandering each other and proving their own progressive values than in stopping the rain.

Similarly, several people want to discuss rumors about an alleged search of the sorcerer Hapandi's bag by some Christian women. Some non-Christians suggest that this incident angered Hapandi and, ultimately, caused the rain; the Christians try to defend themselves by denying the allegations and suggesting ways in which people might have reached this mistaken conclusion by misinterpreting events like a centipede bite and a search for food.

The Inakor villagers apparently feel that rumors are serious business. People like the Councillor and the Christian women are not content to turn the other cheek; they want to clear their names of hidden slander. Others, like those who criticize the Christians for gossiping behind Hapandi's back, seem to think that malicious backbiting can cause problems for the whole community, in this case in the form of too much rain. Indeed, villagers are willing to devote several hours a week to discussion of rumor.

There also seems to be some truth to this dark view of gossip and rumor. Apparently, there is a great deal of gossip in Inakor. Villagers evidently have a suspicious attitude toward each other and have a tendency to find hidden malice and covert plots behind almost any series of events, no matter how trivial. The rain, for instance, has been a popular topic of conversation over the past few weeks, and some people appear to be quite convinced that the Christians are responsible for it. Apparently, trivial events like the centipede bite and the search for food lead to speculation about what lies hidden beneath the surface of community life. Stories about sorcery and secret attack circulate through the community and create alarm and outrage that eventually surfaces in public meetings where accusations fly back and forth. Suspects try to prove their innocence by showing how harmless words and deeds have been misinterpreted. The Inakor villagers evidently think that such speculation creates rumors that can damage reputations, alarm the community, and, ultimately, have serious consequences like the rain that is now preventing them from harvesting their coffee and planting their gardens—and so they hold public meetings to stop the rumors.

Gossip and Power

The Kwanga are not alone in thinking that gossip and rumor should be taken seriously. Gluckman (1963) suggests that "gossip and scandalizing" holds communities together and maintains their values. He notes that when people gossip, they acknowledge each other to be members of the same community—something that quickly becomes apparent when they refuse to exchange similar stories with "outsiders" (Gluckman 1963: 308–309). Furthermore, gossips uphold group norms when they criticize those who break them. Gluckman also suggests that gossiping prevents disagreements or competition for leadership from getting out of hand and destroying the community since "differences of opinion are fought out in behind-the-back tattle, gossip, and scandal, so that many villagers, who are actually at loggerheads, can outwardly maintain the show of harmony and friendship" (Gluckman 1963: 312). In this way, as Bailey (1977: 120–121) puts it, the "irresponsible circulation of information about persons" in gossip allows people to assess their neighbors and criticize digressions without starting fights and breaching surface amity.

Others have taken up various of Gluckman's ideas. Merry (1984) explores the ways in which gossip acts as social control. She suggests that it operates indirectly and is only effective in particular conditions. First, gossip flourishes in dense social networks where people share many acquaintances whom they can "talk about." Second, people only fear gossip when they think it may have more material consequences. Gossip is most likely to cause problems when individuals are dependent on a small group of people for companionship and aid; in this situation, no one can afford a bad reputation within his or her group since this can bring social and economic disaster. Conversely, where people can easily find help and friendship elsewhere, they will be less concerned with what their neighbors think and so will often ignore malicious gossip.

It is perhaps for these reasons that gossip and rumor seem to be particularly feared in small isolated communities where people have relatively few ties with the outside world and so are dependent on their neighbors for many things. Bailey (1971a: 1—see also the other papers in 1971c) notes a morbid preoccupation with gossip among residents of small European villages where people go out of their way to avoid doing things that might provoke malicious backbiting. Other studies have indicated that the fear of gossip is so strong in small communities that people try to keep out of the public eye altogether to avoid becoming the object of backbiting. Mansbridge (1980), for instance, notes that many of the residents of the small Vermont town she studied never spoke in town meetings because they were afraid they would be ridiculed afterward (see also Frankenberg 1957 on a similar fear of gossip in a small Welsh village).

Others have explored the political uses of gossip. Paine (1967) suggests that when people gossip they are less interested in preserving social order than in advancing their own political fortunes and slandering their rivals. Gossip is a particularly effective way of doing this because people can spread all sorts of nasty rumors without having to take responsibility for their words since the rumors may never reach their victim's ears and, in any case, the source of rumors is seldom obvious. Bailey (1977), similarly, suggests that gossiping allows people to influence others without being held accountable. Goodwin (1982), likewise, shows how urban black children in America use gossip to anonymously attack rivals. They tell friends stories about how they have been abused by the absent rival. Although the speaker seldom tells his or her audience what to do the stories are framed in such a way as to encourage the listener to confront the alleged culprit about the incident. In this way, American children and other people can use gossip to influence others without being held responsible.

It is perhaps because gossips can so easily escape responsibility for their words that gossiping is often a "weapon of the weak" (Scott 1985). Relatively powerless people can attack their economic and social superiors indirectly by spreading rumors (Harding 1975; Scott 1985; Spacks 1985: 7, 30). Thus, Scott (1985) argues that peasants in a small Malaysian village are publicly deferential toward their richer neighbors but are much more critical of these people in private gossip circles. Scott also suggests that this covert criticism can have material consequences since poorer peasants often refuse to work for those about whom they have heard bad things in gossip.

Spacks (1985: 46) and Scott (1985) suggest a less direct link between gossip and the empowerment of subordinate groups, as well. They suggest that when "the weak" gossip among themselves they create and maintain interpretations of social relations which challenge the hegemonic ideology fostered by more powerful groups. Thus, Scott (1985) shows that although the richer peasants spoke of charity as an act of voluntary altruism on their part, when their poorer neighbors talked among themselves they were more likely to portray the same charitable acts as social and religious obligations and to criticize those who were not sufficiently generous. Scott argues that such covert interpretations fostered and maintained resistance to the official values and beliefs that chiefly benefited the richer peasants.

Bailey (1971b) and Havilland (1977) suggest that gossip may have a much more pervasive and powerful impact on politics and social interaction in small communities than others have appreciated. Bailey (1971b: 281) suggests that it is through "the spoken word" that people receive much of their information about their social world and so gossip can, ultimately, have a strong impact on their behavior. Havilland (1977) also argues that gossip and reputation are closely linked since villagers compile mental "dossiers" about each other based largely on information received through gossip.

The impact of gossip on people's impressions of their community goes beyond the mere exchange of facts. Gossip also distorts people's impressions of events by adding two kinds of information which are by nature "unseeable," that is, causal connections and moral evaluations (Bailey 1971b: 294). Spacks (1985: 3) suggests that gossip is a form of fiction because in it "fragments of lives [are] transformed into story."

Gossips try to make sense of observed facts by suggesting how they might be related to each other and by relating the particular to more general cultural scenarios. When speakers do this, they transform incidents into stories. Thus, the information people receive through gossip has already been interpreted by the source, and, therefore, hearing gossip tends to influence the way individuals interpret incidents. I will return to this point later.

I will argue (primarily in chapter 7) that because gossips transform events into stories their words have a pervasive impact on people's views of their community. Over time people tend to remember good stories about past events and to forget what actually happened. This is because events are often confusing: people, for instance, were unsure about what had caused the rain, and the best they could do to explain the situation was to make educated guesses based on small things like the Councillor's possible desire for rain to make his yams grow and a rumor that the Christians had angered Hapandi. Stories, however, explain and simplify events and give them meaning by showing how they came about (Brison n.d.) and, for this reason, stories are easy to remember. But because people tend to remember stories and forget the facts, accounts of events, even if they are initially regarded with skepticism, can distort the way people remember the past and also how they interpret the future. Such revisions are especially apparent when people evoke past stories in attempts to understand current crises. Harding (1975: 299), for instance, states: "Gossip about past events reviews and provides background information necessary to gossip about current events." In other words, people make use of stories about past events to try to explain recent incidents, but when they do this, stories that were originally regarded as unsubstantiated speculation can have a powerful influence on the way people interpret the present and future. In fact, Spacks (1985) and Schwartzman (1989) suggest gossip ultimately constitutes much of a community's oral history. I will suggest that when we look at the ways that gossip becomes oral history, it is evident that, as Bailey (1971b: 281) suggests: "The map which a man has of the community around him, of what is going on and of how he should respond to others, is a map created by the spoken word." Consequently, gossip has a powerful impact on behavior.

In short, it seems that the Kwanga are neither unique nor irrational in taking gossip and rumor seriously. Gossip and rumor can affect reputations, social relations, and can help in both maintaining and challenging group norms. Moreover, gossip and rumor are potent political weapons that are particularly dangerous because they are hard to combat. When people become the object of malicious rumors their reputations and social relations suffer, but victims can do little to defend themselves because it is so difficult to find the source of the rumor. For similar reasons, dominant groups can do little to suppress subversive "versions of reality" that are seldom voiced in their presence. Finally, gossip and rumor, are the source of much of people's information about their community and so have a pervasive impact on how individuals view their social world and how they act.

Powerful Words

Studies of gossip speak to a broader concern with the ways in which talking constitutes society. Scholars have suggested that talk is a potent form of political action (Paine 1981) and that we shape and reshape our social and cultural worlds through discussion (Bruner 1984: 2–3). (Bauman and Briggs (1990) review a great deal of recent literature that explores the ways that this "shaping and reshaping" is accomplished through talking.)

Scholars have made several more specific suggestions about how public discussions and other sorts of talk alter the social world. Bailey (1965) and Bloch (1971) suggest that public debates allow participants to negotiate relative rank through displays of oratorical skill. Others (Bloch 1975; Irvine 1979; Myers and Brenneis 1984: 2; Richards 1971: 5, 9) make the broader claim that interactions in meetings constitute political authority and "dominance." The restriction of participation in meetings to certain categories of people (usually adult or initiated men [Bloch 1975: 22; Lederman 1984]), or rules that structure turn-taking (Irvine 1979), display the right of some to lead others and thus reproduce that right. Meetings are like dramas enacted on stage[7] in which masks of ruler and ruled, assumed by speakers and audience respectively, eventually mold the faces that wear them.[8] This is part of a more general view that sees political language as "compel[ling] specific visions of the social world through its own organization" (Myers and Brenneis 1984: 28). Structured styles of speaking and interaction convey a certain message about the relationship between, and the relative power of, the individuals involved and, thus, create a basis for the exercise of power which is "permeated through social intercourse in a totally unconscious and completely accepted way" (Myers and Brenneis 1984: 9, paraphrasing Bloch 1975). The right of some to lead appears to be natural because this right is displayed so consistently in patterns of interaction.

Few scholars would go so far as to claim that patterns of speech are the only thing that creates patterns of dominance; most ethnographers see an interactive relationship between speech styles and other sources of inequality in society such as ideology and access to resources. Rules governing who can speak when both reflect and reinforce political relations (Bowen 1991; Keesing 1990). The distribution of authority in a community will prompt a certain style of public debate; at the same time, when people conform to the rules that reflect a particular configuration of authority they reinforce the status quo by displaying and enacting it. In egalitarian communities, for instance, it is common for speakers to interrupt each other in meetings and these public discussions usually take the form of a debate in which many voices are heard. Such "dialogic" discussion styles both reflect and reinforce egalitarian political relations: it is difficult to suppress debate where power is evenly distributed, and public debate reinforces people's perception that no one has the right to dictate decisions about matters of communal concern. "Dialogic" meeting styles often give way to "monologic" ones in more hierarchical political systems (Bowen 1991: 261). Powerful individuals announce decisions in meetings (though these decisions often represent the end point of much private negotiation [Irvine 1979]); fewer speakers are heard, and interruptions are frowned upon. Monologic styles also tend to stress consensus and conceal differences of opinion (Kuipewrs 1990). Again, this turn-taking style both reflects a political system where some people have the right to dictate decisions to others and reinforces this system by displaying authority and public acceptance of it.

Public discussions may also define social identities and relations in many more subtle ways. Gewertz (1977), for instance, suggests that when big-men among the Chambri of the East Sepik Province of Papua New Guinea discuss recent events in meetings they may be primarily concerned with displaying and, thus, reestablishing the autonomy of small clans that are in danger of being subsumed into larger, more powerful ones (Gewertz 1977: 350). Leaders of small clans make speeches that display their personal power and esoteric knowledge (which they inherit through their clans) and, in this way, reassert their clan identity.

Like turn-taking rules, styles of speech both reflect and create political relations. Various styles of speech are typical of figures of authority. Bloch (1975) suggests that highly formalized speech compels compliance. More recently, Kuipers (1990) has argued that monologic "entextualized" speech that is highly formulaic in style and contains relatively few references to the context tends to be perceived as a highly authoritative perspective on events which transcends individual interests. Kuipers (1990) carefully examines the ritual language in several divination and placation rites among the Weyewa of Indonesia and finds that early debate about how to interpret crises slowly gives way to a stylized official commentary thought to represent the word of the ancestors. People are less inclined to question the final "entextualized" statement because they see it as received wisdom that transcends local political battles. Thus, leaders with a certain amount of authority tend to speak in certain characteristic ways and these typical styles of speech enhance their control over others by making their words authoritative.

Others have noted a connection between highly allusive, "veiled" speech and egalitarian communities. In such places speakers must avoid "hard words"—that is, direct expressions of negative emotions or straightforward revelation of potentially embarrassing and damaging information (Weiner 1984)—which might start fights or destroy relationships (A. Strathern 1975). Allegorical or veiled speech forms, which leave meaning ambiguous, avoid the problems of "hard" words by softening the impact of embarrassing truths or bad feelings and by demonstrating respect for the audience who are free to hear what they will "between the lines" and to feel that they have reached their own conclusions (McKellin 1990; see also Brenneirs 1978, 1986). Poetic speech forms also display the knowledge and wisdom of speakers and, thus, enhance their prestige and influence (Atkinson 1984). Thus, like other styles of speaking, allusive, veiled speech is shaped by the constraints imposed by an egalitarian political environment and, conversely, helps to create and maintain egalitarian relations by demonstrating respect for others' opinions.

"Talk" can also have a political impact by redefining the meaning of events, or, in other words, telling a story about them that changes the way people view and react to these situations. These interpretations may redefine social relations or the meaning of future actions. In fact, Bauman (1986: 113) suggests:

When one looks to the social practices by which social life is accomplished, one finds—with surprising frequency—people telling stories to each other as a means of giving cognitive and emotional coherence to experience, constructing and negotiating social identity. . . investing the experiential landscape with moral significance in a way that can be brought to bear on human behavior . . . generating, interpreting, and transforming the work experience. . . and a host of other reasons.

Telling stories about events gives them new meaning in several ways. First, and most obviously, many stories contain explicit statements about their meaning, commonly known as the "moral of the story." Folk tales often end with a summary of the moral, and Labov (1972) suggests that impromptu stories about experiences also often include "abstracts" and "codas" that sum up the point. Other stories contain less obvious evaluative devices. Many of Labov's American informants, for instance, indicated the significance of each event they described by summarizing their reactions at the time (Labov 1972: 370–372).

As well, storytellers usually send more subtle messages about themselves and about what they think about the characters and behaviors of others involved in the story. Bauman (1986:11–32), for instance, shows how Texans telling stories about dog trading frame their stories so as to impress their honesty upon the audience; at the same time, narrators stress the prevalence of dishonesty in dog trading in order to highlight their own sterling character. Consequently, stories about dog trading prompt the audience to certain conclusions both about the narrator and about the general characteristics of dog trading. The role of stories in "creating" or "constituting" the context of dog trading is particularly powerful because many dog trading stories follow the same form. Thus, people hear over and over again stories that emphasize the dishonesty of dog traders and this contributes both to molding the audience's impression of dog trading and, probably, to reinforcing the dishonest behavior because it is through stories that people become acquainted with the rules and strategies of dog trading (see also Bauman 1986: 33–54, for a similar point about the role of practical joke stories in teaching people the "script" for playing practical jokes).

Second, as noted above, stories give each of their elements meaning by showing how they are related to each other. Storytellers usually impute causal connections between events.

Third, stories give events meaning by engaging the audience's preexisting beliefs and knowledge. Storytellers often leave a great deal unsaid and rely on their audience to "hear" all sorts of related information and to infer causal connections between the lines (Hutchins 1980; Leitch 1986: 34; Price 1987; White 1990) by using their background knowledge. Quinn and Holland (1987), among others, argue that stories give events meaning by relating them to underlying narrative (or knowledge) structures that include

prototypical events, prototypical roles for actors, prototypical entities, and more. They invoke, in effect, whole worlds in which things work, actors perform, and events unfold in a simplified and wholly expectable manner. These events are chained together by shared assumptions about causality. (Quinn and Holland 1987: 20)

Narrative structures, in other words, give us a set of categories, suggest how these categories are related to each other, and often provide a story line that allows us to see the present as a logical culmination of past events and gives us some sense of what is likely to happen in the future (Bruner 1986: 147; Schafer 1983: 235). Listeners "instantiate" specific information into "schemas" that suggest the typical features of that sort of situation. Thus, speakers in the meeting about rain prompted the audience to draw on their schema concerning conflict, magicians, and rain, in order to make sense of recent events.[9]

By giving events new meaning, stories can have an impact on how people perceive and react to events. Discussions can define the meaning of communal action. Lederman (1984) says that that is the case for public discussions among the Mendi of the Eastern Highlands Province of Papua New Guinea. She observed a meeting in which, after a long debate, the members of one clan agreed not to participate in an exchange to be staged by a neighboring clan. When several of the participants in the meeting, nevertheless, contributed to the exchange in question, Lederman concluded that the meeting may not have influenced people's behavior but it did give their actions new meaning; individual participation was viewed by all as informal aid to kinsmen in the neighboring clan instead of as a formal clan contribution.

Casting strategic interpretations of events is also an important part of dispute resolution, particularly in relatively egalitarian communities where people must be careful to demonstrate respect for others' autonomy. Adjudicators, for instance, are often reluctant to impose solutions on others, or even to make suggestions about what to do since this may be seen as a claim to superiority. Instead, they strategically redefine recent events in order to accomplish particular goals. Several ethnographers argue that meetings bring out into the open an "official version" of problematic events (Brenneis 1984; Hayden 1987; Just 1986; Lindstrom 1990a; Myers and Brenneis 1984: 14; White 1990; White and Watson-Gegeo 1990) which does not necessarily reflect reality. Just (1986), for example, argues that the Dou Donngo of Indonesia construct accounts of conflict which reflect their evaluation of everyone's behavior but may present a distorted picture of what actually happened. These accounts hold up before the community the ideals for behavior, and also the consequences of violating these ideals. They also reinforce relations of authority by putting the blame for conflict on subordinate individuals (see also M. Strathern 1974). In other cases, the "official version" is designed to smooth problematic relations by suggesting interpretations of events in which everybody's actions seem honorable, so that people do not have to persist in unreasonable behavior in order to avoid admitting they are wrong (Brenneis 1984; White 1990). For instance, the Fiji Indian *panchayat*, analyzed by Brenneis, distributes blame evenly on both sides of a conflict, reasoning that shaming one person will only lead to further trouble (see also Nader 1969 on Zapotec courts). Participants in moots also try to cast interpretations on events which will best serve their interests. White (1990), for instance, says that disputants among the A'ara of the Solomon Islands stress that they acted out of good intentions in order to pave the way for reconciliation and to protect their reputations. In egalitarian communities, decisions can cause more problems than they resolve: they cannot be enforced in any case; people may resent the adjudicator or they may feel that they have been shamed and should go on the offensive to restore their wounded honor. In this situation, "the transformation of" problematic events into "more ideal constructions" (White and Watson-Gegeo 1990: 5) may be the most effective way of halting the destructive potential of conflict.

Furthermore, audiences often do not notice the ways in which stories add meaning to the events they describe. This makes telling stories an appealing rhetorical device because it allows speakers to comment on events in a veiled and indirect way. For instance, when speakers relate particular events to more general schemas, the audience can infer all sorts of related information. White (1990: 71) argues that many schemas have moral implications.[10] In this way, people reach conclusions about matters that are not explicitly addressed by the narrative when they are able to draw on their more general knowledge. Stories prompt audiences to all sorts of conclusions without the speaker having to state them.

Several ethnographers have shown how speakers make use of stories to comment on events in an oblique way. Basso (1984), for instance, says that the Apache tell historical tales with commonly understood morals to remind people of the consequences of violating social norms and acting in certain undesirable ways (see also Matthews n.d. on a similar use of a Mexican folktale). The "moral" of the story—and its relevance to current events—is not stated. Consequently, storytellers can embarrass culprits into better behavior without having to comment explicitly on their actions.[11] McKellin (1990: 344–345) also suggests that stories are an oblique form of political action. He says that Managalese villagers of Papua New Guinea tell allegorical tales but (like the Apache) do not say how these bear on recent events. This allows people to prompt their audience to certain conclusions without committing themselves to the position. McKellin argues that the Managalase prefer such indirect, allusive forms of communication which allow listeners to reach their own conclusions both because speakers can deny their intent should it prove to be unpopular or controversial and because they believe that one individual should not impose his or her opinion on another.

In short, discussion may accomplish many things even if there is no decision and, in fact, if there is some sort of resolution this may be relatively unimportant. Talk, public and private, conveys certain messages about personalities, the nature of the community, and the relative status of individuals and categories of people within it as well as messages about particular disputes. Moreover, discussion does not passively reflect reality but, instead, actively constructs it; meetings provide a context for people to publicly enact, and thus display, their roles in the community. When people gather to discuss an issue, they show themselves to be a community—and one that can comment on its own affairs. When certain individuals make impressive speeches, they show themselves to be leaders. In fact, in some areas, leaders compel others to comply with their wishes simply by voicing them in formal style (Bloch 1975), and in this sense, talk can be action (Paine 1981). Similarly, when people talk about events, they give them new meaning and alter the audience's impressions of the personalities involved.

Many scholars suggest that this kind of manipulating people's impressions of individuals and events through talk is a particularly important form of political action in egalitarian communities where autocratic assertive action can arouse resentment and resistance. Indeed, in many small, relatively egalitarian communities, politics seems to consist of a great deal of talk and very little action (Myers 1986). Villagers, for instance, hold long community meetings to look into disputes and other matters of common concern but they seldom reach a decision and even less frequently actually implement solutions when participants do agree on them.[12] Read (1959), for instance, suggests that leadership is difficult among the Gahuku-Gama of the Eastern Highlands of Papua New Guinea (and probably more generally in Melanesia) because people resent autocratic attitudes that seem to threaten or to ignore individual autonomy. In such environments, according to Read (1959), leaders must display the necessary force of character to win respect but must also demonstrate respect for others' opinions. One way they can do this is by making forceful speeches in meetings but acting only on the basis of communal consensus. Consequently in egalitarian communities, meetings (and politics more generally) seem to consist of a lot of talk and very little action as people harangue the audience but often end up doing the very opposite of what they seem to recommend so forcefully. "Talk" is largely a matter of impression management and of trying to influence people in veiled indirect ways by altering their impressions of the speaker (cf. Myers and Brenneis 1984: 11, 14, 15, 18).

Myers and Brenneis (1984) also suggest that displaying social relations in public dramas may be particularly important in egalitarian societies where "the polity" is weak and apparently must be reconstructed anew in each meeting.[13] In many areas, meetings may be one of very few contexts in which the community acts as a group and in which people concern themselves with others' affairs. The purpose of meetings, therefore, is to demonstrate the existence of the group, and people's right to comment on each other's problems, as much as to address any particular conflict. Schwartzman similarly says that in the American mental health center that she studied "meetings may be *the* form that generates and maintains the organization as an entity [italics in original]" (Schwartzman 1987: 290). That is, meetings may have the primary purpose of constituting a community by providing a context where people can interact and demonstrate common concern for problems. When a local group is part of a wider political structure, the chief purpose of the meeting may be to display the right of the local community to discuss its own affairs (Pinsker 1986). People prove to themselves and to the outer world that they are a community with some control over their own destiny when they have meetings to discuss local affairs.

Speakers also maneuver in egalitarian communities by casting their remarks in veiled ambiguous forms and leaving the audience to make of them what they wish.[14] Telling stories and dropping hints about current events is one way of influencing people without provoking a negative reaction.

Talking Politics in Inakor and Asanakor

I will also argue that people change their social world when they talk about it and that "just talking" is a preferred form of political action in small, egalitarian Kwanga communities where more direct strategies are both unwise and seldom successful. In fact, as I suggested in the opening pages, spreading rumors and telling other kinds of stories is central to the constitution of power in many Melanesian societies and in small communities everywhere.

Several recent works (Atkinson 1989; Kuipers 1990; Nuckolls 1991) have suggested that divination and other forms of interpretation of misfortunes in supernatural terms are central to the constitution of power in some Indonesian and south Asian societies. Atkinson (1989: 255–257) argues that ambitious men among the Wana of central Sulawesi build followings and enhance their reputations for being men who can control the supernatural world by participating in divination rites. Nuckolls (1991), similarly, shows how the outcome of divination rites can have political consequences in an Indian fishing village. He analyzes a case in which a lineage headman tries to prove that current illnesses are due to neglect of ancestors caused by recent infighting within the lineage, in order to prevent the head of a junior branch of the lineage from breaking away and forming his own, autonomous lineage. Earlier works on African societies (Middleton 1960; Turner 1957; Van Velsen 1964) showed a similar close association between politics and interpretation of misfortune. Although many ethnographers have commented on the close link between oratory and leadership in Melanesia (see, for instance, Bateson 1958; Gewertz 1977; Harrison 1989, 1990; Lederman 1984; Lindstrom 1988, 1990b; Read 1959; Reay 1959; Rumsey 1985; A. Strathern 1975; Tuzin 1980), scholars seldom focus on the way leaders create impressions of power by manipulating interpretations of natural disasters even though it is evident that Melanesians spend a great deal of time in public meetings and in private conversation speculating about the causes of misfortunes.[15] I will argue that this sort of manipulation of public opinion is central to political systems in Melanesia.[16]

Discussion of misfortune is perhaps particularly important, as I have suggested earlier, in societies where leaders claim political power on the basis of control of specialized knowledge. Recently, scholars have suggested that control over things like ritual secrets and magical spells may be more important than success in exchange (emphasized in earlier models such as Sahlins 1963) in at least some areas of Melanesia (Gode-lier 1982, 1986; Harrison 1989, 1990; Lindstrom 1984; Modjeska 1982). This seems to be true of the Sepik region where political author-ity is closely linked with a male initiation cult (Tuzin 1974, 1976, 1980). This type of leadership is perhaps particularly dependent on interpretation of events (Lindstrom 1988). For instance, control over such things as weather magic and sorcery influences others only when particular events are attributed to particular people. Magic may be a coercive sanction but its impact is not straightforward and obvious like, for instance, physical violence. Cause and effect must be linked through a process of discussion in which particular deaths or disasters come to be known to be due to the actions of certain people acting for certain reasons.[17] This discussion may occur in private gossip, as Stephen (1987) suggests is most common in cases of lethal sorcery (see also Bowden 1987 and Young 1971, 1983 on interpretation of natural disasters), or in public gatherings as among the Gebusi (Knauft 1985), the Kalabe (Riebe 1987), the Maya of the Madang Province (Dar-rouzet 1985), and the Kwanga (Brison 1988, 1989). As scholars such as Turner (1957), Middleton (1960), and Van Velsen (1964) estab-lished, the link between various types of magical powers and influence over others is the process of interpreting natural events.

Similarly, other kinds of knowledge, such as information about genealogies and histories of land tenure, only bring prestige and in-fluence when they are used in meetings and in more private conversa-tions to demonstrate wisdom or to win cases (Harrison 1989, 1990; Lindstrom 1988). Indeed, Lindstrom (1988, 1990b) and Harrison (1990) both suggest that in knowledge-based Melanesian polities the exchange and display of knowledge in public and private talk may play a similar role to the exchange of material items such as pigs and yams in other Melanesian societies where leadership is based on success in com-petitive exchange; thus public debates may be a functional equivalent to large competitive exchanges.

The link between "talk" and "power" is complex in Inakor since, as the example of the rain suggests, speakers seem to spend more time denying complicity in supernatural activities (and blaming misfortunes on others) than in claiming credit for these occurrences. I will argue that although speakers generally deny involvement in magic and sorcery in public, their stories do reproduce general beliefs that sorcerers act at the bidding of initiated men and that they often punish those, like the Christians, who disrupt the community. Thus, although it is never clear who is responsible for what calamity, when people hear over and over again that misfortune results from insubordination and disruptive behavior, this has the overall effect of discouraging them from challenging initiated men and making other sorts of trouble. In this way, sorcery stories, like Texan dog trading stories, reinforce general beliefs about and characteristics of their social environment, even though the audience takes each individual story with a grain of salt.

Discussion of misfortune also provides an opportunity for oblique expression of opinions about events and personalities. We have seen that, like people in other areas, when the Inakor and Asanakor people discuss recent events they tell stories about them. Sometimes people do this in order to reassure themselves that they understand and, therefore, can control ambiguous and potentially dangerous circumstances.[18] But most often, people are less disinterested than this: they try to shape their interpretations of events to deliver particular messages and to prompt people to certain (often unstated) conclusions. The rumors about the rain, for instance, conceal a larger debate about a Christian revival movement that had been a source of tension in the community for several months. In recent months, Mary[19] and several other Christian women had claimed to have received prophetic powers from the Holy Spirit. These so-called "prophet women" had caused a great deal of commotion by telling everyone to throw out sorcery implements and other magical paraphernalia. The Christians had claimed that getting rid of all their magic would stop untimely death and pave the way to an era of peace and prosperity. They had declared themselves to be well on the way to achieving this goal after Hapandi had converted to Christianity and had renounced his evil ways. When the non-Christians speculated that the Christians were responsible for the rain, then, the non-Christians were arguing that, far from having rid the community of harmful magic, the Christians, in fact, had aggravated Hapandi so much with their suspicions about him that he had returned to his nefarious ways. Rain was a problem in its own right but, more importantly, it was an example of the consequences of a general pattern of behavior—that is, Christian abuse of Hapandi—which could lead to other problems. People tried to interpret the current crisis in such a way as to support their own view of the revival and to prompt others to either support or abandon it. If the non-Christians could persuade their fellow community members that Mary and the other Christian women had caused the rain this might help to undermine the revival and to humble the revival leaders. Thus, participants in Kwanga meetings try to influence others by suggesting particular interpretations of recent events.

Moreover, when speakers criticized the revival indirectly by implying that it had caused the rain, they could prompt their audience to the conclusion that the revival was bad without seeming to do so. In this way they could influence events in ways they could not be held accountable for: no one said that the revival should be stopped; they just suggested that the Christians were responsible for the rain and left others to draw their own conclusions. If anyone had pushed them to do something about the rain or the revival, speakers could have said that they were "just talking" or "just guessing" and had no real knowledge of either the cause of the rain or of the revivalists' activities. In that way, they could try to persuade people to stop the revival without incurring the Christians' wrath. Others did not even come right out and say that the Christians were responsible for the rain. Instead, they dropped strategic hints and left others to draw their own conclusions. Ambwambuli, for instance, suggested that there had been no rain when Hapandi was out of town; but he left others to infer that the Christians must be behind the current bad weather. By doing that, Ambwambuli and others like him suggested to the audience that the revival caused problems and prompted them toward the conclusion that it should be stopped, or at least controlled. Still others, like Bwalaka, remained silent in the meetings but had evidently had a great deal to say about the topic of rain in private conversation. Gossiping is another way in which people can influence others without being held accountable. No one can be really sure of who said what to whom in gossip, and so people can plant suspicions in others' minds by spreading rumors without fearing reprisals. In this way, gossiping and telling stories allows people to exercise "power without responsibility" and, thus, to escape the straitjacket imposed by an egalitarian community where everyone resents autocratic attitudes and where leaders can do little to force people to do as they say.

My analysis will differ from others that focus on the power of words to define situations and to constitute relations of authority in that I will suggest that we cannot fully understand the political impact of public words without examining the fate of stories over time, and without taking into account both public discussions and the more private conversations that surround them. That is important for several reasons. First, as was apparent in the meeting about the rain, public talk often addresses private discussions preceding the meetings and only makes sense when those earlier theories are taken into account. Furthermore, as Bailey (1977) and Murphy (1990) argue, "front stage" discussion in public meetings usually gives a distorted impression of the state of community opinion. "Front stage" discussion generally appeals to shared norms (Bailey 1977, 1983) and, in many societies, is designed to convey an impression of consensus (Kuipers 1990; Murphy 1990). Concurrent discussions in "backstage" or more private contexts, however, may be much more cynical and self-interested and may also show a great deal more disagreement among individuals than is evident in public. Scott (1985), for instance, suggests that public deference on the part of subordinate groups masks a critical attitude toward dominant individuals which is only evident if one examines less visible discussions between peers. In Inakor and Asanakor public discussions were also deceptive; people generally denied complicity with sorcerers in public but did drop hints that they had influence over, and knowledge of, sorcerers' activities in private. Furthermore, the interpretations of events produced in public meetings were by no means definitive. Instead, Inakor and Asanakor meetings tended to produce many stories about events, none of which was ever conclusively judged true or false, and subsequent discussions in more private contexts produced still more stories. Thus, we cannot assume that when public speakers redefine situations that theirs is the prevalent view. Looking at public meetings gives, at best, a partial and distorted view of the continual work of defining situations and constructing social relations which takes place in private conversations.

Second, tracing stories over time allows us to study the process through which they become authoritative and influential. Kuipers (1990) argues that commentary on events among the Weyewa of Indonesia becomes authoritative only after it has undergone a process of "entextualization." In Inakor and Asanakor, stories underwent a similar process of conversion. They went from being regarded as from unsubstantiated just-so stories to being viewed almost as well-established truth. Public meetings generally prompted further speculation about events in private conversations. Such discussions created rumors. Often if people heard the same rumor from several different sources, they would come to think it was true simply because so many people were saying it. Indeed, I will argue that, universally, people have a tendency to assume that something is true if they hear it from several different people—and to overlook the fact that these people could all be repeating a groundless rumor that they all heard from the same source. This situation is particularly likely to occur in small communities where networks of friendship and kinship are dense and overlapping and, therefore, people can easily hear a rumor from several different people who all originally heard it from a common acquaintance. I will suggest that people come to believe stories in situations where they suspect that there is good but concealed evidence to support them. This is often true of stories that circulate in gossip—since most people hear gossip second- or thirdhand and have reason to suspect that they do not have the full story. Consequently, when considering the way "talk" defines situations and relationships, it is important to pay attention to the process by which stories are incorporated into people's "map" or "history" of their community.

It is particulary important to take this process into account because only some of the many stories told about any event become authoritative. Audiences do not believe everything they hear. Presumably, many opinions voiced in Weyewa meetings do not become entextualized (and authoritative), although Kuipers provides little information on this point. It was also evident in Inakor and Asanakor that only a few of the many accounts of events voiced in meetings had substantial influence on the way people interpreted situations. The only way to determine what kind of stories are influential, and how they come to be so, is to look at what people say afterwards, in other contexts.

Third, looking at the fate of stories over time shows that the process of defining a situation is in general a communal one. As Brenneis (1986, 1988) and Duranti (1986) argue, audiences are not passive recipients of speakers' messages. Instead, audiences interpret what they hear in light of their own beliefs and interests and so, in a sense, speaker and audience are "coauthors" (Duranti 1986) of any account; that is, both speaker and listener contribute to an interpretation. This process is particularly evident if one follows the fate of stories over time. Among the Kwanga, people use stories they have heard in one context to interpret other events and it is in this process that accounts become persuasive. But each successive speaker and listener changes the story. Thus, the accounts that ultimately become part of a community's oral history and come to define social reality are always shaped by multiple voices as they are told and retold in different contexts. It is important to take this process of distortion into account when considering the way storytelling can be an act "of power" because it is evident that although speakers do maneuver to influence others by casting strategic interpretations of events, storytellers cannot control the impact of their own words (see Duranti 1986). As interpretations circulate through a community, they can take on a life of their own and have results that the original speaker neither anticipated nor desired. As rumors spread through Inakor and Asanakor they are distorted in certain systematic and predictable ways (which I will outline in chapter 7). In this way, the "truth" or "definition of reality" that emerges from public and private discussion is, to a large extent, produced by a group and is beyond the control of any single person. Consequently, in order to understand how our "map" of the social world is created by "the spoken word" one must look beyond the strategic interests of particular speakers and consider the ways in which information circulates through the community and how it tends to be distorted in the process.

In short, I will suggest that "talk," public and private, has a much more profound impact on people's impressions of their community than has previously been appreciated and that the Kwanga, and other members of small communities everywhere, have reason to think that "names" may very well "hurt them" and reason to make sure they deny rumored charges in public meetings.

Big-Men and Small Communities

Examining rumors will provide an entry point into a broader exploration of politics in small, relatively egalitarian communities, particularly in Melanesia.

It is not immediately apparent why Kwanga leaders prefer dropping hints and spreading rumors to more straightforward means of influencing people. Melanesian societies are often described as "egalitarian" (Forge 1972; Sahlins 1963), but Kwanga society also is not entirely lacking in concepts of rightful hierarchy or in legitimate means of coercion. In fact, it could be argued that Kwanga communities are permeated by a sense of rightful hierarchy. The genealogically senior men of lineages have authority over their juniors, allocate group resources, make decisions on communal exchange obligations, speak for their lineages in public gatherings, and control hunting and gardening magic. Furthermore, Kwanga men are initiated into a multigraded cult in which they are taught hunting, gardening, and war magic necessary to the well-being of the community. The cult also creates hierarchy within the group of initiated men since initiates of the higher grades have authority over their cult juniors.[20] Initiated men not only have authority but are also believed to have coercive powers to punish violations of social norms and cult rules, in the form of sorcerers who act at their bidding. In short, Kwanga society has both legitimate hierarchy and (at least in local belief) leaders with power since, whether or not magic is practiced or effective, as long as people believe that it is, this amounts to a coercive sanction.

The Kwanga political system is not unusual. In many areas, particularly in lowland and insular Melanesia, lineage headmen, hereditary chiefs (Hau'ofa 1971), and male cult initiates are believed to control magical powers such as sorcery, and gardening and weather magic, and can use their powers both to benefit the community and to punish misbehavior (see, for instance Chowning 1979, 1987; Forge 1970b; Hau'ofa 1981; Knauft 1985; Malinowski 1926; Patterson 1974–1975; Stephen 1987; Tuzin 1974, 1976; Young 1971, 1983). Furthermore, the Abelam villagers described by Forge recognize the role of leaders in defending the community from outside attack and take pride in their achievements (Forge 1970b: 269), and this recognition of the benefits of superior power and achievement is also found among Goodenough Islanders who acknowledge the authority of magicians (Young 1983) and Arapesh people who believe that the power of male cult initiates is necessary for communal prosperity and survival (Tuzin 1976). So these leaders seem to have both legitimacy and power.

Still, as the opening examples indicate, there does seem to be something about Kwanga society which limits the power of leaders, makes consensus necessary, and evokes the label "egalitarian." For some reason, despite their powers, people like the Councillor and Hapandi become scapegoats, and others make impressive speeches but are reluctant to act on their own words. Possession of superior powers, particularly magical ones, seems to invite suspicion that they are being misused (see chap. 10).

The "egalitarianism" explanation, therefore, seems not wrong, but too simple. Vague labels like "egalitarian" seem often to be used in a relatively unreflective way and they may mask a number of different constraints on the actions of leaders. These only become apparent if processes of communal decision making, such as meetings and the more private discussions that surround them, are made the focus of study. Something seems to be constraining assertive leadership, but what is it? I will examine the dense network of social relationships in a small village society and argue that these create a situation in which almost anything anybody does provokes a negative reaction. Consequently, people seek ways to influence events without incurring the personal costs of taking responsibility for leadership. Spreading malicious rumors is one such strategy; making speeches in meetings is another. Similar behaviors are found wherever people live in small, isolated, "face-to-face" communities, and also in institutional settings, like academia, which artificially create similar relationships by forcing people to deal with each other as "moral beings," or "persons in the round" (Bailey 1977).

But I will also argue that spreading rumors and dropping strategic hints can have dangerous consequences. People like to drop hints and to spread malicious rumors in small communities because it is a way of influencing events without facing the consequences; but everyone realizes that since individuals prefer such covert strategies, nothing anyone says or does can be taken at face value. Indeed, I will suggest that small communities like Kwanga villages are characterized by a pervasive spirit of distrust in which everyone looks for nefarious hidden plots behind apparently innocuous surfaces. This spirit of distrust, in turn, both creates rumors as people speculate about what lies hidden from view and makes villagers particularly prone to believing inflammatory gossip—because they are predisposed to think that their neighbors are up to no good. In short, suspicion and distrust create a preference for gossiping which increases suspicion and distrust and so on.

The result is an environment where it is difficult for anyone to attain or consolidate power. Almost anything leaders do creates resentment and rumors; some try to influence events in covert ways to escape the criticism and backbiting; but such strategies increase the people's distrust of leaders and can blacken the reputations of particular leaders to the point where they may be attacked or ostracized. Thus, ironically, the same leaders who hint and gossip to attain "power without responsibility" ultimately become the victims of rumors themselves. Talk, then does more than reflect egalitarian social conditions created by political ideology or the economy; patterns of talk in many ways create and maintain the egalitarian ethos by making it difficult for anyone to consolidate power.

In the following chapters I will examine various kinds of meetings and suggest that stories which emerge from meetings and gossip are an important part of the Kwanga political system. Chapter 3 shows how initiated men spread rumors that suggest that they are closely associated sorcerers and could evoke their potent force to punish challenges from younger men and women. Rumors about sorcery, thus, reinforce and create the dominance of initiated men in Kwanga society by creating a diffuse fear of sorcerers. Spreading rumors also allows "power without responsibility" since people cannot take reprisals against initiated men because no one can be really sure if the rumors are true or not. In chapter 4 I examine village court cases and suggest, again, that people spread rumors in order to influence others and slander their enemies. They always make their charges in private, or avoid spelling them out, so that, if challenged, they can deny their words or say they have been misinterpreted. But, in chapter 5 I will suggest that these strategies create rumors that can get out of hand and have unintended and harmful consequence for the perpetrators. I will examine several cases in which people suffer from bad reputations created by rumors and suggest that often individuals try to stop slanderous rumors and clear their names by denying the charges in public meetings and trying to convince people that they have misinterpreted events and come to erroneous conclusions. In fact, speakers in meetings are often more interested in stopping rumors than in trying to explain the crisis that prompted the discussion. Chapters 6 and 7 will continue the examination of the way in which rumors can get out of hand and, over the long run, create unanticipated problems. Chapter 6 investigates kin and exchange relationships and shows how the dense web of kin ties, crosscutting group divisions, acts both to escalate conflict and to prevent it from resulting in violence or village fission. The same network of communication ensures that rumors spread easily in the community and that they rapidly distort the facts and create alarm and conflict. Chapter 7 shows how "stories" about events can have a pervasive impact on people's impressions of their natural and social world.

Chapters 8, 9, and 10 attempt a broader examination of leadership in small egalitarian Kwanga villages by investigating the distribution of power and authority in Kwanga villages and the constraints on assertive leadership. I suggest that although initiated men spread rumors about sorcery to enhance their own position of authority these rumors eventually come back to haunt them and, ultimately, lead to their downfall. People develop such a dark image of leaders that they suspect them of all sorts of nefarious deeds. Most leaders get tired of the malicious gossip that ensues and attempt to divest themselves of their powers; those who ignore the gossip increasingly alienate their supporters and often meet violent ends. Finally, in the conclusion, I suggest that the prevalent preoccupation with gossip, rumors, and other forms of talking in small communities reflects a social situation in which stories about events have a powerful impact on people's impressions of their community and, ultimately, on what they do.

CHAPTER TWO

The Kwanga

Standing at the highest point in Inakor, I could see for miles over what always looked to me like a vast unoccupied forest, though the local people would invariably point out signs of human habitation like smoke from fires burning off garden plots, coconut palms marking distant villages, and the sole visible corrugated iron roof in the administrative town of Dreikikir more than twenty miles away. I never ceased to be impressed by the beauty of the area and found other parts of the country, even the more dramatic highlands, disappointing in comparison. The Kwanga inhabit a landscape of ravines and ridges in which flat land is restricted to small areas along the tops of ridges where villages are built, and most gardens are cut on sloping hillsides. They live in the foothills of the Torricelli Mountain range, in the north-western part of Papua New Guinea, an area best known to the world through the work of Mead (1938, 1940, 1947) and Fortune (1939, 1942) among the Mountain Arapesh who live some distance to the northeast.

The apparent physical isolation of Inakor is illusory. The Maprik district, just to the east of Inakor, is one of the most densely populated areas in the country. Inakor has neighbors no more than three or four miles away in several directions, and the village of Asanakor is less than a mile down the road. Traditionally, a complex system of alliances and enmities associated with warfare, a trading network, a ritual complex, and intermarriage linked the villages in an area. Migrations were frequent in a region where endemic warfare produced many refugees, and the majority of Inakor and Asanakor residents claim immigrant ancestry.

Still, the world of "the ancestors" must have been a limited one. The Inakor and Asanakor ritual and trade networks did not even extend as far as the village of Ilahita (Tuzin 1976, 1980), about six miles away. One man, after describing how his ancestors migrated to Inakor from a vast distance to the west, shook his head and said something to the effect of: "Well, nowadays we could walk there in a day but before it seemed much further away and if you went there you would surely be killed on the way."

Kwanga villages are typically compact and large. Inakor had a population of 390 in September 1984 (when I took a census), whereas Asanakor had a population of 310. Houses are grouped around the edges of clearings scraped bare of grass because people think it looks better that way and find it easier to keep clean. Villages are divided into named hamlets (fourteen in Inakor, seven in Asanakor) but these hamlets often merge together so that it is difficult for an outsider to tell where one ends and the other begins. Patrilineal descent groups are localized in these hamlets, and each hamlet is occupied by two or three lineages.

Socially each Kwanga village seems in many ways to be a world unto itself. Marriages are concentrated within the village (78.9 percent of Inakor wives are local women; of the remaining 21.1 percent, 16.7 percent are from Asanakor, and 4.4 percent from places beyond). Children from several villages attend the same school but, during recess, they generally play in groups that are segregated by village. News is slow to travel between villages.

The eastern Kwanga villages are grouped in pairs; Inakor and Asanakor are less than a mile apart but are at least three miles from their next nearest neighbors (see map 1). To the south, the villages of Apangai and Yubanakor form another such pair, as do Sunahu and Kamanakor to the east. The village of Apos, to the west, is paired with the Urat village, Musendai. Local people do not remark on any special relationship between proximal villages, though, in fact, intermarriage is much greater between close villages and so is the rate of interaction. Legend has it that Inakor and Asanakor were once one village that divided when overcrowding led to frequent fights.

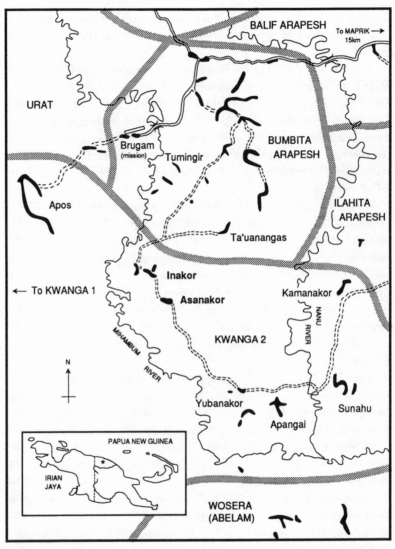

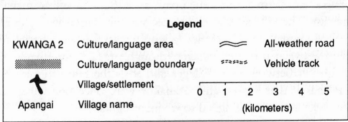

Map 1. The Kwanga and surrounding groups

Language

The Kwanga language is part of the Nukuma family of the Sepik-Ramu language phylum (see Laycock 1973) which stretches from the Sepik River northward to the coast. The Kwoma, the other member of the Nukuma family, live on the Sepik River and have been studied by Whiting (1941), Bowden (1982, 1983a, 1983b, 1987), and Williamson (1975, 1979). Other members of the Sepik-Ramu phylum include the Abelam, who live to the east and have been the subject of numerous studies since before World War II including research by Kaberry (1941, 1941–1942, 1966, 1967, 1971); Forge (1965, 1967, 1970a, 1970b, 1972, 1973); Scaglion (1976, 1978, 1979, 1981, 1983a, 1983b, 1985, 1986, 1987; 1979 with Richard Condon); Condon and Scaglion (1982); Losche (1978, 1982a, 1982b); geographer David Lea (1964); and Gorlin (1974).

The Kwanga are on the edge of the Sepik-Ramu language region and all of their neighbors, save the Wosera Abelam to the south, speak languages of the Torricelli phylum, which extends south to the area from the coastal mountain range. These include the Bumbita Arapesh directly to the north (Leavitt 1989), the Urat to the north and west (B. Allen 1976; Eyre 1988), and the Ilahita Arapesh to the east (Tuzin 1972, 1974, 1975, 1976, 1977, 1978a, 1978b, 1980, 1982, 1983). Tuzin (1976; following Laycock 1965) hypothesizes that the Kwanga were originally a Sepik River group who pushed north into an area originally occupied by Torricelli groups when overcultivation destroyed their own land. Local legend among both members of the Nukuma family, the Kwanga and Kwoma (Bowden 1983), has it that the Nukuma groups originated in the Torricelli foothills. Probably these contradictions between local and scholarly accounts are more apparent than real. Laycock (1965) argues that many of the Sepik River language groups originally migrated south to the river from the northwest, and the Kwoma and Kwanga origin myths may reflect this earlier migration. The Kwanga were pushed northward by the Wosera-Abelam speakers from the village of Nungwaiya to the south,[1] and many Inakor and Asanakor people claim that their ancestors came to their present homes from villages to the west at this time.

The Kwanga language has two dialects, locally known as "Kwanga One" and "Kwanga Two," located to the west and east, respectively, of a wide expanse of unoccupied bush (Manabe 1982a). The western

Kwanga villages are numerous and have been studied by Markus Schindlbeck (1981, 1984, 1986). Brigit Obrist (1987, 1990) has conducted research on health care for children in a western Kwanga village and Nigel Stephenson (Basel, Museum für Volkerkunde) has also studied a western Kwanga group. Speakers of the eastern Kwanga dialect number about 3,500 and live in seven villages[2] including Inakor and Asanakor. The information presented in the following chapters comes almost exclusively from these two villages. Summer Institute of Linguistics translators, Takashi and Kezue Manabe, based in the eastern Kwanga village, Yubanakor, five miles south of Inakor, have done extensive studies of the Kwanga language (1979*a*, 1979*b*, 1982*a*, 1982*b*).

At the time of my research, fluency in Neo-Melanesian was almost universal among adults (the exceptions being some elderly people) and adolescents. Neo-Melanesian was sprinkled through public meetings and informal conversations and was the primary means of communication with Europeans and neighboring language groups. Children under the age of twelve (particularly if they had not started school) often had limited proficiency in the language.

Subsistence

The Kwanga are horticulturalists who practice slash and burn cultivation. The chief crops are several varieties of short yam (*Dioscorea esculenta*), supplemented by taro, several varieties of bananas, sweet potatoes, and many kinds of leafy greens. Sago, pandanas, breadfruit, and several types of fruit trees are also cultivated. Long yams (*Dioscorea alata*) are grown in small quantities, mostly for ceremonial purposes. But the cult of the long yam, so striking among the nearby Arapesh and Abelam, in which prize specimens often exceeding six feet in length are decorated to resemble humans and displayed, is attenuated among the Kwanga. Indeed, several people told me that their own fathers had learned the techniques and magic necessary to grow long yams from the Bumbita Arapesh. Kwanga men are more concerned with their short yam harvest, which was traditionally displayed in large bins.

New gardens are cut from the bush each year from September to December, and often people have not yet finished cutting and burning their new garden plots when the rainy season begins; this leads to further delays in planting and usually to a poor harvest. New garden plots are planted once. At the first harvest some people leave a few yams in the ground and reap a very meager second crop of yams from the plot the next year. They also harvest sugar cane and bananas in the second year before the plot is allowed to revert to bush.

People work most often in family groups but also sometimes exchange labor with other families. Men are responsible for cutting down large trees and the high branches of smaller trees which are left standing to support the luxuriant yam vines. Women cut and burn the underbrush and excavate tree roots near the surface. Once the ground is prepared, men plant the varieties of yams that must be buried underground, whereas women take charge of the less prestigious kinds that are planted in mounds of ashes and litter above the surface. They also plant bananas, taro, and greens.

When the yams start growing the men cut forest vines and train the young yam vines to climb these ropes to the supporting trees; the work of weeding falls to the women. Well-established gardens require relatively little work and people spend time building new houses or processing sago to eat during the lean season before the yam harvest. The final harvest is again shared work. Men dig the tubers from the ground, and women scrape the dirt away and carry the yams, often for several miles, to the village.

The typical fallow period is long, about twenty years, and the grasslands that have taken over so many areas of the East Sepik Province, due to overcultivation, have made little headway in Kwanga territory. Recently, however, much prime land near the village has been permanently planted in the cash crops, coffee and cocoa, and this may disturb the traditional fallow cycle, since people are reluctant to plant gardens further than an hour's walk from the village.

The Tambaran Cult

Initiation of males into the tambaran cult is widespread in the Sepik area. The Kwanga cult differs only in detail from that described by Tuzin (1980) among the neighboring Ilahita Arapesh. Males are initiated successively into six grades, ideally starting in late childhood and finishing in their late prime.[3] As an individual progresses through the various initiation grades he gains knowledge of, and the rights to use, hunting and yam growing magic, oratorical techniques, and secret myths. Initiation also brings the knowledge that many of the things told to women and children about cult activities are lies. Thus, for instance, the initiates find that what they formerly believed were the "voices" of cult spirits are really flutes, bullroarers, and trumpets played by men.

The tambaran cult is underpinned by a complex set of social relations that, again, closely resemble those described by Tuzin (1976) for the Ilahita Arapesh.[4] Villages are divided into crosscutting moieties and initiation classes.[5] Initiation classes initiate each other's sons into the tambaran cult. Localized moieties compete in associated food exchanges. Each adult man inherits two exchange partners, one in the opposite moiety and the other in the opposite initiation class.

Initiations have been sporadic for the last thirty years and the last initiation was performed in Inakor in 1978.[6] Revelation of cult secrets in a Christian revival movement and general disinterest have severely undermined the cult and many believe it will never be performed again.

Recent History

Inakor and Asanakor probably had their first direct experience with white people when an Australian patrol visited their villages in 1929 (B. Allen 1976: 66) but European implements such as steel tools and rifles had preceded their owners.[7] The Australians banned all warfare and fighting in the 1920s, and they also appointed village headmen (known in Neo-Melanesian as "luluai" and "tultul"). The Australian colonial adminstration started making sporadic patrols to the villages at this time to take censuses and to make sure that villagers were maintaining footpaths and following hygenic practices like digging and using toilets (B. Allen 1976: 67–68).

Labor recruiters also came seeking young men to work on plantations. The first group of men to leave the village are now in their midsixties. They contracted for periods of two to three years to work in Morobe gold mines and then returned to the village. In subsequent years, "going to the station," (as the local people refer to plantation labor) became a tradition. Some men stayed away from the village for many years, and most returned to the plantations two or three times. A few emigrated permanently, but most returned to the village eventually.

After cash crops were introduced there were ways to earn money locally, and plantation labor became less attractive. So although plantation labor experience is virtually universal for men over thirty, many of the younger men have never undergone this rite of passage.

The most dramatic exposure to the outside world came with World War II. A few men who were working on plantations when the war broke out were employed by the Japanese army. But the majority of the villagers had their first experience with the war when Japanese soldiers entered inland areas of the Sepik region in 1944 (B. Allen 1976: 86). They arrived in Inakor in the middle of a tambaran initiation. The villagers fled to bush settlements where they lived until the Japanese left. The Japanese established an administration that had one of its bases in Asanakor (B. Allen 1976: 89). Several young men were equipped with grenades and rifles by the Australians—and now love to boast of their exploits in fighting the Japanese. A few people died in the course of the struggles, one killed by gunfire from an Australian fighter plane. The Japanese took two women with them when they left but these women later managed to return home relatively unharmed.

Missionization, Schools, and the "Revival"

By the time I arrived in the field in 1984, the majority of Inakor and Asanakor residents had been baptized. Many had lapsed back into "heathenism." The eastern Kwanga region has been influenced chiefly by the South Sea Evangelical Church (SSEC), a Protestant mission. The SSEC (then the South Sea Evangelical Mission) received permission to expand activities to the Sepik in 1948 and by 1951 had opened a station in Ilahita, about six miles to the northeast of Inakor. An airstrip and mission center were established in Brugam (about a two hour walk to the west of Inakor) in 1958 and, in the same year, another station was opened in Yubanakor, an eastern Kwanga village three or four miles south of Asanakor. Inakor and Asanakor villagers attended a weekly "afternoon school," and, as a result, many of the men and women between thirty and forty-five are at least partly literate in Neo-Melanesian. In 1973, the Yubanakor Community School opened, and the children of the eastern Kwanga villages Inakor, Asanakor, Yubanakor, and Apangai now receive six years of primary schooling there. A handful of people, the oldest of whom are now in their late twenties, did well enough on the nationwide competitive examination that all Grade Six students write, to go on to high school. Two of the high school graduates are now schoolteachers in the Highlands of Papua New Guinea, and two have become policemen. But more recent graduates have found few employment opportunities and have returned to the village to live much as their parents do.

In the early years of the afternoon school, a few promising young men including the current village magistrate, Ronald; the Asanakor pastor, George; and Sam, the head of the Asanakor business group, were taken to the nearby mission base at Brugam for Bible study courses of varying lengths. These men were then told to return to the village and "spread the good news" in weekly church services. Some people were baptized in these early years. More conversions and baptisms occurred in the late 1970s and in the 1980s in waves associated with "revivals." Revivals are periods of intense Christian activity; people attend church services twice daily. In all-night hymn singing and prayer meetings, people (usually women) fall to the ground in faints and wake sobbing and moaning (they sometimes continue for days) and claiming that they have been possessed by the Holy Spirit. These "prophet women/men" have visions and dreams that often reveal such "sins" of their neighbors as possession of hunting and gardening magic, tambaran-related objects, and sorcery implements. Revivals are also often associated with a millenarian ideology. People believe that Christ's return is imminent and that He will bring to the New Guineans the material wealth of the white men. Peaks of revival activities bring great increases in church attendance and mass baptisms, but generally within a few months the new converts stop going to church leaving a small core of committed Christians, consisting mostly of elderly and middle-aged women and a few men.

I witnessed the tail end of one wave of the revival that reached its peak in late 1984, in which tambaran secrets were revealed to women and children. In Inakor and Asanakor this revelation was, according to several informants, more symbolic than real since the two pastors merely alluded to the secrets without "explaining." Nevertheless, it had a profound impact and many non-Christians claimed that the Christians had no right to act this way without unanimous support. Many felt that the revelation of secrets was too early and that the Papua New Guineans should not give up the "power" of their ancestors (in the form of healing rites and magic insuring good harvests and successful hunts) until they had learned the ways, and achieved the power, of the white men.

The 1984 wave of the revival ended in Inakor when Hilanda, an elderly and prominent Christian, berated the young people in church for always singing the new hymns, which he had been unable to master, instead of the old familiar ones. After this incident most of the younger people, who had joined the church with the revival, stopped attending services. Spirit possessions and nightly church services came to an end.

In February 1985 the revival returned to Inakor. Suroho, an elderly man and a leader of the Christian community, allegedly discovered that a rival had asked the local sorcerer, Hapandi, to kill him and his children. Hapandi, a classificatory brother, refused the money and warned Suroho who asked a "revival team" from a nearby Urat village, Emul, to come and bring the Holy Spirit back to Inakor and rid the community of sorcery. "Revival teams" of enthusiastic Christians, a few of whom have been possessed by the Holy Spirit, are asked to visit other villages, usually to divine the location of traditional magical items, particularly sorcery spears. During their two days in Inakor, the Emul team managed to convert Hapandi who confessed his sins (in highly abbreviated form) in a large public meeting and declared himself a new man. Mary, the wife of a prominent Inakor man, Bwalaka, was possessed by the Holy Spirit at the same meeting. Up to this time, most of those possessed (known locally as "propet meri," which translates as "prophet women"), had been adolescent girls who had little influence. Mary caused a great commotion during the following three months, regularly reporting that she had divined the presence of traditional magical items and demanding that the owners destroy them. But after a number of her divinations were proven false, many of the non-Christian villagers grew skeptical of her claims and recent converts, once again, began to fall away from the church. Although spirit possessions continued through the duration of my fieldwork, church attendance and general enthusiasm about the church never again achieved the levels of late 1984 and early 1985.

Local Government

In 1966, the Dreikikir Local Government Council replaced the old system of indirect rule through village headmen. This was a move toward representative democracy, which was a prelude to Papua New Guinean independence. Each village (or sometimes a number of small villages together) elects one representative, the Councillor, to attend monthly meetings of the local government Council. Inakor and Asanakor jointly elect one man to sit on the Dreikikir Council.

Councillors are responsible for conveying information on new laws and programs to their villages and also vote on the disbursement of funds allocated to that Council area for building aid posts and schools and for maintaining roads. They also assign government labor on Mondays in community meetings. In the past they also held mediation sessions to resolve disputes within the village and still are encouraged to deal with land disputes.

The introduction of the village court system followed shortly after national independence in 1975. Several villages comprise a court area with four magistrates who (theoretically) meet once every two weeks to hear cases. Inakor and Asanakor, along with the Kwanga villages of Yubanakor, Apangai, and Apos, form the Kwanga Two court area. The court has four magistrates, one each from Yubanakor, Apangai, Apos and Inakor, two "peace officers" (one from Asanakor and one from Apos); and a court clerk from Asanakor. Ronald, the Inakor magistrate, is the chairman of the Kwanga Two court area.

Villagers report grievances to their local court official. Magistrates can, and usually do, deal with cases in informal mediation sessions, where participants try to find a solution they can all agree on. If this fails, the matter is referred to full or "inside" court where it is heard by a panel of three magistrates.[8] Court fines (paid to the court) of up to fifty kina can be set as well as compensation payments (paid to the plaintiff) of up to three hundred kina. People who fail to pay fines can be sent to jail or forced to perform community service such as cutting the grass along roads or digging community toilets. Villagers can appeal their case to a higher level court in Maprik or Dreikikir. People often threaten to do this but seldom do because of difficulties in finding transportation and because Maprik and Dreikikir judges often refuse to hear village cases that they consider to be trivial.

"Business": Cash Cropping, Coffee Buying Cooperatives, and Trade Stores

The first cash crop, dry rice, was introduced into the Sepik area in the late 1940s (Allen 1976: 190). But villagers complained that rice cultivation required much labor and brought little monetary return.[9] Since there were few roads, women had to carry the rice on their backs to Maprik, a distance of some thirty miles.

The extension of an all-weather road, the Sepik Highway, to Dreiki-kir in 1970 greatly improved the situation. Villages located off the highway cooperated to build, manually, rough dirt roads to the highway, and government bulldozers later improved these roads. Inakor and Asanakor are approximately nine miles from the Sepik Highway and the branch road is passable in dry weather, though even then a team of men is usually needed to push a truck out of the inevitable mud holes.

Coffee was introduced in the Sepik area in the early 1950s and had reached the Maprik and Dreikikir districts by the early 1960s (Allen 1976: 208–210) where it quickly supplanted rice as the main cash crop. Unfortunately climatic and soil conditions in the area are unsuitable for arabica coffee so villagers grow the less valuable robustus variety. Most villagers have, or have access to, a coffee garden.[10] The average yearly income from coffee sales is about 145 kina per family, with some villagers making as little as 20 kina and the most successful coffee grower realizing almost 500 kina. Many villagers have recently planted cocoa gardens believing the monetary returns to be greater, whereas the labor is much less, but few of these gardens had reached maturity in 1986.

Coffee can be sold directly to buyers near Maprik but most villagers do not do this since transporting beans is expensive and time consuming. Most coffee is sold through the village representatives of the two coffee buyers, the SPCA (Sepik Producers Cooperative Association) and the Lus Development Corporation. The SPCA representative in the village runs a small business group formed with his own money and donations from his close kinsmen. He buys coffee from villagers and then transports it to the SPCA headquarters near Maprik where he sells it for a slight profit. The return is not great since transportation costs are high but what little profit there is is used to run, sporadically, a small trade store that sells tinned mackerel and rice, newspapers for rolling cigarettes, and occasionally such luxury items as soap, razor blades, flour, and sugar. The trade store also realizes little profit because of transportation costs and because of the tendency of villagers to buy on credit and never pay their debts. The other trade store in the village, run by one man, Hilanda, is similarly unsuccessful, and both stores are only occasionally stocked.

Most coffee is sold through Lus. The Lus Development Corporation was established with an eye toward promoting grassroots development. Buying contracts are given to community groups instead of individuals or families and the profits are supposed to be used for projects that benefit the community such as trade stores and trucks. The Corporation provides loans for such ventures. In Inakor and Asanakor (each of which has its own group), individual families bought memberships in the Lus Corporation[11] and also contributed capital to start the village group. In the early years, when coffee prices were unusually high, the Inakor group had some success, and coffee profits, as well as contributions from the villagers, were used to buy a Toyota pickup truck that was to be hired out for profit. But due to bad drivers and bad roads, it broke down frequently, and repair costs were a constant drain on resources. This soon proved to be the undoing of the five-man board of the group who were accused (perhaps with some justice) of stealing communal funds and were replaced. The new board, however, met a similar fate and, by the time I left the village, the village truck was broken down, the business group was flat broke, and people were talking of disbanding it and forming separate family groups.

Meetings

Meetings such as the one described in chapter 1, organized by the village Councillor, were introduced along with the local government council system. But there is a tradition of holding meetings among the Kwanga. Tambaran initiations required the cooperation of everyone in the village, and also of surrounding villages, so numerous meetings were held to plan them. In addition, Scaglion (1983a: 260), working on dispute settlement and courts among the neighboring Abelam people, says informal meetings led by big-men were one of three major traditional ways of dealing with disputes.

The number of meetings has probably increased in number in recent years due to suppression of other means of dealing with problems. Traditionally, conflict often resulted in competitive food exchanges (within a village), warfare and raiding (between villages), and tambaran initiations (also within the village) (see also Scaglion 1976, 1983a: 260). But now people are reluctant to perform initiations or become involved in competitive food exchanges since both are expensive in time and resources and many people are more interested in devoting their energies to development and cash cropping. Meetings are an alternative way of dealing peaceably with problematic situations.

CHAPTER THREE

Gossip, Innuendo, and Sorcery: Power without Responsibility

The Kwanga believe that almost all deaths are due to sorcery and they spend a great deal of time speculating about the activities of sorcerers. They hold long public inquests after most deaths (the exceptions being those of young children) to find the cause, and these meetings are just the most public moment in a great deal of discussion that starts before the inquest is convened and continues long after it has ended. Generally people continue to speculate about the cause for years after someone dies, and they almost always come up with many theories about the death which were not considered in the inquests.

In this chapter I will argue that although such discussion seems to accomplish very little—people seldom come to any agreement about the identity of the murderer and almost never achieve their stated objective of punishing him—it is through spreading rumors and dropping hints about sorcery that initiated men maintain their authority over their fellow villagers.

Furthermore, talking about sorcery allows people to influence events in ways for which they cannot be held accountable. Speakers show themselves to be wise, knowledgeable, and powerful when they hint that they have inside information about the cause of a death; they can also damage their rivals' reputations by implying that they might have been involved in the murder. But by leaving their remarks ambiguous, speakers make sure that, if challenged, they can always say that their words have been misinterpreted, and, in this way, they avoid dealing with angry suspects and their families. Thus, hinting in public and spreading rumors in more private contexts is an ideal way of influencing others in a relatively egalitarian community where forceful actions provoke resentment and resistance.

Sorcery Talk

Inakor and Asanakor deaths are almost invariably attributed to assault sorcery (Neo-Melanesian: *sangguma*; Kwanga: *wasi*). It is theoretically possible to die a natural death. But it is felt that only very old people or very young babies could die from illness, and accidents are almost always considered disguised sorcery. When a girl died after falling from a tree, for example, people quickly concluded that she had been "shot" by a sorcerer the day before and instructed to fall out of a tree to make the death look natural.

Another possible cause of death is parcel sorcery (Neo-Melanesian: *poisin*; Kwanga: *sawa*), but the only death I heard of that was attributed to this was of a baby. Someone, usually an initiate of a high tambaran grade, takes a leaving such as a scrap from some food the victim has eaten and ties it in a parcel with some magical items. The parcel is carefully hidden and may be suspended above a fire. Unless found and destroyed, it will kill the victim. The "poison" theory that will be described below in the Naifuku and Ambusuroho case was atypical because it involved actual poison rather than parcel sorcery. I heard of no other deaths that were explained this way and it was probably because the death of two brothers on the same night was considered so odd that people looked for an unusual cause.

Knowledge of sorcery techniques is restricted to a few men who have been selected by the village to undergo training as curers and assassins. The whole village pays for the training. Inakor and Asanakor hired some Bumbita Arapesh and Urat sorcerers to teach some men sorcery so they could attack enemy villages and could prevent similar counterattacks. Sorcerers are also believed to preserve law and order within the village by punishing disorderly conduct and violations of male cult rules. But people think that sorcerers sometimes kill maliciously or for money so the legitimacy of a murder is always open to question.

Since sorcerers may either act of their own volition or be hired, inquests attempt to identify both sorcerer and employer. The first meeting is on the day following the burial and involves the village of the dead person, the neighboring village,[1] and also kin from other places. The guests are given soup, yams, and coconuts in appreciation for their help and to give them "strength" for the discussion. But in accordance with general notions of reciprocity which emphasize exchange of equivalents, this food is also viewed as a debt that will be returned at future funerals. The next day brings an intravillage discussion. Moieties attend each other's inquests and exchange food much as neighboring villages do.

Meetings after the deaths of young children usually draw only close kin. The deaths of adults, however, particularly in their prime, result in numerous meetings attended by people from many villages, though occasionally, as when the dead person had a long-standing fight with a sorcerer, the cause of the death is considered obvious from the start, and meetings are brief and poorly attended. Generally, various theories are discussed in the first two meetings, and further meetings—often involving suspects from other villages—may be scheduled to investigate them.

First, participants determine who had a motive for murder by examining the quarrels that involved the dead person or members of his family. Possible violations of tambaran laws are also discussed. Suspects are asked to touch the leg of the corpse in the belief that the body will give some "sign" (such as urination, defecation, twitching of limbs, opening or closing of eyes) in the presence of the murderer. But the results are not conclusive since sorcerers can cast spells to prevent their victims from identifying them and may argue that signs from the corpse are actually a response to a bystander. For instance, when a woman died, people from a neighboring village were asked to perform this divination and later when some women washed the body for burial they discovered that she had defecated. For several months this was considered evidence of the guilt of the people from the neighboring village. But later people claimed that the corpse had been responding to one of the women who washed her, the daughter of a local sorcerer, indicating that that sorcerer was the murderer. People also believe that the murderer and his family will avoid going near the corpse to escape identification, and so they watch the movements of suspects closely.

Evidence of the recent activities of sorcerers is considered as well. Sorcerers making their rounds are believed to use whistles to emit a characteristic bird cry. After a death people discuss the recent activities of birds, particularly at night (when everyone agrees that real birds are asleep), and try to trace the direction of these cries to find the home of the assassin. But since it is believed that sorcerers can purposely throw their cries from misleading directions, this is not very conclusive.

Unusual statements made by the victim before dying are also discussed. Before the little girl fell to her death, she told her companions not to look up at her since she was brushing ants off the tree and did not want them to fall into the other children's eyes. Since this prevented the other children from observing the circumstances of her fall, it was considered part of the sorcerer's "cover up." Similarly, people examine remarks that might indicate a motive for murder or foreknowledge of the death. But such statements are, at best, only suggestive.

The evidence that seems to carry the most weight is gossip and rumor. Sorcerers are believed to talk to each other about their activities and also to tell kinsmen, particularly those in other villages who are unlikely to warn the victim. The kin of the victim will seek information from these sources, and this is one of the reasons for inviting people from other villages to the inquests.

Several courses of redress are possible if the murderer is identified. If people think the murder was justified they do nothing. But in other cases the sorcerer and the person who hired him may be taken to court.[2] Alternatively, the villagers can force the person suspected of hiring the sorcerer to give him a prestation of yams, pigs, shell valuables, and money to prevent him from killing others in the same village or family. This payment is usually given to all the sorcerers in the area but the culprit, whose identity is often unknown, will distribute it.[3] For this reason people are not usually allowed to watch the distribution. Other methods of redress are counter-sorcery and murder in ambush.

But usually people conclude that the evidence is not sufficient to justify prosecuting a suspect, and most often new rumors replace the original theories as people continue to speculate about the deaths in the following months and years.

The Deaths of Naifuku and Ambusuroho

About a month after I arrived in Inakor, two brothers from the village of Asanakor, Naifuku and Ambusuroho, died on the same night. They had been sick for less than a week. The deaths shocked the people of Inakor and Asanakor. The two men had been in the prime of life (in their late thirties or early forties), a time when the body is thought to be too strong to be killed by illness or accident. And no one could remember two full brothers dying at the same time. For both these reasons people immediately concluded that not only was foul play involved but the culprit must have been an uncommonly abhorrent character. An unusual number of meetings were held weekly for months, and the case was even taken to court.

I joined a crowd of my Inakor neighbors going down to view the bodies on the morning after the men died. The bodies lay side by side in the central plaza of their hamlet surrounded by mourners. The aged mother of the two men lay on the ground by their bodies keening and Deborah, the pregnant wife of one of the men, sat in her house crying. People examined the bodies looking closely for signs that might indicate the cause of death: "Look at the way his wrists are swollen as if all the bones were broken!" "Look, both wrists are that way!" They also discussed the burial. This is usually done on the day after the death but many people, including the children of one of the men, were away at a revival meeting in another village and many thought that they should be given a chance to see the men one last time before the burial. A messenger was dispatched to summon them.

The bodies lay in the hamlet for a day so that all those who had known the men could see them one last time. The kin and exchange partners of the dead men slept in the hamlet (as is customary) to give support to the bereaved family, and in the morning women washed and clothed the bodies while men dug the graves in the cemetery. The exchange partners of the two men entered the hamlet and pulled the bodies on their bark mats away from the crowd of weeping women. The wives and mother of the dead men, abandoning keening for outright tears, had to be forcibly restrained as the bodies were removed and carried to the graveyard where they were lowered into the waiting graves and covered with banana leaves to protect them from the soil. A crowd of mourners watched, wept, and keened, and Deborah lay on the ground next to her husband's grave. As the first shovelfuls of earth went to cover him she tried to scramble into the grave but was restrained by several kinswomen.[4] After the graves had been filled they were carefully covered by palm fronds bound in place with vines and stakes to prevent sorcerers from exhuming the bodies to obtain the fluids necessary for their potions. People gradually returned to their homes.

The following day I returned to the hamlet of the dead men with my Inakor neighbors. The Asanakor people were also gathering in the hamlet, each man bringing yams and green coconuts for the Inakor

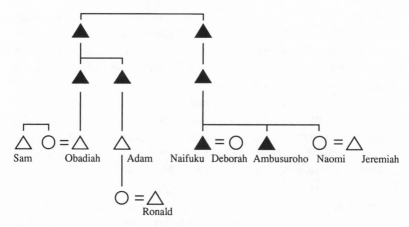

Figure 1: The two brothers and their family

guests. The women of Asanakor had already gone to their gardens in the morning to get yams and greens and were now preparing soup for the visitors. People sat under temporary shelters made of palm fronds, and on the verandas of houses, to escape the sun while they waited for the discussion to begin.

After the food had been presented and distributed, Adam (see fig. 1), a classificatory brother of the dead men, rose and stood in the middle of the plaza. The close agnates of the deceased set the agenda by voicing their suspicions. Adam opened by stating that the two brothers were good and peaceable men and had fought with only two men, Arawapi, a man from the neighboring village of Ta'uanangas, and Jeremiah, their sister's husband. These men had performed the customary divination but there had been no sign of guilt. This, however, did not exonerate them since evidence from divinations is inconclusive, and following Adam's lead, the discussion focused on these two suspects.

Arawapi had a land dispute with the brothers and the history of this fight was discussed at length. Much was made of the fact that Naifuku had allegedly said in his dying breath that he had been "shot by a bamboo from Pilimbi," the land over which he and Arawapi had disputed. Several people also pointed out that lately many birds had been heard flying to Asanakor from Ta'uanangas.

Jeremiah and his wife Naomi had a stormy marriage. Jeremiah was noted for his violent temper, and he frequently beat his wife and accused her of being lazy. He claimed that he had been forced to marry her and had never liked her. Naomi had often run away from Jeremiah and taken refuge with her two brothers, Naifuku and Ambusuroho. Jeremiah alternately accused the brothers of trying to keep Naomi away from her husband and of trying to prevent a divorce. The affair reached village court several times. The consensus among the villagers whom I talked to was that Jeremiah was unreasonably brutal with his wife and that he was wrong in trying to "hook" his two brothers-in-law into his marital squabbles. Naifuku and Ambusuroho, people said, had no desire to interfere in their sister's marriage; it was Jeremiah and Naomi herself who were always trying to involve her brothers. A recent violent eruption in this long-standing conflict between Jeremiah and his brothers-in-law made him a prime suspect in their deaths.

In the meeting, person after person got up and commented on the violent quarrel between Jeremiah and Naifuku and Ambusuroho. The consensus seemed to be that Jeremiah and Arawapi (who were distantly related to each other) had conspired in the murders. In sleuth style, people tried to prove that Jeremiah and Arawapi had met on several occasions, implying that the two had had ample opportunity to hatch their plot. For instance, Adam questioned the two men about a time when Arawapi had visited a kinsman in Asanakor and allegedly sat and talked with Jeremiah. The suspects finally admitted that they did have a conversation on this occasion but denied that they talked about Naifuku and Ambusuroho. Adam commented, "Yesterday I made this point and you guys said no that you did not meet on the occasion in question. Now I ask you again and you say yes, you did talk. This is wrong. What you talked about, I don't know. Now I will ask for witnesses: Who saw them sitting together?"[5]

The implication of Adam's remarks was made explicit by Ronald, who said, "Why did you two meet? Yesterday you said you didn't talk that day. You said he was lying. Now you have changed. We are not happy about this. You are trying to cover something up."

At the end of the day an Inakor man summarized what had been the general theme of the day's discussions, that Arawapi and Jeremiah had conspired to kill the two brothers. Ronald, the village magistrate, followed, saying, "If you want to meet tomorrow, you can. But don't discuss this anymore. Just sit and tell stories of things the two men did when they were alive. This will go to the law now." He was trying to end the discussion of the deaths, by claiming that Jeremiah and Arawapi were guilty and would be taken to court. And his words were supported by others who spoke of the hazards of endless discussion and recommended that Ronald take immediate action.

Despite these closing words and the apparent consensus displayed at the first discussion, new theories about the deaths proliferated in the following weeks and were investigated in weekly meetings. Many people suspected Richard, a sorcerer from a nearby village, and his fellow villagers were invited to several meetings to discuss these theories. Later, people remembered that Naifuku had worked on a plantation with an Inakor man who had been killed in an accident and the Asanakor people suggested that Naifuku might have been implicated in the death and perhaps had been killed by counter-sorcery. George, the Asanakor pastor, felt that Inakor people angered by his public revelation of tambaran secrets might be involved, and there was also a rumor that some Inakor men had recently undergone secret sorcery training. Most of these theories were quickly rejected. They also rejected the theories concerning Arawapi.

The criteria for evaluating theories were a little mysterious. When I asked Andrew, an Asanakor court official, why Arawapi was cleared of suspicion, he replied that this was because the charges against Arawpi were untrue. When pressed, Andrew suggested that when that theory had been discussed people had felt that sorcery was probably not the cause of death since a sorcerer would be unwilling, and perhaps unable, to kill two men in their prime at the same time. This made poison[6] a more probable cause of death, and Arawapi had been suspected of practicing sorcery. Furthermore, only a local person who had to deal with people on a daily basis would find it necessary to kill both brothers, realizing that if one died the other would remain to continue the quarrel. Someone from another village would kill only one of them. On logical grounds this makes little sense as Arawapi could just as easily have conspired with Jeremiah to poison the two brothers as to ensorcel them, and he also had reason to kill both brothers since if only one died the other would surely continue to fight with Arawapi over land.

In February of 1985, months after the deaths, there was an informal court hearing to look into rumors that it was not Jeremiah who had killed the two brothers, but Adam. He had allegedly hired a sorcerer from the neighboring Bumbita Arapesh language group to kill the two men over a land dispute. These theories were said to have originated with Richard, who had privately told some Inakor men that he had seen Adam give two hundred kina to a Bumbita Arapesh sorcerer. This was not the only rumor started by Richard who had also made the wonderfully ambiguous statement that the two brothers had "fallen in Subumu," a hamlet of Asanakor. People told me that they thought this implicated Richard's wife's father, Ezra, who lived in Subumu. Another popular rumor was that an Asanakor man, Brian, had seen a group of sorcerers from Ta'uanangas (also a Bumbita Arapesh village) while he was hunting in the bush and had called out to them to come. People thought that he must have hired the sorcerers since otherwise he would have avoided them.

Bumbita Arapesh magistrates were invited to participate in the court hearing because Bumbita Arapesh sorcerers had been implicated in the murder. The Kwanga were trying to solicit information from the Bumbita officials and also would have needed their cooperation if they had decided to prosecute Bumbita people. With the aid of Ronald, the Inakor magistrate who was also married to Adam's daughter, the Bumbita magistrates quickly rejected the new theories as foundationless rumor and reasserted that Jeremiah must have killed the two brothers. Brian said that he had not called to the Ta'uanangas sorcerers; they had called to him. Even if he did want to hire a sorcerer he would not have done it then as this would have endangered his young son, who was with him. Jeremiah said Brian was lying and had previously confessed to having called the sorcerers. But when the magistrates asked for witnesses to this statement none came forward, and Brian said that he had warned Jeremiah not to spread rumors as this would only be seen as an attempt to conceal his own guilt and would make people more suspicious.

Ronald said several times that Jeremiah had made up all the new theories in order to cover up his own guilt. The rumors about Adam were eventually traced to Richard, but Ronald said he had been present when Richard made the allegation and had told the others not to bring these rumors back to the village because everyone knew Richard was a liar. Ronald said that it must have been Jeremiah who had spread this talk to distract people's attention from his own role in the murders.

The discussion then turned to a theory that Jeremiah had put poison in the lime tin of his brothers-in-law. Several people said that no sorcerer was strong enough to kill two men in their prime at the same time; this was not the "law" of sorcery. But poison in something like the lime that both brothers consumed could easily have this effect. Men often share lime, which is chewed with betel nut, and so people thought it probable that the two brothers had both consumed poison meant for one of them. They focused on times when Jeremiah could have acquired the poison to kill his brothers-in-law and slipped it into their lime tin. Naomi told of an incident when her two brothers had asked Jeremiah to help them harvest their yams and he had first refused and then changed his mind after going into his house to get something. People speculated that he had reconsidered when he realized that this would be a good time to poison the men and had gone into his house to get the poison. There was also a great deal of discussion of a time when, enraged by a fight with Naomi, Jeremiah had broken his radio, cut his seedling coconut palms, and left the village claiming he was going to go to work on a plantation in another part of the country. But he got only as far as the provincial capital, Wewak, and then returned home. Again, people suggested that he had changed his plans because he had hatched the plot in Wewak to kill his brothers-in-law and had acquired the poison there. When Jeremiah tried to protest, saying that there was no better evidence against him than against the Bumbita sorcerer, Brian, or Adam, he was summarily silenced by Ronald and the Bumbita magistrates who said there was never any good evidence in such cases since people always worked secretly to avoid suspicion.

No one supported Jeremiah. And when the magistrates asked about other suspects the only response was from Ezra, an old man from Asanakor, who made some mysterious remarks about a time when Naifuku had found a pig snared in a trap at Pilimbi. When he turned to ask his son for the gun, the pig escaped. Ezra did not explain the significance of this incident, and the discussion turned to other matters. Finally, the Bumbita magistrates, impatient with the long and confusing stories, asked if anyone wanted to charge Jeremiah with the crime, and Naifuku's eldest sons, both young married men, stepped forward.

A few months later, Jeremiah was officially convicted in the village court and told to pay two pigs and 800 kina compensation to the widows of the two men (a huge amount in an area where the average annual income from coffee sales is about 145 kina).

No sooner was this decision made than new rumors began to circulate in Asanakor. Gossips claimed that Adam and his son-in-law, Ronald, had conspired with Obadiah, an Asanakor sorcerer, to kill Naifuku and Ambusuroho. I later found out that the new rumors had started with an Asanakor man, Sam. He told me that he had seen Obadiah making a fire to cook a yam even though his wife was already cooking food at another fire. Sam concluded that Obadiah was avoiding contact with women in order to build the necessary magical "heat" to practice sorcery. Sam also said that he had helped Obadiah make a particularly powerful sorcery implement several years before. Since that time, Obadiah had publicly declared himself a Christian and had revealed and destroyed many sorcery implements to prove that he had given up his evil ways. But Sam had noticed that Obadiah had never destroyed the implement he and Sam had made together, and so Sam told me that he did not believe Obadiah had really given up sorcery.

Obadiah, however, was Sam's sister's husband and so Sam said that he had kept quiet except that he told the two Asanakor court officials, Andrew and Bruce, what he had seen. According to Sam, when Naifuku and Ambusuroho died some weeks later, the three men quickly concluded that Obadiah must have been responsible. But they continued to hide what they knew, and Sam even made an impassioned speech at an early funeral meeting accusing Jeremiah of the crime. Sam told me that later, however, Bruce told his classificatory father, Ezra, what he knew; Ezra, in turn, spread the rumor of Obadiah's involvement to the rest of the community and, as the new rumors spread, Adam and Ronald were also implicated. People told me that they were particularly suspicious of Ronald given the active role he had taken in attempting to stop discussion and have Jeremiah convicted of the crime; people suspected that Ronald was trying to blame Jeremiah to cover up his own guilt.

When Ronald heard of the new rumors, he quickly reassembled the magistrates for a hearing. He said the new rumors would not be investigated in their own right; instead, the person who was the source of the rumor must be found and charged with illegally gossiping about a case already resolved in court. Ronald accused Jeremiah of starting the rumors and the Bumbita magistrates supported Ronald in his attempts to fine Jeremiah. It was late in the day, however, and they decided to reconvene in the morning.

The next morning the tone of the hearing had changed. It was clear that some Asanakor men had talked to the Bumbita magistrates during the night and had persuaded them to investigate the rumors. (Sam later confirmed that this had occurred.) Ronald was told to step down as magistrate since he was implicated. Sam opened the discussion with a long account of the various signs that indicated that an Asanakor sorcerer had been involved. Interestingly, one of these signs was a new interpretation of Naifuku's dying words about Pilimbi. Originally thought to refer to Arawapi, people now thought these words pointed to another incident that had occurred at the same place, Pilimbi, and had, in fact, been mentioned by Ezra at the first meeting with the Bumbita magistrates. A pig snared in a trap at Pilimbi had escaped when Naifuku turned to ask his son for the gun to shoot it. Since everyone agreed that pigs cannot escape from snares, this meant that it had really been a sorcerer lying in wait. Furthermore, since he had understood when Naifuku spoke in Kwanga (rather than Neo-Melanesian), the sorcerer must have been a local man, and people strongly suspected Obadiah. Sam did not mention the incident of the separate cooking fire which had originally led him to conclude that Obadiah was guilty, nor did he directly accuse Obadiah, but rather argued that it was "an Asanakor sorcerer"[7] who had killed the two brothers.

After hours of discussion, the magistrates asked Deborah to come forward and tell them who she thought had killed Naifuku and Ambusuroho. She said that she felt that Obadiah, Adam, and Jeremiah, should all be accused. The magistrates rejected the charge against Adam, saying that there was no real proof, but said that Jeremiah and Obadiah should pay compensation to the widows. Since, however, there were no witnesses to the alleged killing, the magistrates continued, no one could really know who did it, so the whole community should aid Obadiah and Jeremiah in paying the compensation.

The last discussion occurred in July 1985. When I left the field in October 1986, no compensation had been paid to the widows. Indeed, Deborah had been forced to leave Naifuku's hamlet to live with her brothers because Naifuku's patrilineage was angry with her for having accused two of their number, Adam and Obadiah.

Some months later I interviewed Andrew, an Asanakor court official. I asked if any action would be taken against Jeremiah and Obadiah. He replied that he was uncertain what should be done as he felt that higher courts would not support the village court decision since the hearing had not been properly conducted. There was, therefore, nothing the village court could do to force Obadiah and Jeremiah to pay their fines. Moreover, Andrew was doubtful whether the charges against Obadiah and Jeremiah were justified. He said, "Yes, me too, I think about this a lot. We men of the earth can't know the truth. Only God knows. Yes, I too think that this charge wasn't right. We didn't actually see them do anything."[8] But he went on to say that perhaps the charge against Jeremiah was justified just because of his fight with his brothers-in-law:

Jeremiah carried the blame because he fought with his two brothers-in-law for a long time. So when he wanted to [defend himself in court] the magistrates shut him up and said he was a troublemaker. You fought like that and they died so you can carry the blame. . . . That's the way of the village: they look at the fights the dead person had and they accuse the person who fought with him. Sometimes it's true and sometimes it isn't. They just carry the blame because of the fight. If I don't fight with you then when you die I won't carry the blame.

In other words, troublemakers deserve to be accused of sorcery.

I interviewed Jeremiah some months after the final court hearing. He was firmly convinced that he had been framed by the murderer. Jeremiah claimed that the murderer had waited to kill the two brothers until their fight with Jeremiah had reached a peak of violence so everyone would suspect him. He even thought that the murderer had prevented the two brothers from settling their differences with Jeremiah so that this fight would divert attention from the real motive:

Now I am going to tell you [the truth]. The enemy was there before. He wanted to kill [Naifuku and Ambusuroho] so they wouldn't go to court in Maprik when I brought the summons paper [to court to divorce Naomi].[9] They knew. They knew this. But me, I didn't know about this attack they were going to make so I thought that we were just fighting. They were thinking of this and they kept us here. Before in our law, our custom, we did it like that. It doesn't matter if it has been one month or two months since I fought with you. You don't know first and later I will kill you. This is our law in Papua New Guinea. This plan they made before and it was there. [Members of Naifuku and Ambusuroho's patrilineage] didn't want us to go to court and settle our differences so we would live peacefully afterwards. No, they knew, this fight of theirs was from a long time ago and they wanted to kill Naifuku and Ambusuroho. . . . So all these court orders I kept bringing, they said: "Forget it; we aren't going to obey this court order. Throw it away." Because, they had made this plan a long time ago to kill these two men. This is our law from before. . . . They thought: "We are going to put the blame on him now."

In Jeremiah's view he was the victim of a long-standing conspiracy. The clever killer will wait until everyone has forgotten about his fight with the victim and will encourage the victim's disputes with others to conceal the murderer's role in the murder when he eventually strikes. I asked Jeremiah about those who had accused him in the early funeral discussions and he replied, "They were trying to find out. When they are trying to find out what happened then they speak forcefully like that." I then asked him if he thought his accusers had believed their charges, and he answered:

Some of them believed it. The children will think that it is true but all the really big-men will say we are just guessing. . . . It's like this, they have heard with their ears but they haven't really seen this man killing this other man. They don't really know so they will speak angrily and they will watch you. If it's true then you will tremble. If it's not true then you will just sit there and you won't tremble. They are evaluating you: the big-men and the law men will evaluate your thoughts. They will watch your body and your talk. If they accuse you and accuse you and you hold firm then they will say: "What is this man here?" They will accuse you and accuse you and say: "If he really did it he will shake." If they accuse you and accuse you and you don't shake, they will say: "I guess not," and then they will talk calmly [Neo-Melanesian: *tok isi*].

I then asked Jeremiah whether he thought that the Bumbita court officials who had accused him of murdering his brothers-in-law had really thought he was guilty. He answered:

Like I said before, they knew who did it. They were clear. . . . In the beginning, all the big-men know. Because some man has told them somewhere. For instance, if Richard [a local sorcerer] came and killed me, later he would tell you. They do it like that and they know but then when the meeting comes up they won't tell. They will just lie. They will know but they will accuse some other man. This time they accused me; they were tricking everyone but the real thing was there. If you hear who killed my child you won't come and tell me at first. If you do that a spear will go through you. They will wait till the talk is old. . . . They will accuse lots of men so the discussions will have to go on and on. Then after a few years the truth will come out. So you saw how all these different points came up in the funeral discussions. Not you: it is us black skins who do it this way. We are different.

Jeremiah claimed that murderers leaked information about their crime but people hid what they knew in public meetings and waited until a few years later to hint about their information in private conversations. Jeremiah was not alone in his views about public speech. In fact, when I interviewed Sam he admitted that he had accused Jeremiah in an inquest but had really suspected Obadiah all along:

I never believed Jeremiah did it. I yelled at him because it was his fault. He had a big fight with his brothers-in-law and Obadiah killed them under the cover of that. If he had been a good brother-in-law and they had died we would have found out right away who their enemy was. Obadiah saw the fight and thought: "All right. I'll do it now and they will all think Jeremiah did it." But I saw him so I knew it wasn't true. He was just hiding under the other fight.

In other words, Obadiah made use of Jeremiah's fight with the two brothers to kill them without being suspected.

I also asked Sam why he, Andrew, and Bruce had hidden what they knew about Obadiah in the first inquests. He replied:

We felt that it was none of our business. It was the business of Naifuku and Ambusuroho's patrilineage. It wasn't our own family who had died. Andrew said: "It's not my family, my child, who died that I will start the talk." Me too, the same. Obadiah is my sister's husband. If it was my wife or my child [who had died] then I would have taken him to court. But it was them so I said it was their problem. We didn't want to start the talk. Like I said before, it was something for them to worry about. If we had some of the poison he used or the spear [i.e., some conclusive evidence] then we would have taken him to court. The law wouldn't convict someone on just the evidence we had so we didn't say anything. . . . We left it like that . . . but then Bruce went and told Ezra and Ezra told all his children and a lot of people. So there was a lot of gossip around. . . . So Ronald called the Bumbita magistrates down. We talked to the Bumbita at night and told them what we had seen and they know all about the ways of sorcery so they felt that it was true so the decision was changed.

Later he continued:

Our law is like this. If a sorcerer kills my wife or my child or if I die, my wife will start the talk or I will open the talk: "This is who came and killed my family." I can't help other families with their talk. It's their business. If I did that it would come back on me. The death might come back on me. If I talked the death would come back on me. This sorcerer will come and kill me. I have exposed his sin. He will be ashamed and will come back and kill me.

Murder and Conspiracy

After the two brothers died, many meetings were held but little was apparently accomplished. Many suspects were questioned; court hearings were held, and, after months of debate, two men were charged. But when they did not pay their fines nothing was done.

The difficulties that plagued the affair seemed to stem from the fact that it was hard to find the truth. Evidence from divination was ambiguous and could be interpreted in various ways as were other signs such as the bird calls from Ta'uanangas and Naifuku's dying words about Pilimbi. Compounding these problems were suspicions that people were engaged in elaborate cover-up schemes. Jeremiah and Sam both said that the murderer had made use of Jeremiah's quarrel with the two brothers to kill them and escape suspicion. Others agreed that assassins behave this way, and one man even suggested that a sorcerer will wait until the victim has had fights with so many people that it will be impossible to determine which of them is the murderer. This compounds the intrinsic ambiguity of the evidence since anything that seems to point to one person's guilt could easily be part of someone else's cover-up.

Jeremiah also suspected that people were lying, hiding what they knew, and making false accusations in public meetings, and his suspicions were widely shared. People told me that directly after a death the murderer will tell others of his deed. But they will not reveal what they know in public discussions, and, instead, will make accusations they know to be false in order to conceal the truth for fear of retaliation from the sorcerer or from the family of the victim.[10] Others will be genuinely ignorant and will make strong accusations in order to test the reaction of the suspect. The guilty person will "shake" or reply angrily whereas the innocent one will present a calm, reasoned defense. Since people may be using any of these several strategies, speeches in inquests cannot be taken at face value, and the ordinary person will be more confused than enlightened by them. At the same time, sorcerers brag about their deeds in conversations with kin and friends—particularly with those from other villages who will be unlikely to tell what they know to the victim's family—and those who hear such tales keep quiet for a little while but then begin to drop hints and spread rumors that reveal their suspicions. In this way, the "truth" of the matter eventually leaks out to the whole community.

Furthermore, the local view seemed to be an accurate description of at least one of the main actors in the case, Sam, who accused Jeremiah in a meeting but also started a rumor about Obadiah which eventually led to the latter's conviction.

The Benefits of Ambiguity

The Inakor and Asanakor people say that individuals hide their knowledge in public and spread rumors about what they know, and the events that followed on Naifuku and Ambusuroho's deaths suggest that there is a lot of truth to the local ideas about people's behavior.

The case also sheds light on why people might hint and spread rumors but avoid prosecuting suspects. Spreading rumors seems to have been quite an effective strategy in this case. It allowed people to mobilize the community without having to face reprisals. Sam, for instance, avoided openly accusing Obadiah and instead made veiled allusions to the possible complicity of "an Asanakor sorcerer" in the final court hearing and disseminated his most damning evidence (the incident of Obadiah cooking his own yam) through gossip networks. In this way, he was able to preserve a proper "face" of goodwill toward

his sister's husband, Obadiah, and, at the same time, bring about a conviction. Public sentiment against Obadiah was mobilized through
innuendo and rumor so that the eventual accusation came from the
whole village: Sam's role was not obvious and he suffered no reprisals.

Keenan (1974: 129) describes a similar process among Malagasy
speakers in Madagascar. Here people are reluctant to accuse others even
when they have good evidence against them. Instead, they gossip about
it and when everyone is saying the same thing, the accusation seems to
come from the whole community and nobody is held responsible.

Furthermore, Sam's methods of revealing his information increased
its eventual impact. Sam observed Obadiah practicing female avoidance rules and noticed that he had never thrown away a particular
sorcery implement, and concluded that he was the murderer. When I
asked Sam why he did not publicize this information, he said that it was
not sufficient evidence to convict Obadiah in court. Indeed, when the
Bumbita magistrates were told of it privately, they agreed that the evidence was convincing but still decided that everyone should contribute
to compensation payments to the widows, since no one could be sure
who had killed Naifuku and Ambusuroho. In its own right, Sam's
information was evidently not definitive. But spread through the
community as rumor the same information created public pressure for
a new meeting and eventually brought about Obadiah's conviction.
Thus, rumor and innuendo can make evidence that, if told outright, is
at best suggestive, seem much more impressive, especially since everyone thinks that people actually know much more than they say and
there must be a hidden meaning behind every remark.

Conversely, those who were more open about their suspicions suffered unpleasant consequences. Adam and Ronald, for instance, tried
to prosecute Jeremiah and ended up being accused of the murder.
Ronald's frequent attempts to stop discussion and convict Jeremiah
were seen as proof of his own guilt: he was trying to frame Jeremiah
to cover up his own complicity. Similarly, when Deborah asked that
Obadiah and Jeremiah be charged at the final court hearing this not
only brought her no benefit (the fines were never paid) but actually
harmed her: she was expelled by the outraged family of the men.
Direct action against culprits is apparently both difficult (if not impossible) since any action produces opposition and can also have undesirable consequences.

This seems to be due to the fact that people have large local kin
networks who support them, and so attempts to prosecute suspects

inevitably meet opposition. For example, when I asked Jeremiah whether anyone had supported him when he was accused of murdering Naifuku and Ambusuroho, he answered, "Only a few supported me: my brother-in-law, . . . my mother's brother . . . my sister's child. . . . They supported me. They said: 'Everyone is against him, we will stay and shield him. Whatever he has done, we must protect him.'"

There will be opposition to any accusation that cannot be definitively proven, and few can be. Perhaps this is why people left it to Deborah to decide in the final court hearing who should be charged (and so left her to bear the consequences of this charge). It is safer to accuse people by dropping hints in private conversations.

Innuendo is not confined to gossip. Speakers in inquests also hinted that they had information about the murder, and sometimes they even spelled out their suspicions—but they said that they did not want to prosecute the suspect since there was no good evidence to support the charges. As long as they confined themselves to suggestions and innuendo and did not try to prosecute suspects, speakers in meetings, like rumor-mongers, were also able to influence events without facing reprisals.

In fact, it was evident that all the public talk did have an impact on the community even if people never reached much consensus about the identity of the murderer. In the inquests, many theories were constructed and examined. Apparently trivial words and deeds such as the meetings between Arawapi and Jeremiah and their subsequent denial that it took place became signs of darker acts and intentions. Although these accounts could not be proven either true or false, they did convey certain messages to the community. For instance, people could not prove that Jeremiah had killed the two men, but they did make use of various suspicious things like the fact that Arawapi and Jeremiah had at first denied, then admitted to, meeting, to construct accounts of how and when he might have killed them. In the first inquest, Adam and Ronald were unable to extract a confession from the two men but the process of articulating and examining the theory cast suspicions about Jeremiah in everybody's mind. People looked for other proof against him and came up with incidents that displayed both his ill-will toward his two brothers-in-law and the fact that he had had an opportunity to poison them. For instance, in the first court hearing, the magistrates discussed a time when, after a violent fight with his brothers-in-law, Jeremiah had destroyed all of his possessions in the village and said that he was leaving to go and work on a plantation in a distant part of the country. But he went only as far as Wewak and then mysteriously returned to the village. People suggested that this incident showed that Jeremiah had had both a motive for murder and an opportunity to obtain poison: he could have purchased this in Wewak and then decided to return to the village and wreak his vengeance on his brothers-in-law instead of going to the plantation as he had originally planned. The story of the time when Jeremiah first refused to help harvest Naifuku and Ambusuroho's yams and then inexplicably changed his mind after going into his house and, people guessed, picking up the poison there, was interpreted in similar ways.

None of these incidents conclusively proved Jeremiah's guilt and, indeed, Andrew said that the villagers could not take Jeremiah to district court on the basis of such evidence. But the Asanakor people did make Jeremiah very uncomfortable for almost a year by telling of such incidents and drawing out their implications. They shamed him by suggesting that he was a violent and irrational character who might kill his brothers-in-law. He became a social outcast for several months, and he told me that he had feared for his life.

These theories also contained messages for others in the community. People learned that unreasonable hotheads who fight with others were prime suspects in sorcery cases. Andrew maintained that Jeremiah deserved to be accused even if he were innocent because he was a troublemaker, and Sam later echoed these views. As Andrew said: "If I don't fight with you then when you die I won't carry the blame." Fear of being accused of sorcery discourages people from fighting even when they feel they are in the right. My neighbor, for instance, frequently chastised his classificatory son for fighting with other families, saying that fights led to sorcery accusations and, indeed, the son's name was frequently raised in inquests. Sorcery accusations are both unpleasant and can lead to fears of counter-sorcery.

Men who voiced such theories in public meetings also made claims about themselves. People, like Sam, who made accusations in meetings presented themselves as guardians of law and order who brought troublemakers before the public eye.

Finally, the meetings were somewhat more effective in exonerating suspects than in proving guilt. People, like Brian, were able to defend themselves against suspicions and could convincingly, if not conclusively, argue that they were innocent particularly if they presented themselves well, making well-reasoned statements, and avoiding angry outbursts or brooding silences. In fact, many people seemed more concerned with proving their own innocence than with establishing the truth in the discussions. This is not surprising since anyone suspected of sorcery fears counter-sorcery.

In short, by talking about sorcery in inquests and in more private conversations, Inakor and Asanakor men try to enhance their own reputations, clear their names, and mobilize the community. But as soon as they move beyond suggestion and innuendo and try to prosecute suspects, leaders are liable to lose the support of the rest of the community and may even come under suspicion themselves. Thus, rumor and innuendo are not just effective political tools; they seem almost to be necessary strategies since more direct, public action is seldom successful and can even be dangerous.

How the Truth Emerges: Gossip and Innuendo

The Kwanga say that a murderer, and those who know of his crime, will carefully cover his tracks by planting false leads. In inquests, confusion will reign and the true cause of death is unlikely to come to light. After a few years the "truth" will leak out, but by then no one will care enough to do anything about it, and, in any case, there will never be enough definitive information to justify prosecuting a suspect.

The Naifuku and Ambusuroho case seemed to confirm this general scenario. The evidence was, from the beginning, ambiguous. The inquests made little progress toward finding a murderer until rumors reputedly spread by Sam led to Obadiah and Jeremiah's conviction. But evidence against the two men was not conclusive and the charges were not enforced. People continued to gossip about the affair and to develop new ideas about it. When I was preparing leave, over a year after the final public hearing, some people told me that they thought the truth about the two deaths had not yet emerged.

It also seemed in this case that the confusion about the affair was, at least in part, intentioally fostered, as my informants told me is generally true. People like Sam hid what they thought was definitive information and made misleading accusations in public. When Sam did hint at his real opinion in public, he did not disclose the name of his prime suspect nor what he considered to be the best evidence against him. Instead he mentioned suggestive incidents like the unsuccessful pig snaring at Pilimbi which could have meant any number of things. Sam seemed to be willing to plant suspicions in people's minds but was reluctant to offer up all of his evidence to the cold light of public scrutiny.

Informants' accounts of how they discovered what they believed to be the true causes of particular deaths revealed that the Naifuku and Ambusuroho case was typical. Information about sorcery deaths comes largely from rumor and innuendo. People said there were several ways to get information about sorcerers. Traditionally, hints about the causes of recent deaths were dropped in the course of tambaran initiations. Songs included verses commenting on current events, and sorcerers could include veiled references to the cause of deaths. Hints were also dropped in conversations among men secluded in the cult house. People seeking information would listen carefully for clues.

In others cases, people purposely seek out sorcerers for information about the deaths of family members since sorcerers are believed to be in league and to know of each others' activities, and I heard of several instances where people had formed their final interpretation of a death from information from a sorcerer. But sorcerers' hints are suggestive at best.

For instance, Henry told me that several years after the death of his older brother Walafuku, Henry went to the local sorcerer, Hapandi, for information. Hapandi said that Walafuku had been one of three men who had given money to a sorcerer from another village to kill Semaina, a man with whom they all had quarrels over land. After killing Semaina, the sorcerers turned back and killed Walafuku.[11] Henry concluded that Hapandi himself had killed Walafuku because of his role in the death of Semaina.

In another case, when Arumbwai, a young Inakor woman, died her kinsmen sought information from sorcerers from the neighboring village of Ta'uanangas who had recently been in jail with Inakor sorcerer Hapandi.[12] People often go to other villages, thinking that sorcerers might speak more freely to friends there since they would be unlikely to pass information on to the victim's family. Arumbwai's husband and her mother's brother heard from kin in Ta'uanangas that Hapandi had said that Arumbwai was "his rubbish," a statement that was taken to mean that he had killed her.

In a third incident, after several deaths in Inakor, Hapandi suggested to his daughter's husband, Ronald, that it might be a good idea to give some pigs, yams, and money to the sorcerers in the Bumbita and Urat villages to the north, and the Inakor people did this. Some months later, one of the Bumbita sorcerers privately told Ronald that he and the other Bumbita and Urat sorcerers had had nothing to do with the Inakor murders. He said that Hapandi had hinted that Bumbita and Urat sorcerers might be attacking Inakor because Hapandi wanted to divert suspicion from himself. This was generally thought to mean that Bumbita people had commissioned Hapandi to kill his fellow villagers and he had later tried to conceal his role.

In a fourth case, after the death of an Asanakor child, Ronald told the girl's father that a sorcerer had privately told him that the little girl was killed by sorcerers from Apangai because her father had revealed tambaran secrets there. Ronald said that the sorcerer claimed that a teenage boy who had died some months before had been killed by the same sorcerers over a land dispute. Ronald revealed this information in the inquest but he did not name his informant or the specific sorcerers implicated.

Finally, a fifth incident also illustrated the way in which sorcerers and others prompt people toward a certain interpretation of a death but avoid straightforward public accusations. When a two-year-old boy died people immediately suspected Hapandi who had a long-standing fight with the child's father, Karalanda. Karalanda and some young men tried to kill Hapandi, but he escaped into the bush and reappeared a few days later at the home of his daughter and her husband, Ronald, who suggested that the two sides exchange compensation payments of pigs, yams, and money. Later, I heard from an informant who claimed to have overheard the conversation that Hapandi quietly told his wife's brother, Gwarambu, that he had killed the child at the request of Suroho, who was angry because Karalanda had tried to plant coffee on some land Suroho thought was his own. When Karalanda presented his compensation to Hapandi in a public gathering, Gwarambu called together several men, including Suroho, and gave each of them a sprouted coconut, traditionally exchanged as a declaration of peace. Gwarambu made some general remarks about how the older men should not try to stop young men from planting coffee gardens and mentioned the name of the land over which Suroho and Karalanda had fought.

There was general confusion in the village on the following day. Some people thought that Suroho had hired Hapandi to kill the child and had been given the sprouted coconut to warn him against taking such measures in the future.[13] Others were unaware of these suspicions and thought that Suroho and the others had received part of the prestation because they had supported Hapandi when the young men attacked him. They had a village meeting to look into the matter but Gwarambu and Hapandi refused to explain their intentions.

In each of these cases people said they found the cause of death through interpreting hints dropped by sorcerers in private conversations. These usually implicated other sorcerers but (as in the last case) sometimes amounted to confessions. Information from sorcerers is usually taken seriously but it can be interpreted in various ways, particularly since hints are usually cast in veiled forms and sorcerers are believed to lie. Often, for instance, Hapandi hinted that a sorcerer from another village was responsible and people concluded that he, himself, was the murderer. People say that sorcerers protect each other by planting false leads so their words cannot be taken at face value.

The way these hints are passed on increases the confusion. In the death of the two-year-old boy, for instance, Gwarambu provided enough information in his speech (the name of the plot of land Suroho and Karalanda fought over, and that the fight was over a coffee garden) for those who knew about the fight between Suroho and Karalanda to guess that Suroho was involved. Giving him a sprouted coconut confirmed this suspicion. But since Gwarambu did not openly accuse Suroho, many people—including Suroho himself—did not even realize he had been implicated until they heard the rumors later. After the deaths of the Asanakor children, Ronald similarly passed on only part of his information, refusing to name his source or exactly what had been said.

In all the cases people said that information circulated largely through kin networks. When Arumbwai died the Inakor men sought out Ta'uanangas kin. Hapandi may or may not have intended his alleged veiled confession to reach Inakor ears through these networks. Likewise, after the Asanakor girl's death, the Yubanakor sorcerer supposedly spoke to Ronald who passed the information on to his classificatory brother, George, the girl's father. Finally, in the last case, Hapandi told his wife's brother, Gwarambu, of Suroho's involvement in the death.

The Kwanga recognize the importance of kin networks in spreading gossip. That is why the family of the victim goes to kin in other villages after a death. People who have talked to sorcerers often tell others what they know, and as the information moves further and further from its source people become more willing to reveal it to the victim's family. But by this time it is so diluted through hint, figurative speech, and partial omission that it is at best suggestive. In short, information about deaths leaks out in such a way that there is always doubt about the identity of the murderer.

Gossip, Innuendo, and Sorcery as a Political System

Evidently, ambiguity in attributions of sorcery is not an accidental result of inconclusive evidence. It is intentionally fostered. In fact, the confusion and inaction fostered by rumor and hint are necessary for the political use of sorcery beliefs among the Kwanga. Gossip, innuendo, and sorcery together form a system of social control and political power. There are benefits to speculating about the cause of deaths. To proceed beyond speculation is dangerous.

When people speculate about deaths they convey certain messages about themselves and about the community, all of which tend to enhance the authority of initiated men. First, individuals enhance their prestige and influence when they hint that they know about the activities of sorcerers. Forge (1970b), writing of the neighboring Abelam, says that those who aspire to leadership must claim knowledge about the activities of sorcerers. Because sorcery is the major source of power among the Abelam (and Kwanga), only those who are believed to have the ability to control it look to others to be able to maintain order and to protect the community from enemy attack. Tuzin (1974, 1976: 321) also shows how sorcery beliefs reinforce the position of leaders.

The Kwanga think there is a close relationship between community leaders and sorcery. Henry, for instance, described in an interview the kind of man who is closely associated with sorcery; "He is a big-man. All he has to do is talk and the sorcerer will kill someone. He gives prestations to other men to kill people. He is a leader of sorcerers." I asked him if anyone in Inakor fit this description and he replied, "Yes: Hilanda, Narombor, Bwalaka, Ronald, myself too. They always accuse us. They say that we support sorcery, that we lead sorcerers."

Henry's list included most of the leaders of the community. Ronald is the village magistrate and the head of the business group. Hilanda was Councillor of the village for many years and before that was village headman under the Australian colonial administration. Bwalaka had also served as village Councillor, had taken the lead in forming the business group, and is currently prominent in the Christian church. Henry is the head of a second business group and has one of the few trade stores in the community. All of these men are initiates of the highest grade of the tambaran cult, and also dominate village meetings.

Theories about deaths also enhance the power of all initiated men by suggesting that sorcerers act at their bidding and that, consequently, challenging the authority of tambaran initiates can be dangerous. I collected information on some forty deaths and in none of them was an uninitiated man or a woman implicated. By implying that they control sorcery and have exclusive knowledge of it, initiated men enhance their position as leaders of society and guardians of order. Deaths are often attributed to violations of tambaran laws. Possible violations range from such things as revealing tambaran secrets to planting varieties of yams inconsistent with tambaran status. Uninitiated men who display greater prowess than their initiated seniors at pig hunting and yam growing also risk attack. In general, the tambaran system places initiated men in a superior position giving them access to gardening and hunting magic, secret myths, and other things forbidden to the uninitiated.

Moreover, only initiated men are thought to know about the activities of sorcerers. Traditionally, funeral discussions were conducted in a stylized rhetoric that was learned by men in the course of initiation. Women did not participate in these meetings (as they did not know, and would not have been allowed to use, this rhetorical style). They did not even listen to the meetings (though they do now). Contexts such as tambaran festivals, in which hints were dropped about recent deaths, were controlled by men. Thus, initiated men largely control the interpretation of particular deaths. This enables them to ensure that deaths are interpreted in such a way as to reinforce their authority.

Another way that sorcery talk enhances the authority of initiated men is by (often) portraying sorcery as a moral force; initiated men and the sorcerers they control are, thus, shown to be guardians of law and order in the community. Sorcery is commonly described as the "police force of the ancestors," and community leaders, like Ronald, the magistrate, and Gwarambu, the Councillor, often made speeches in funeral discussions suggesting sorcery would stop if people behaved themselves and followed the law. Ronald said in one inquest:

Custom [i.e., the traditional ways] has its own law. The big-men made these laws a long time ago. It's just like the [modem] law. You can't break the laws of custom. You can't beat the power of the ancestors who did custom before. . . . Our government stands on the back of custom now. If [here he names a woman who recently died] broke a custom law, what can I say? If you are a troublemaker you will die. . . . Satan [that is, sorcery] wouldn't come and kill us for no reason. He will come to the troublemakers and the sinners. If you are good, you won't die.

Gwarambu voiced similar ideas in another inquest when he said, "What brings sorcery up are these fights over women and bush ground. People are troublemakers and sorcery comes up. . . . If everyone behaved themselves we wouldn't have sorcery here."

An informant told me the putative cause of all the deaths he could remember. In many of the cases (twenty-one out of thirty-four), the person was said to have died for a legitimate reason such as: violations of tambaran rules (seven cases); that the victim was a noted troublemaker (four cases); and retaliation for another death with which the victim was somehow associated (ten cases). Of the remaining thirteen deaths, four were not clearly illegitimate. Discussions of the cause of death also discourage misbehavior by raising the specter of punishment through sorcery (see also Tuzin 1974, 1976: 324).

Sorcery talk not only enhances the authority of initiated men but does it in such a way as to prevent challenges. Because theories about deaths are almost always cast in gossip and hint, people can deny statements attributed to them or say that they were misinterpreted. For instance, Adam took Richard to court for slander when he said that he had seen Adam give two hundred kina to a Bumbita sorcerer. But Richard denied he had said this and it proved impossible to find witnesses who could remember exactly what had been said.

These processes also protect the person who is accused. In the Naifuku and Ambusuroho case several people said that they were uncertain about the truth of accusations. For example, Andrew said that he was not sure if he would take Obadiah and Jeremiah to a higher court to enforce the charges against them because he was not certain that they were guilty. "We talk back and forth and it comes to nothing," a common complaint about inquests, implicitly recognizes the way discussion ultimately prevents action. Indeed, the local people say that big-men will purposefully create confusion in order to protect sorcerers. Cynics say that this is because sorcerers give part of their commissions to big-men. But others say that there would be chaos if there was no sorcery

since people are not afraid of courts and jail; only sorcery keeps troublemakers in line.

There is evidence that community leaders protect sorcerers. Hapandi
was frequently accused of murder and threatened with violent death but
received considerable support when there was an attempt on his life.
Earlier, when Hapandi's life was in danger after he was accused of killing a man, his daughter's husband, Ronald, escorted him to Maprik
and told him to stay there.[14] Later, when people decided that the murder was justified, Hapandi came back to the village. Hapandi also took
refuge in Maprik several years earlier after he was blamed for several
deaths. But then when the village decided to perform a tambaran initiation, they asked Hapandi to come back. Although people publicly de-
plore the institution of sorcery and support its abolition, privately they
are more ambivalent.

Keeping the cause of death ambiguous also benefits the community.
The local people acknowledge the role of confusion created by inquests
in preventing violence. People told me that the truth must be kept from
the family of the victim until a few years after the death. Right after the
death the family is so "angry" that if they discovered the identity of the
murderer they would kill him on the spot. So they must be kept in the
dark. They should hear so many theories about the death that they
cannot be certain of the truth. After a few years, when feelings have
cooled, they will be able to act more rationally, recognizing that they
cannot be sure who the murderer is, or that he might have acted for
good reasons. This is important since violence would probably provoke
retaliation from the kin of the victim, and this could start a feud. Thus,
paradoxically, a process that on the surface seems designed to label and
punish a culprit in fact prevents this. Hearing discussions of sorcery
prompts people to obey their leaders and to behave themselves.
Prosecuting suspects could only cause trouble for everyone.

Ethnofunctionalism

In the past decades, scholars have tended to shy away
from analyses that show how particular customs or patterns of behavior
help hold social groups together and preserve order in society. They
argue, with some justification, that individuals are often less interested

in the well-being of the community than in pursuing private goals and that, therefore, we cannot explain why people do things by showing how that behavior preserves the community.

Examining Kwanga inquests and talking with my informants, however, convinced me that they, themselves, took a functionalist view of their own community. Villagers stressed that customs like keeping the cause of death ambiguous in inquests kept people from killing each other and maintained order in the village. Furthermore, although Kwanga big-men wanted to enhance their own power they also were interested in the well-being and survival of the community. People, for instance, said that sorcery was a severe system of justice but feared that their communities would quickly become chaotic without its regulatory influence. In short, my Kwanga informants were inclined to think that it was important to keep their community together and to think about ways of maintaining order in the village; they were "ethnofunctionalists" and so, in this case, functionalist explanations did account for their behavior.

Furthermore, this may be true in many small acephalous communities such as those examined by the early proponents of structural-functionalist approaches in anthropology. When there is no central authority, people may fear chaos and disorder and may realize that their customs, by preserving order, keep life from being "nasty, brutish, and short." Consequently, people in many small communities are worried about problems of maintaining order and keeping their community together and so in such contexts, structural-functionalist arguments do describe both the causes and consequences of people's behavior. Thus, though we should not assume functionalist approaches are useful in all contexts, we should not avoid them where they are relevant.

Ambiguity and Power

Jeremiah's comments on inquests reveal another aspect of ambiguity. He stresses the fact that only the big-men will really know what is going on in funeral discussions; "children" will believe the lies and will be unable to recognize the truth. Since people purposely lie and hide the truth in public discussions, only those who know the truth ahead of time will be able to distinguish fact from fiction. Furthermore, most people do not have access to the privileged information through which the truth is revealed, that is, gossip from sorcerers. A sorcerer, of course, would not tell just anyone; he confides primarily in initiated men. And when people listen to gossip about a death they take the words of such men more seriously because they are believed to know what they are talking about. Women and uninitiated men would not have access to privileged information from sorcerers and, in any case, would not possess the necessary knowledge to interpret the sorcerer's words, which always allude to rather than directly reveal his deed. Therefore, when women and uninitiated men speak of sorcery, everyone knows that they are just guessing and, consequently, their speculations have little impact.

The complicated process of communication creates the impression of a complex social reality that only the big-men can fully understand. Just as the reputation for consorting with sorcerers enhances a man's prestige and influence, the complicated process of hint and gossip through which information is revealed displays to the community that only big-men really know about the activities of sorcerers and, therefore, can control them. Women and uninitiated men can neither correctly identify assassins nor challenge the interpretations of initiated men. The only way they can escape sorcery attacks is to follow the rules and not make trouble. Furthermore, by disseminating rumors of sorcery in veiled forms and in private conversations, men avoid being challenged and having to prove their charges. The power of Kwanga leaders, in fact, seems to be dependent on ambiguity and confusion. This is truly power without responsibility.

It may be that keeping attributions ambiguous is necessary for the political use of sorcery. Tuzin (1974, 1976) and Forge (1970b) both say that leaders are careful to keep the nature of their relationship with sorcerers ambiguous. Ilahita big-men claim that sorcerers act at the request of cult spirits (Tuzin 1976: 320–321). Among the Abelam, big-men accept shell rings from families of sick people implying that they "may know another who may know the sorcerer" (Forge 1970b: 265).

People will be reluctant to do things that they believe will invite sorcery attacks. As a result, individuals can opportunistically make use of deaths to hint at responsibility and gain power. Once this attribution has been made, however, the same person may be blamed for future deaths for which he has no desire to take credit. Acquiring a reputation for frequently practicing sorcery is highly disadvantageous. I heard of sorcerers who were ambushed and murdered after being accused of killing many of their fellow villagers. Hapandi may soon meet a similar fate. Informants said that when there were several sorcerers in the village they were never sure who was responsible for any particular death. But now that Hapandi is the only sorcerer, this protective doubt is eroding and he had been jailed several times on sorcery charges. In short, in hinting that one consorts with sorcerers, ambiguity is desirable.

Scholars such as Scott (1985), Harding (1975), and Rogers (1975) have suggested that gossip is often a "weapon of the weak"; relatively powerless groups can influence events in ways they cannot be held accountable for when they gossip. But the Kwanga material shows that in some situations gossip can also be a tool controlled by more powerful groups in a community.

There is also evidence that gossip is used by powerful groups to enhance their position in other places. Weatherford (1981), for instance, describing the American Congress, says that the more TV cameras make congressional meetings and hearings public, the more they become an empty show. Congressmen make impressive public speeches to score points with the public. But decisions are made elsewhere in more veiled private contexts where people cannot be held accountable for their words. Likewise, Bailey (1977), when describing university politics finds it necessary to discriminate between "front stage," "backstage," and "under the stage" contexts in which people try to influence the events. Thus not one, but two levels of covert action are recognized. And he devotes a chapter to the political uses of gossip. Where people do not necessarily act on their public words and can deny their private ones, they can influence events without being held accountable because no one can be really sure who said or did what, when, and how.

When influence is exercised in such ambiguous ways it is very hard to undermine. In America, for instance, laws govern the formal visible processes of decision making in various institutions but the ambiguous nature of informal influence is hard to control. After all, who can be really sure if X spoke to Y or even if he did if that had any influence on the final decision. Similarly, the ambiguity surrounding Kwanga sorcery preserves the institution and its power to influence behavior. Thus, gossip and rumor are not always weapons of the weak; they can also be used to reinforce existing power relations and to prevent people from challenging them.

Kwanga inquests seem to go on and on and come to nothing: people hide their best evidence, say that they were "just guessing" and have no proof of the charges they made so forcefully in public meetings, and are reluctant to act on their own words; indeed, they say one thing about a death in public and quite another in private conversations. But closer examination has revealed that this apparently pointless talk about deaths helps to keep the community in order and reinforce the position of leaders. Indeed, the very ambiguity that surrounds their words and seems to prevent action enhances the power of Kwanga leaders and allows them power without responsibility.

CHAPTER FOUR

Village Courts and the Art of Bluffing

The Inakor and Asanakor people spend a great deal of time commenting on styles of communication in inquests: they complain that others are hiding the truth or spreading slanderous rumors and that these behaviors both damage individual reputations and protect culprits. As my fieldwork progressed, it became evident that there was a great deal of truth to these complaints: people did drop hints and spread rumors about sorcery; they also often refused to make the same charges in a straightforward public manner. Furthermore, these behaviors could damage the reputations of suspects and did, ultimately, seem to protect culprits since hints and gossip fostered confusion about the evidence and prevented people from being sure enough about the validity of charges to take suspects to court. But I have argued that people preferred to drop hints and spread rumors because this gave them "power without responsibility," and there were ways in which this behavior benefited the rest of the community as well.

Examining court hearings revealed that initiated men were not the only ones who dropped hints and spread rumors. In fact, almost everyone in the community preferred to avoid open confrontation and criticism and to cast their complaints about their neighbors and kin in veiled, ambiguous language. In this way, people could mobilize public opinion against those they did not like, or could try to get people to behave better. But speakers could (and frequently did) escape being held accountable for their words by denying them if challenged. Indeed, court hearings frequently failed when plaintiffs could only offer rumor and veiled remarks as proof of their charges, and witnesses either denied the statements attributed to them or said their words had been misconstrued.

But although the pervasive duplicity seemed to hamper the court's ability to deal with disputes, it was evident that, like inquests, court hearings did have an impact on people's behavior. Although both magistrates and witnesses tried to preserve ambiguity, hide information, and avoid controversial actions, court hearings did allow people to voice their opinions and try to frighten others into changing their ways. Thus, in court hearings and in everyday life, as in inquests, people tried to influence others by dropping hints, spreading rumors, and making public strong recommendations that they later refused to act on.

Gossip, Innuendo, and Lies

The courts explicitly challenged the system of gossip and innuendo so prevalent in other contexts. Witnesses were frequently told to say clearly what they knew and not to be "ashamed" to testify against kin or affines. Furthermore, at least in theory, gossip was not considered valid evidence. In fact, gossiping was, itself, an indictable offense, and those carrying rumors could be fined even if the rumors turned out to be true. Nor were the various signs of hidden malice such as suspicious statements and odd behaviors, which figured so prominently in more loosely structured discussions like inquests, considered acceptable evidence in court. The magistrates theoretically insisted on eyewitness accounts.

If the magistrates had adhered strictly to these rules, the village court would have been unable to address most conflicts in the community since people were usually careful to criticize and make accusations against their neighbors in ambiguous ways so that they could deny their words later.

But, in fact, the magistrates' treatment of rumor and suspicious circumstance was inconsistent and sometimes they did accept this kind of evidence. Just as in other kinds of meetings, they heard long accounts of suspicious signs and ambiguous comments and tried to make sense of this kind of evidence.

The following cases will illustrate both the pervasive use of innuendo and rumor in Kwanga social interaction and the court's inconsistent treatment of this sort of information.

Ekwa

Ekwa, an Asanakor woman, was married to Ian, a man who had just returned to the village after having been away for several years performing wage labor in another part of the country. Ekwa's father, Obadiah, brought Ian to court claiming that he was threatening to take a second wife and leave the village without Ekwa. The magistrates found that Ekwa's suspicions had been aroused by veiled threats made by Ian in the course of marital squabbles. Ian claimed that she had misinterpreted his words and that he had no intention of either remarrying or leaving the village. The magistrates dismissed the case, chastising Obadiah for interfering with his daughter's marriage and scolding Ekwa for leaping to false conclusions. About a month later Ian took a second wife and soon afterwards left the village in the middle of the night with this woman and one of Ekwa's children. They later discovered he had gone to another part of the country.

The Adulterous Wife

Wanbwai, an Asanakor woman, had been married to Bwainjeri for several years and the couple had three children when she had a nervous breakdown. She had a fourth child but proved incapable of looking after the baby or her older children. Bwainjeri took care of the children but stopped having sexual relations with Wanbwai so that she would have no more children. When she bore three more children, Bwainjeri claimed he was not the father. According to rumor, Wanbwai had three lovers but there was no good evidence of these allegations. When the case came to court, people refused to testify because (as one of them told me later) they felt that the court might fine them for gossiping since they had only circumstantial evidence.

An Insulting Remark Is Discussed in Mediation

Satapi, a young woman recently married to Ken, was brought to court by a single woman, Mewamwa, for allegedly saying that she smelled because of a skin condition (Mewamwa had a skin fungus, quite common in the area, which is considered disfiguring and does, indeed, have an unpleasant odor). When both young women had attended a recent Christian revival meeting in a neighboring village, they and several other women slept overnight in an empty house. Walking home the next day, Satapi was reported to have said that she had slept the night before with some women who smelled because they had fungus. Mewamwa heard this and thought it referred to her.

When Ronald opened the mediation session he was seemingly already aware that the apparent cause of the dispute concealed another issue. Satapi's husband, Ken, had had an affair with Mewamwa before marrying Satapi. Satapi did not find out about this until after her marriage, and she became convinced (probably with the aid of gossip from neighboring women) that Ken intended to take Mewamwa as a second wife, something that Satapi strongly opposed. She made several insulting remarks about Mewamwa after this, and the latter's sister Susan, who lived nearby, faithfully passed on these comments to Mewamwa, who was furious.

Ronald opened the discussion by trying to find out who had told Satapi that Ken was going to marry Mewamwa and if it was, indeed, true. After much discussion, including criticism of Susan for trying to force Ken to marry her sister, and of Satapi for being so ready to jump to the conclusion that Ken wanted to marry Mewamwa, Ronald decided that the rumor was untrue. Ken's parents had long ago asked him if he wanted to marry Mewamwa, and he had said no.

Ronald then turned his attention to the remark about women with skin fungus. Satapi, predictably, admitted she had said it, but denied that she had meant Mewamwa. A neighbor of Satapi's supported her by saying that she had overheard the comment and taken it to be a general one. After a long discussion of various other things Satapi was reported to have said about Mewamwa, Ronald seemed inclined to think that Satapi had not intended to insult Mewamwa. But then Mewamwa's mother walked away shaking her fist and saying that Satapi had maligned her daughter and must pay for this. Seeing how upset Mewamwa's family was, Ronald told Satapi to pay a ten kina fine and ended with a general caution against people who spread rumors.

A Discussion of an Alleged Threat from a Sorcerer

Wangembor, an Inakor man, scheduled a court hearing to find out if Richard, a sorcerer from the village of Tumingir, had a grudge against him. Wangembor had been married to Richard's ex-wife, Gwarsumwa, for about a year and although Richard had publicly given his blessing to the match, Wangembor's family continued to suspect a hidden grievance and to fear attack. Wangembor said in court that renewed fears of imminent attack broke out when Gwarsumwa was told that her children, who had remained in the custody of their father, were being mistreated by his new wife. Gwarsumwa stormed up to Tumingir saying that she was going to take her children but Richard's new wife said that Gwarsumwa had no right to take the children or even to interfere on their behalf. Nengekwa, an Inakor woman married into Tumingir, said in court that Richard's wife mistakenly believed that she (Nengekwa) was responsible for the trouble. After Gwarsumwa left, Richard's wife said to Nengekwa something to the effect of "It was you who persuaded Gwarsumwa to leave Richard and go marry your [classificatory] brother Wangembor. So now you can't make trouble!" Nengekwa said that she feared that this remark indicated that Richard harbored a grudge against her, and that she had hastened to assure him that she had had no part in the marriage of Gwarsumwa and Wangembor. She also went to warn Wangembor that Richard was angry about losing Gwarsumwa. Wangembor brought the matter to court to forestall an attack.

In court, Richard denied that he had any grievance against either Nengekwa or Wangembor. The magistrates chastised Nengekwa for carrying alarmist rumors and dismissed the matter saying that it was wrong to gossip about sorcerers without good evidence.

A Man Is Prosecuted for Spreading Rumors of Sorcery

Ronald charged Marauri, a man from a neighboring village, Ta'uanangas, with saying that Ronald had paid a sorcerer to kill his classificatory brother's wife, Arumbwai (who had died almost a year before this case appeared in court). In court, Marauri claimed he was not the source of this rumor and had, in fact, heard it himself in Inakor. When the magistrates pressed him to be specific and provide witnesses, Marauri said he had heard the rumor from his classificatory brother, Nakumini. When summoned, however, Nakumini said that it was Marauri who had told him not the other way around. After several young men came forward to say they first heard the rumor from Marauri, the magistrates concluded that he was guilty and charged him seventy kina for spreading false rumors.

Later Nakumini told me privately that he had lied in court. He had heard the rumors about Ronald from other Inakor people and had, in fact, told Marauri about it himself.

A Rumor of Adultery

Loposumbwai charged her husband, Ricky, and a young single woman, Handala, with flirting. The case was discussed in two mediation sessions, the first directed by Andrew, the court clerk from Asanakor, and the second by Ronald, Handala's sister's husband. Andrew, a neighbor of Ricky and Loposumbwai, concluded that the rumors were true. He knew from living near them that Loposumbwai and Ricky had never gotten along very well, and Ricky's family had not yet paid brideprice even though the couple had been married for several years. Andrew told me that Ricky continued to flirt with the single girls as if he were unmarried and, therefore, Andrew felt that it was likely that the rumors about Handala were true. In the second mediation session, Ronald decided that there was no proof of flirtation between Handala and Ricky. Loposumbwai's evidence consisted of rumors and of having once seen Handala and Ricky speak to each other when a number of young people were picking coffee. Ronald dismissed this evidence saying that it was not strong enough proof as there were no eyewitnesses of anything but one conversation which could have been quite innocent.

Gossip about an Affair

People in Inakor had been telling me for months that Harold's wife, Hamekwa, was having an affair with his younger brother, Larry. When Harold heard of this he asked Andrew to look into the matter. At the hearing, person after person was questioned and each admitted to having gossiped about Hamekwa and Larry, but claimed to have heard about the affair secondhand and to have no direct evidence. Finally, one woman said that she had once seen Hamekwa and Larry, alone, talking at a garden house. Larry quickly admitted to having propositioned Hamekwa at this time but said that she had refused him. Hamekwa agreed with this account, and Andrew closed the hearing after fining Larry twenty kina for propositioning a married woman.

A few months later I was discussing the case with my neighbor and she said that she knew that Larry and Hamekwa were having an affair since she often saw Hamekwa going to her garden alone, with Larry following at a discreet distance behind. On one such occasion, my neighbor said that she had called out to Larry (who was her classificatory brother): "Oh are you going pig hunting?", playing on common metaphorical association between pigs and women. Larry had laughed and replied: "Oh yes, but not because I want to. It's the pig who is eager to be shot!" My informant felt this was conclusive proof of adultery (as it probably was) and claimed that many of the women questioned in court had similar evidence. My neighbor said that they had been reluctant to reveal what they knew, however, because they had no wish to harm Hamekwa and were, in any case, angry with Harold who had publicly lambasted "gossipy women" shortly before the hearing.

Dealing with Ambiguity

In each of these cases, the magistrates had to find the truth behind rumors. Evidently, initiated men were not alone in preferring to cast their criticisms and threats in veiled, ambiguous forms or to make their allegations in private conversations and allow them to reach the ears of the rest of the community as rumor. Everyone else also dropped hints and speculated about their neighbors in private conversations—but were reluctant to make the same charges in more straightforward public ways.

It was also apparent that the preference for rumor and innuendo created a pervasive suspicious attitude between villagers: because rumors and ambiguous remarks so often did conceal a potentially dangerous charge, people feared that any remark that was even the least bit out of the ordinary might have a deeper, darker message. Thus, most court hearings involved trying to decipher the intent behind rumors and veiled remarks.

It was not hard to figure out why people preferred not to spell out their criticisms of their neighbors and kin. Dropping hints and spreading rumors did sometimes allow them to escape the consequences of their words. Richard, Ekwa's husband, and the people who gossiped about Wanbwai and Hamekwa, for instance, were able to claim that veiled remarks had an innocuous meaning although this strategy did not work for Satapi and Ricky. People could avoid giving evidence against their neighbors by saying that their words had been misinterpreted or that they had no evidence to support their charges. Similarly, they could claim that seemingly slanderous remarks had had a more innocent intent. In this way, they could avoid taking responsibility for their words.

Magistrates also seemed to exploit the ambiguity of the evidence presented to them. When they did not want to take responsibility for controversial decisions, they insisted on eyewitness evidence; conversely, when they wanted to further their own interests, or did not feel threatened, they accepted gossip and suspicious circumstance as adequate proof.

There were several situations in which magistrates seemed reluctant to take a public stand on issues. First, they were reluctant to make decisions against powerful defendants. In case 3, Satapi, a young woman, was unlikely to protest Ronald's decision or take covert action against him, but in case 4 it was much more risky to decide against the sorcerer, Richard. Ronald, therefore, fined Satapi but insisted on direct evidence in Richard's case.

Magistrates were also swayed by the support groups of litigants. Disputants were often backed by kin, or fellow moiety members. Such support groups discouraged the magistrates from making decisions on the basis of evidence that was less than clear-cut or, conversely, as in Satapi's case, pushed them into finding defendants guilty on the basis of scant evidence if the plaintiff had a lot of public support.

The magistrates' behavior was also influenced by their own interests. In case 6, Andrew and Ronald reached opposite decisions about the same evidence because Ronald, married to Handala's sister, insisted on direct proof, whereas Andrew, who had no particular connection with either side, was willing to accept rumor and observations of suspicious behavior as sufficient indication of guilt. A similar process was at work in case 5 when Ronald, judging a case of a rumor about himself, fined Marauri.

In short, people were able to criticize their neighbors in relatively cost-free ways by casting their remarks in veiled forms and by speaking only to trusted family and friends. Magistrates, similarly, took advantage of the ambiguous evidence to avoid taking stands when they thought that doing so might be dangerous. Thus, in courts, as in inquests, people sought ways of influencing events for which they would not be held accountable.

Social Pressures on Magistrates and Witnesses

Social pressures on magistrates and witnesses encourage them to act this way. The village court charter officially gives magistrates the authority to make decisions and the power to enforce them through appeal to extra-local law enforcement agencies such as district-level courts and police departments. In reality, these agencies often refuse to deal with village disputes, claiming that they are too trivial or that village court hearings were improperly conducted and, therefore, reached invalid decisions. It is also difficult to make sure that everyone involved goes to town on the appointed court day, especially if people do not feel this to be in their interests. So magistrates have little power to enforce unpopular decisions.

Magistrates fear sorcery attacks and also complain that people neither respect their authority nor believe that they have the power to enforce decisions, and their fears are not without foundation: people do complain about magistrates frequently and often say nasty things about them behind their backs. These pressures discourage magistrates from making controversial decisions.

There were several ways that magistrates lessened the impact of decisions to avoid offending people. They imposed fines (court fines as payment for wrongdoing, and compensation payments to injured party) instead of jail sentences. This was standard practice in village courts but people who failed to pay fines promptly were supposed to be sent to jail. Kwanga magistrates, however, routinely gave people a grace period of six months to pay and would also grant extensions. As a result, no one went to jail or performed community service (the alternative to jail) during my two years in the field even though magistrates in the neighboring Bumbita and Ilahita Arapesh court areas (Stephen Leavitt and Donald Tuzin, personal communication) frequently sent people to jail.

Magistrates often referred cases to other court bodies (claiming, for instance, in the case of repeat offenders that the culprit had refused to listen to village court officials in the past so must be dealt with by extralocal courts that had more power), or postponed hearings because witnesses were absent. Disputes were first reported to the village magistrate who often attempted to get everyone to agree on a solution in mediation. If this failed, the magistrate could delay hearing the case or "forget" about it altogether. Ronald was fond of saying that it was impossible to settle a conflict until time had elapsed and feelings had cooled and people would be prepared to hear reason. In accordance with this philosophy, he often put off court hearings until the participants had lost all interest in the affair.

Third, if court decisions were disputed or proved ineffective they were often not enforced, and sometimes cases were brought back for a second hearing.

Magistrates also avoided making decisions that favored one side of a dispute because of a realistic perception that they would do little to restore harmonious relations between litigants and might even subject the winner to covert attack. For instance, although Andrew knew that the law was on the side of his classificatory daughter, Waimele, in her attempt to obtain a divorce, he told her to wait. Her husband had been absent from the village for several years, working on a plantation in another part of the country and had no apparent intention of returning. Everyone knew that under the national law if a man had been away for more than three years his wife was free to remarry. But, although Waimele's husband had been gone for longer than that, Andrew urged her to wait a few months longer so her husband's family could try to contact him. Magistrates also tried to find hidden grievances in court so no one would be dissatisfied with the decision.

Witnesses, similarly, were reluctant to alienate their neighbors by testifying against them or even by directly criticizing them in day-to-day life. Through spreading nasty rumors and casting their criticism in ambiguous, veiled forms, people could mobilize social pressure against others and could avoid the opposition and resentment that they would inevitably incur if they phrased their criticisms and complaints in a more open fashion.

Dealing with Disputes

If witnesses can avoid giving evidence and magistrates can avoid making decisions, how do courts contribute to the resolution of conflict? In many trivial matters, like the case of Satapi and Mewamwa, decisions are made and implemented, and disputes are settled to the satisfaction of all. In other cases decisions are not made, are not enforced, or turn out to be ineffective. Disputes reemerge, perhaps in a new form, and are, once again, discussed in community meetings or court. What is the role of court hearings in such situations?

THE UNFAITHFUL WIFE

Tewamwa, an Asanakor woman, married Suahopo, a young Inakor man, but after the couple had two children he left the village to work on a plantation in another part of the country. After he had been gone for several years Tewamwa got pregnant and said Wolanda, a married man who lived nearby, was the father. Wolanda admitted to having slept with her on a number of occasions and the two were taken to the district capital, Dreikikir, to be jailed for adultery. But the Dreikikir officials told them to go back home since Tewamwa had children to look after.

Ronald (who was married to one of Suahopo's close classificatory sisters) held a mediation session and decided that Wolanda should pay Suahopo's family 1500 kina compensation for destroying their son's marriage. It was unlikely that Wolanda would ever be able to pay such a large fine, but those involved seemed to agree to its justice. They discussed the possibility of Tewamwa marrying Wolanda but his wife objected so strenuously that the idea was dropped.

Tewamwa went to live with her classificatory brother, Rangu. After a few months, Suahopo sent a letter saying that he would not return to the village until he and Tewamwa were divorced, and she had married another man. His parents suggested that she marry Tasamba, a young man of their lineage whose wife was terminally ill and was unable to work, saying that if Tewamwa agreed to this they would drop the 1500 kina fine. This way Tewamwa's child would not be lost to their lineage. They went to court and on threat of jail, Tewamwa agreed to this solution, and a court order was written, saying that she would marry Tasamba and could not divorce him without good cause.

Tewamwa and Tasamba were married, and her child was born. But Tasamba's family complained that Tewamwa was always criticizing Tasamba and saying that she had been forced to marry him. Tasamba, himself, was a mild-mannered man, and he suffered Tewamwa's complaints in silence but his brother and mother were furious on his behalf and they beat Tewamwa on several occasions and often said she could not eat food from Tasamba's gardens. This conflict came to my attention, and that of the rest of the village, when Suahopo's classificatory sister (and Ronald's wife), Meka, witnessed one such altercation on the way to her garden. She was outraged by the mistreatment of her former sister-in-law and took Tewamwa home with her. Ronald held a mediation session in which people described the conflicts between Tewamwa and Tasamba's family.

After a while, Tewamwa went to stay with her brother in Asanakor. The case was brought to court, and the magistrates offered to write a court order to Tasamba's family to stop them from mistreating her. But Tewamwa insisted that she had never wanted to marry Tasamba and now intended to divorce him. The magistrates said that if she violated the previous court order by leaving Tasamba she would have to pay the standard two hundred kina fine for breaking a court order or go to jail. But she held firm.

Tewamwa returned to her brother's house (and did not paid the fine) and lived there for several months until Tasamba brought the matter to court once more, claiming he should be compensated for the pollution he had suffered when her baby was born in his house. The magistrates first suggested that she return to Tasamba but, when she refused, asked her to give him the child in compensation, and she agreed.[1]

One of the judges then brought up the two hundred kina fine at the insistence of Tewamwa's brother, Warabu. Warabu later told me that Tewamwa had married Suahopo against Warabu's wishes and he had, therefore, not supported her until he thought that he might have to pay the two hundred kina fine on her behalf. He then took the initiative in arguing that this fine was unjust since Tewamwa had been forced to sign the original court order against her will. Furthermore, he said in court that since Suahopo had been away from the village for more than three years, Tewamwa was free to do as she liked and should never have been punished for her affair with Wolanda. The magistrates seemed to be persuaded by this until a group of Inakor men entered the court and asked to be heard. They each said that Tewamwa must go back to Tasamba. They said that several years before, Suahopo had plotted to incapacitate Hapandi by polluting his food with the feces of one of his classificatory grandchildren, a child of Tasamba's. But Tewamwa was angry with Suahopo because he was having an affair, and so she warned Hapandi of the plot. Suahopo was afraid for his life and fled the village. Several subsequent deaths, including those of two of Tasamba's children, were attributed to the ill feelings created by this incident. So the Inakor men said that Tewamwa must marry Tasamba and replace the children who had died. Faced with this consensus, the magistrates and Tewamwa's brother advised her to go back to Tasamba. If she married anyone else, sorcery would surely strike. She returned to Tasamba but fought bitterly with his first wife in the following months.

Just Talk

Like many of the cases presented so far, the dispute over Tewamwa was difficult to resolve because so many people with conflicting interests were involved. The behavior of the court in this situation was notable in several ways. First, the magistrates made decisions that were beyond their jurisdiction as, for instance, when Ronald imposed the 1500 kina fine on Wolanda in the first mediation session. But there was never any attempt to enforce these decisions; for example, fines were not collected from Tewamwa or Wolanda. The magistrates seemed to be bluffing. When solutions did not work, or people refused to comply, the matter was forgotten until a new fight brought it to the attention of the court again.

Second, the magistrates, particularly Ronald, were not impartial. Ronald generally made decisions that favored his wife's classificatory brother, Suahopo. He had been away from the village for more than three years and so Tewamwa was free to divorce him. But the magistrates consistently ignored this.

Third, the court was swayed by outside pressure. This was most obvious in the final decision but was also evident in the inconsistency in the treatment of Tewamwa. When no one supported her, decisions went against her. But when her brother and Meka defended her, the magistrates were more sympathetic.

Court proceedings are evidently part of a process of negotiation. Gulliver (1979) suggests that negotiation is a process of learning in which each side tries to convey an impression of inflexibility and power while trying to judge the other side's strength and willingness to compromise. If the magistrates are viewed as participants in a process of negotiation actively pursuing the interests of one side and swayed by the relative power of the support groups of those involved, instead of as impartial adjudicators, many of their actions are easier to understand. Magistrates made threats, and imposed exorbitant fines, in order to convince Tewamwa that her options were limited and there would be consequences for acting against their will. But they did little to enforce the decisions and even ignored them in subsequent hearings. Like Gulliver's model negotiator, Kwanga magistrates try to convince the other side that dire consequences will result from noncompliance, but they are often unwilling or unable to act on their words.

This system of negotiation means that no one bears the responsibility for decisions. In the case of Tewamwa, resolution (such as it was) came through expression of consensus so everyone was responsible and no one could be singled out for retribution. Courts become a tool in a traditional system of resolution through negotiation.

The case of Tewamwa, and indeed most of the other court cases presented in this chapter, share many features with community meetings and inquests. In meetings and in court, people announce decisions and make extravagant threats. But there is little expectation that their words will be implemented. If the dispute persists and comes to public attention again, the previous decision is often ignored or even apparently forgotten. When and if action is taken, it is usually the result of widespread consensus. This was true in the case of Naifuku and

Ambusuroho (chapter 3) when suspicions about Obadiah were only acted upon after gossip had turned community opinion against him; similarly, in Tewamwa's case a final solution (or at least one that lasted longer than the previous ones) came after the display of consensus by the Inakor men.

Until such consensus is achieved, people avoid direct action. Strong statements in public contexts, whether court or less structured meetings, are but one move in an extended process of negotiation in which people attempt to convince others of their power, knowledge, and inflexibility of purpose. What appears to be a decision is actually a part of this presentation of self. When people explain away contradictions between words and actions by saying that statements were "just talk," they implicitly recognize the applicability of the negotiation model to their actions.

Likewise, those on the receiving end of this "talk" sometimes see it as an attempt to intimidate them into compliance. I remarked to a young woman, Kenuku, that there always seemed to be a great deal of discussion about widows and she responded, "Yes, that is true. All kinds of talk will come up over her. The men of Inakor will all be dying over this woman. . . . That is the way of the men of Inakor, that you have just said. If a woman is single, they will talk and talk, all kinds of talk, and try to trick her."

I then asked Kenuku what the men would do to try to trick the widow, and she answered, "They will guess about who she wants to marry. But it isn't true, they are just guessing. . . . They are just talking among themselves. We women, when our first husband dies, it's over."

I followed up by asking if a woman would be able to prevail if she did not want to remarry and Kenuku answered, "Yes, they will just talk and talk and finally they will leave it. If she listens to them she will remarry. If she doesn't, she will stay as she is."

I asked Kenuku next if the men would try to force the widow to remarry. She responded, "Before they did, not now. Now they follow her wishes. . . . They will try to trick you so you will be afraid for your life and you will go. If you stay single, forget it, they will kill you and bury you. Right away. It's not true: they are just lying so you will be afraid for your life."

Just as decisions in courts and community meetings create the impression of inflexibility and authority, the display of knowledge in inquests enhances the prestige of initiated men. The object of the exercise is not making decisions but creating a particular picture of individual personalities and of the abilities of initiated men. What Kwanga politics is "about" is manipulating presentation of self and interpretation of events so as to enhance the impression that you, or those like you, have power and wisdom and should be obeyed. When force is inadvisable and perhaps impossible, impression management becomes the primary political weapon.

Impression management in meetings and courts is, of course, just the most public moment in a great deal of similar discussion, and the Tewamwa case also illustrates the power of the less visible gossip and rumor in shaping public opinion and, ultimately, also influencing individual fates. Tewamwa had to marry her second husband against her wishes because of an earlier interpretation about her role in a number of deaths. The ambiguity of the attribution was central to its power over her. She could argue about matters for which there was evidence such as the status of her marriage but could do nothing to counter a rumor that everyone believed but for which the evidence was obscure. Undoubtedly, for instance, there was little evidence that Tewamwa had warned Hapandi of the attack on him, or that he had killed the children as a result. Had these allegations been made in court they probably would have come to nothing. But hidden in the context of hints dropped in private conversations, the rumors circulated unchecked around the community and came to be accepted as truth. Consensus was shaped through a diffuse and hidden process of hint and private discussion and once formed there was little Tewamwa could do to argue against it. Anyone could speak in court and observe other types of meetings; only those who had heard beforehand in private gossip, and who had access to such privileged sources of information, could assess the "truth." Thus interpretations of events, shaped through gossip and innuendo, have a powerful impact on people's lives in Inakor and Asanakor.

CHAPTER FIVE

Getting It All Out into the Open

Kwanga villagers drop hints and spread rumors in order to influence events in ways they cannot be held accountable for. This kind of talk (particularly when it concerns sorcery) constitutes the authority of initiated men and allows both leaders and others to maneuver within the straightjacket of a small, inbred, relatively egalitarian community where almost anything anybody does or says might arouse resentment and resistance.

In this chapter, and in the next two, I will further explore the way people use gossip and innuendo to influence others but will also argue that such talk can get out of hand and create problems that no one anticipated or desired. Rumors fly around the community and seem to take on a life of their own; they are distorted in certain predictable ways and can cause problems both for the perpetrator and for everyone else. Rumors can also escalate conflict so that trivial disputes can eventually become big fights involving most of the people in a village, or even members of more than one village.

To check these destructive rumors, villagers hold long weekly meetings in which people sift through the evidence to try to figure out how much truth there is to rumors, and speakers try to deny whispered charges against themselves.

In this chapter, I will explore the ways in which meetings check rumors and why this is necessary, and in the next two chapters I will show how "talk" can have dangerous consequences. Throughout, I will be concerned with demonstrating that studies of the ways in which talk alters social reality must look beyond speakers' intentions to the way in which information is distorted as it travels through a community.

Getting It All Out into the Open in Meetings

Villagers frequently bypassed the village courts and discussed disputes in less structured community meetings in which anyone could participate. These discussions had no adjudicator and no formal verdict. Like inquests and court hearings, weekly community meetings often seemed to accomplish very little. Often there was no decision, and if participants did reach one no one tried to enforce it. Disputes would reemerge in superficially altered form later and frequently were discussed again either in court or in community meetings. But although meetings seemed ineffective, many people apparently preferred them to village court hearings, and magistrates encouraged public discussions of certain types of disputes.

Similar community discussions coexist with village courts in many areas of Papua New Guinea. Indeed, Epstein (1974*a*: 28, 1974*b*: 94; see also Counts and Counts 1974) says that such meetings are preferred to courts in many Melanesian societies. Likewise, Scaglion (1983*a*) notes that the Abelam think that wide-ranging, open-ended debates involving large numbers of people produce more satisfactory resolutions to conflict than do narrower more focused discussions.

In many areas, the local people say that the purpose of such meetings is to get hidden grievances "out into the open" rather than to punish culprits or even to suggest solutions to conflict (Epstein 1974*a*: 14). But at the same time it is clear that participants and adjudicators are very selective about the information they reveal in public moots. Marilyn Strathern (1974), for instance, says that Hagen big-men realize that their groups' bargaining position could be weakened if certain kinds of information come to light, and so they carefully manage the presentation of evidence in public discussions. White (1990) also argues that although the A'ara of the Solomon Islands hold mediation sessions to get hidden anger "out into the open," they realize that cathartic displays of emotion can cause more problems than they resolve, and so participants usually avoid them. In short, it is unclear what exactly is brought "out into the open" in public discussions.

We have seen (chap. 1) that scholars have argued that often what adjudicators and participants bring "out into the open" is not the facts of the case but an official version of events which is in some way less problematic than the truth. Brenneis (1984) suggests that after people hear an official public version of a conflict, they stop speculating in private gossip about what happened. This is important because when people gossip about a dispute they run the risk of being drawn into the conflict. If they side with one of the disputants this could start quarrels if one of the listeners favors the other side. The official public version stops this private speculation and, thus, dampens the potential of conflicts to escalate.

Such analyses have given valuable insights into the logic of conflict management in small communities. But they leave many questions unanswered. Why, for instance, is gossip of such concern in some communities that people feel the need to create an official version of problematic events whereas in other areas rumors circulate unchecked? Do official versions of conflicts, in fact, stop people from gossiping about events? The fact that authors of the Papua New Guinea law code felt the need to make gossiping about cases that have been resolved in court an indictable offense suggests that public discussion does not necessarily stop private speculation.

In this chapter I will examine several community meetings and suggest that the concern with stopping rumors is part of a more pervasive concern about hidden aggression which, in turn, stems from a real preference for attacking people in covert ways. I will examine the ways in which rumors can be destructive and how constructing public versions helps check them.

The Remarriage of the Widow Haumele

Haumele, a woman in her early fifties, was widowed by the death of her husband, Tana, a little over a year before this conflict arose. A widowed woman is supposed to show respect for her late husband by waiting a year before remarrying. After that there is almost always a great deal of speculation about who will marry her.

The decision is complicated. Men wishing to marry the widow often have to deal with opposition from their wives. As well, several not always mutually consistent rules govern who the widow can marry. A leviratic rule states that her late husband's brothers have first right to the widow, with true and close classificatory brothers having a stronger claim than distant classificatory brothers. Because the kinship system reckons ties bilaterally, most people have a great number of brothers both inside and outside their patrilineage. Another rule is that the widow should marry into the initiation class of her deceased husband. Since many of the husband's brothers will be in the opposite initiation class, the first and second rule often conflict. In short, discussion of the remarriage of a widow involves determining not only who wants to marry her (and whose wife will allow the marriage), and who she wants to marry, but also who has the strongest claim. Further complications arise because some people believe that all the rules are "ways of the past" and that now the widow can marry anyone she wants provided her first husband's lineage is compensated.

The case of the widow Haumele involved all of these complications. People I talked to claimed that four men wanted to marry her. According to traditional rules, her husband's younger brother Gara had the right of first refusal. But his wife Apsambwai was opposed to the marriage and so was Haumele's son Bemba, a young married man of about thirty who thought Gara would be a bad stepfather. Gara himself said that he did not want to marry Haumele. But some people told me that he was lying because he was embarrassed by opposition from Bemba, Apsambwai, and others. All the other suitors were more distantly related to Haumele's husband and so were reluctant to marry her without being sure of Gara's approval.

The second candidate, Ambwambuli, was from the appropriate initiation class and was also a distant classificatory brother of Haumele's husband. Bemba said in a mediation session that he wanted his mother to marry Ambwambuli. But Ambwambuli repeatedly said he did not want to marry Haumele unless he could be sure that Gara and his close classificatory brothers approved.

A third candidate, Tunumu, was from the wrong initiation class but many thought he was Haumele's first choice since he was the only single man of her age group and many women are reluctant to marry a man who already has a wife because co-wives often fight. People claimed that Tunumu had been trying to win Haumele's affection by bringing her frequent gifts of meat. Finally, the fourth candidate, Mwanchambor, was another distant classificatory brother of Tana's from the appropriate initiation class.

The case was first discussed in an informal mediation session held by the village Councillor, Gwarambu.[1] The case was brought to Gwarambu's attention by Gara who was angered by all the gossip about Haumele's remarriage. As the true brother of Haumele's husband, Gara felt that her remarriage was his business and no one else's. In mediation, Haumele said she wanted to marry Gara. But his wife Apsambwai was against it, and there was a fight between the two women. Adding to the confusion, Bemba struck his mother and said she should not marry Gara because he was lazy and never helped Haumele or her children. She should marry Ambwambuli, instead, since he was a hard worker and often helped Bemba. Amidst the resultant chaos, Gwarambu concluded that resolution was impossible until everyone had calmed down.

About a month later, the case came up in a Monday community meeting. Hilanda, who was married to Haumele's sister and was a classificatory father of Tana and Gara, introduced the topic:

This is a big thing. The big brother died and the little brother is here. This is a big law of the ancestors. You can't go over the head of the little brother. If he says you should go to marry another man then you must go. If he says you can't, then you can't. If you disobey him then you and your husband will run into trouble. This is the law of the ancestors. Now under the new law [i.e., the national law] it is whomever the woman likes. Her new husband can give compensation to the little brother. Haumele herself has said that all the married men are flirting with her but later if she marries them she and the first wife will fight all the time. This is all I am going to say. You [from Gara's initiation class] talk about it and work it out, and I will just sit and listen.

Hilanda's words pointed to the contradiction between the "new law," under which Haumele could marry whomever she wished as long as Gara received compensation, and tradition, which gave Gara ultimate power to decide her fate. But Hilanda did not say which applied in this case and said that, as a member of the other initiation class, he would not interfere, beyond suggesting that Haumele wanted to marry a single man, but would sit and listen while Gara's initiation class worked it out.

The wives of Mwanchambor, Gara, and Ambwambuli followed and each said that she would go along with whatever Haumele wanted although, at least in the case of Gara's wife, this had already been proven false in mediation. Ronald, the village magistrate, scornfully pointed this out, saying that Haumele would never reveal her desires for fear of adverse reactions from the wives.

Ambwambuli tried to explain his role in the conflict. He said that he was offended because he had heard a rumor that Gara had told Apsambwai to say that she did not want Haumele as a co-wife. Gara allegedly told Apsambwai: "Just leave Haumele there and we will see; Ambwambuli and Tunumu can fight it out," implying that both men were pressing equally unjustifiable claims. But Ambwambuli felt that as a member of Gara's initiation class, his claims were stronger than Tunumu's and that Gara should have recognized this. Gara explained that he had spoken in anger, provoked by all the speculation about Haumele's remarriage which he felt ignored his right as her brother-in-law to decide her fate. But this comment enraged Ambwambuli's wife, Ilikopika, who argued that Gara had forfeited his rights over Haumele by never helping her with work or bringing her food. She said that people only talked about Haumele's remarriage because they felt she needed a man to look after her. This in turn provoked Hilanda who said that Gara was too embarrassed to help Haumele because of Bemba's hostility, and then warned everyone that Haumele could easily end up in the same situation as another woman who had run away to marry in another village because her husband's kin could not agree about who should marry her. Ambwambuli and Ilikopika, responding to what was possibly a veiled implication in Hilanda's remark, said that they had not told Bemba to oppose his mother's marriage to Gara. He had done this entirely on his own accord. Ambwambuli said that he had no inappropriate designs on Haumele and that he was only looking out for his initiation class' interests by trying to prevent Tunumu from stealing her:

If Haumele didn't object, and Bemba was tired of looking after her, then I would marry her. But if everyone is arguing about this woman, then I won't marry her. I am not talking for my own benefit when I talk about Haumele; I am doing it to help Gara. All the time I see that Tunumu catches game and brings it to Haumele. So I say: "She's not your woman that you should look after her this way. She belongs to [my initiation class]."

Haumele herself spoke for the first time and said that she would marry no one but Gara since one of her classificatory sisters had been killed by sorcery when she had married outside the lineage of her first husband. But an agitated Apsambwai responded, "Why are you so determined to marry Gara!? He never does any work that you should be so determined to marry him. You go marry this man who works hard [i.e., Ambwambuli]!"

As the discussion continued, Haumele's brother interrupted to say that Gara should decide the issue, and Tunumu denied that he was trying to win Haumele's affections by bringing her meat and said he was only helping a needy neighbor as the Bible said he should. Finally Apsambwai said that Gara could marry Haumele if this would prevent a fight over her, and everyone murmured approval. But Ronald, after a whispered consultation with his classificatory brother, Gara, stood up and said, "Gara says that he doesn't want to marry her. When she was newly widowed and when her husband was still alive, Haumele slept with other men. Gara does not want to marry her because of this."

After Haumele repeated that she would marry no one but Gara, the discussion gradually turned to other issues.

That night Gara and Apsambwai had a fight. Neighbors said that Gara had berated Apsambwai for putting him in an awkward position by publicly saying he could marry Haumele without consulting him first. A fight broke out when Bemba rushed in to defend her. The next morning Ronald held a mediation session. It was decided that Haumele should marry Ambwambuli, and word was sent to Tana's classificatory brothers in two nearby villages, Apos and Ta'uanangas, to ask if they had any objections. Ronald was married to Ambwambuli's foster daughter and so he was probably biased.

Soon word came back that Haumele could marry anyone as long as Gara approved. But three months later, someone announced in a community meeting that the Ta'uanangas relatives had sent a new message demanding a pig and four hundred kina (a large sum in local reckoning) from any man other than Gara who married Haumele. When I asked an informant about this change, she speculated that Gara must be behind it all. She claimed that Gara wanted to marry Haumele, but had denied it in public because everyone was saying that the marriage would be inappropriate since she was older and had taken care of him like a mother after his parents died. Now he was using his Ta'uanangas kin to covertly oppose her marriage to Ambwambuli.

Disputes and the Fear of Covert Aggression

The attempts to arrange the remarriage of Haumele were reminiscent of cases in previous chapters: the discussions were long, drawn out, and met with little apparent success. As in the discussion of rain in chapter 1, suspicion and bickering seemed to prevent resolution. There were several other obstacles. First, and most simply, many people with conflicting desires were involved. Haumele, her children, and her late husband Tana's immediate family had a say, and so did Tana's extended kindred (from Apos and Ta'uanangas) and the members of his initiation class (Ambwambuli, Mwanchambor, and their wives).

Furthermore, though it was difficult to negotiate consensus among so many people, it was necessary to do so because of a general anxiety that anyone dissatisfied with the result would take covert revenge. People were reluctant to do anything unless they could be sure that everyone approved. Neither Gara nor Ambwambuli, for instance, would marry Haumele unless they could be sure that everyone was in favor and Haumele, likewise, refused to marry anyone but Gara because she was afraid that he would resent her decision and would seek revenge in some way. It appeared later that her fears were well founded when it was rumored that Gara was behind his Ta'uanangas kins' demand for an exorbitant compensation payment. A majority decision would not have worked because people would have feared secret attack from those whose wishes had been ignored.

Third, people were trying to avoid appearing to interfere in others' affairs. Hilanda opened the discussion by saying that he would just watch while the other initiation class settled the affair and Haumele's brother Wanjeri, similarly, spoke of his reluctance to interfere in the matter. Ambwambuli and Ilikopika also took pains to explain why they had taken an interest in Haumele's remarriage. Furthermore, this reluctance to interfere seemed to be well founded since people (principally Gara) clearly resented it when they felt others were interfering inappropriately.

To add to the difficulties, people were worried that others were hiding their true desires in public and would pursue them through covert means such as sorcery. Gara said several times that he did not want to marry Haumele but her continued fears of sorcery revealed that she suspected he was not being truthful. My informant's comments about Gara and his Ta'uanangas kin showed that at least one other person shared Haumele's fears. Furthermore, it was clear that, indeed, some people were not being totally open, as when the four wives said they would agree to anything Haumele wanted even though this had been shown false by Apsambwai's earlier reaction when Haumele said she wanted to marry Gara. In fact, in the meeting, all of those who were rumored to want to marry Haumele denied it (Gara, Ambwambuli, Tunumu), and all of those who had previously opposed particular marriages denied their opposition (the wives of these men), or remained silent (Bemba). Taking these people's statements at face value, one might wonder why there was conflict over Haumele at all and so one suspects that at least some people were lying. It is not difficult to understand why the attempt to resolve the affair required several inconclusive meetings.

But a closer examination of the community meeting reveals more than a frustrated attempt to resolve the conflict. The matter was taken to mediation because Gara thought people should not be discussing Haumele's remarriage behind his back. When Ambwambuli later brought the matter up in the community meeting, he was worried about an insulting remark Gara had made behind his back, and the possibility that others might suspect him of instigating Bemba's actions (though no one had accused him of this). Apparently many of the participants were more interested in addressing gossip, suspicions, and insults than with resolving Haumele's status. People feared covert attack but were just as concerned about the possibility that others might suspect them of similar secret maneuvering. Thus Ambwambuli went out of his way to deny that he had put Bemba up to hitting his mother. People's suspicions about each others' motives and fears that they, themselves, were the object of similar suspicions seemed to create more anxiety and concern than did the issue of who Haumele should marry.

An Alleged Plot to Ensorcel Gara

A second, unrelated incident, coincidentally involving many of the same people, occurred some months later. The topic came up when the Councillor told his sister's son, Karalanda, to hurry up and pay compensation to Hapandi for leading an attack on him the month before. Karalanda protested that the Christians should pay the compensation since they had provoked his attack by saying that his son had been killed by Hapandi. The Councillor told Karalanda to pay the compensation first and then take the Christians to court, a remark that irritated Abel, the Inakor pastor, who retorted that the Christians were not afraid of court. Fuku'asa, then spoke:

Abel, you can't get up and oppose this talk of ours. All this talk comes up in your [that is, the Christians'] mouths. We have a point about you. You said that when the Christians went to Yubanakor [for an Easter celebration] someone would die. First you brought up this talk of Hapandi killing [Karalanda's son] and now this talk first of fifty kina and then of seventy kina came up with you. This talk of killing Gara.

This was a reference to a recent rumor. Gara's wife Apsambwai rose and described three dreams that had started the talk. In the first she had seen Hilanda giving fifty kina to Hapandi saying: "So he thinks money is worthless. He'll see my hand now." In a second dream, Hilanda and his wife gave Hapandi twenty kina.[2] Finally, in the third dream, Apsambwai met George, the Asanakor pastor, who told her, "You get up and run away. You are in the middle of a big fight now. They are angry over this money and they are going to shoot Gara now."

My translator told me that these dreams referred to a recent controversy over the Inakor coffee buying cooperative, or "business group" as it is locally known (and the subsequent course of the discussion confirmed this interpretation). The group was formed with contributions from all the villagers, and profits were supposed to be used to fund communal ventures. But under the management of Gara and four other board members money mysteriously and regularly disappeared, and the group was perpetually broke. Eventually, two of the board were accused of stealing the money and, though Gara was not himself accused of theft in the many community discussions about the group, the whole board was replaced under suspicion of theft and incompetence. My translator told me that a few months later, Gara asked for the return of 150 kina that he said he had lent the group during the final months of his management. The new board gave him 100 kina and said that the remaining 50 would "die with the group" as compensation for his bad management. Apsambwai had her dreams soon after and, because she was one of a number of women who had been "possessed by the Holy Spirit" in the recent Christian revival, her dreams were given a special significance. Gara and Apsambwai had since several times heard suspicious rustling outside their house at night, and this confirmed their fears that sorcerers were after them.

After Apsambwai, Nakukwiya, her neighbor and a member of Gara's lineage, spoke:

All the time I hear [Gara and Apsambwai] talking about this fifty kina. Every afternoon, every night. I hear them talking about this and it makes me angry. I heard them talking about this all the time and I went to my [classificatory] mother and said: "Do you hear these two talking about this fifty kina all the time? They never say who it is who gave the money to the sorcerer but always just talk about the money. Who are they guessing about [that is, accusing of hiring a sorcerer]? Is it the new board of the business group?" Gara heard [what

Nakukwiya had said] from [Nakukwiya's classificatory mother] and said: "I don't know anything about this talk. You tell me what boy it was who came and told you this and I will break his house and throw him out." But you can't deny this. I hear you all the time. Later I went and asked Mwachambor [another neighbor] about this: "These two talk about this all the time. We must get it out into the open [Neo-Melanesian: *putim long ples klia*] and investigate this fifty kina." Gara heard that and said: "Why are you talking about this fifty kina all the time? It's your fault. You and Apwelaka scold me all the time and now you have given fifty kina to Hapandi to kill me." Well, thanks a lot Gara. That's it. I gave Hapandi fifty kina to kill you.

My translator said that Nakukwiya was referring to a related incident. When Gara asked for the return of his 150 kina, Nakukwiya and Apwelaka demanded that he show them receipts from his personal coffee sales to prove that he had made that much money, implying that he must have stolen the money from the business group. Gara refused, and Nakukwiya was apparently worried that he might be suspected of complicity in the plot to kill Gara because of this incident.

After Nakukwiya, Fuku'asa, a member of the new business group board, questioned the prophetic powers of Apsambwai and the other Christian women and demanded proof that someone was trying to kill Gara.

But Henry objected:

If you want to talk like this you can't call the name of the Spirit. The Spirit is something of God. If you want to talk, talk about these people who have dreams. They make up these thoughts in their own heads. So if you want to talk, talk about the prophet women. They make these things up when they talk with each other. . . . When you guys talk you always talk of the Spirit and put this blame on the mission but that isn't right. You should talk about politics. It's politics that fouls you up. The Spirit is something of God. If we believe in God we can straighten out our lives and go to Heaven. So if you want to talk, talk about these prophet women and men. It is their own politics, their own dreams. . . . So when you talk you can't go calling the name of the Spirit all the time. You must call it the politics of men. That's all it is.

Henry was also questioning the Christians' prophetic powers. What they claimed God revealed to them was really a product of the "politics," or discussion, among men and women in the church. An old man, Saimbor, took up Henry's theme and suggested that the church was so surrounded by rumors that it resembled a tree completely obscured by vines:

It's not us non-Christians who make all this talk. It's you Christians. This church of yours isn't a house. It's like a tree in the bush that is covered with vines. You go under these vines and you can't get back out so you are in the dark all the time. You are always trying to get out to where it is clear and you can walk around. We outside men [that is, non-Christians], we walk properly. We don't have complaints or problems. We are free. You in the church are in the dark trying to get out.

And others followed, complaining that the church people always spread rumors. Finally, Gara's neighbor Mwanchambor interrupted impatiently to explain the history of the rumors and the meeting. He said that the rumors had started when Gara heard suspicious noises on his roof one night and had thought it was a sorcerer. In the morning he told Mwanchambor: "If I die they can't [investigate] a lot of different causes of my death. If I die it will be over this 150 kina. If I die you must get up [in the inquest] and say this." Mwanchambor suggested that they discuss the issue in the next weekly community meeting but Gara said he was going to put the matter "in God's hands." Later that day Nakukwiya asked Mwanchambor if he had heard the rumors about the plot to kill Gara and Mwanchambor repeated what Gara had told him. Fuku'asa overheard the conversation and brought the issue up in the community meeting.

Ignoring Mwanchambor, Hilanda responded angrily to the charges against him implied in Apsambwai's dreams, saying that dreams could not be taken as literal truth and that, although he was a Christian, he would support the non-Christians in court. Following suit, two members of the new board of the business group, Kewangu and Fuku'asa, denied the veiled accusation that they had refused to return Gara's fifty kina because they intended to use the money to ensorcel him. They said that they had no reason to kill the men they had replaced; it was more likely that the old board resented them. But Walafuku, a member of the old board, indignantly denied that he was involved in sorcery plots and said he was happy to be replaced since managing the business group was hard work. The Christians defended their claims to prophetic powers by quoting the Bible. The discussion continued with little resolution until Hilanda interrupted to introduce a new issue.

Nakukwiya, in an effort to prove to Gara that he was not involved in a plot to ensorcel him, took the case to village court about a month later. But the magistrates postponed the hearing because several of the participants were not there. The case had not yet been heard when I left the village in October 1986, six months after the issue was discussed in the Monday meeting.

Rumors, Covert Violence, and the "Politics of Men"

The discussion appears at first to be an attempt to stop a sorcery attack but closer inspection reveals a greater concern with the possibility of being accused of sorcery. Apparently, the potential victim, Gara, did not want the matter discussed in a community meeting; instead, those who thought they were under suspicion (Nakukwiya, Fuku'asa, Hilanda, and the rest of the business group) brought it up. In the first case, Ambwambuli denied that he had told Bemba to hit his mother before anyone suggested this; similarly, in the second discussion, each man inferred from circumstance and veiled statements that he might be a suspect and described the possible charges against himself before answering them. Nakukwiya told the story of how Gara accused him; Fuku'asa and the other members of the new board inferred that they might be suspects from the fact that the alleged motive for killing Gara was a dispute over the business group. They were probably trying to avoid being accused of sorcery if Gara or a member of his family were to die. And their fears were realistic since Gara had evidently told Mwanchambor to accuse those involved in the affair of the 150 kina at his funeral.

Rumors and hidden suspicions were apparently also of more general concern. Fuku'asa opened the discussion with the allegation that "all the talk comes up with the Christians." Henry and Fuku'asa later commented on the role of the church in propagating rumors; when Fuku'asa seemed to accuse the Holy Spirit of lying and causing trouble, Henry objected that it was not the Spirit but the "politics of men" which were at fault. Hilanda later echoed these sentiments when he protested that it was not right to discuss dreams about sorcery in church as such conversations were the source of many false rumors (about himself in this case). Finally, Saimbor provided the crowning metaphor when he described the church as like a tree so covered with vines that the light could never penetrate underneath. This is an image of the Christians surrounded by a web of rumor and lies which prevents them from seeing the truth. Saimbor's rhetoric also neatly reverses the conventional imagery of local Christian speeches, which portray "heathens" as covered up by "darkness" and sin, whereas Christians stand in the "light" of truth and goodness. Henry, Saimbor, and the others seem to be saying that when people discuss things their "talk" inevitably distorts the truth and causes problems for everyone. Indeed, suspicion and rumor did often seem to complicate things. The villagers attempted to pull rumor and suspicion into the public eye and this was, in itself, apparently thought to be beneficial since after the discussion there was no urgency about resolving the matter in court.

Hidden grievances are apparently associated with the risk of covert attack. In the first case, Gara was suspected of hiding his intentions in public and later taking secret revenge. Because his feelings were unknown, he could secretly try to prevent Haumele's marriage without being suspected. If he had revealed his desire (perhaps) to marry her, people would have ridiculed him because Haumele was so much older, Bemba and Apsambwai would have opposed him, and the other suitors would have resented him. Indeed, some of these things had already happened with the mere suggestion that Gara and Haumele might wish to marry. Others tried to block Gara's covert maneuvering by getting him to state his true desires.

In the second case, Nakukwiya was also worried by Gara's refusal to discuss his suspicions openly. Gara and Apsambwai evidently did not confront anyone but planted seeds of suspicion by reporting Apsambwai's dreams in church and hinting to neighbors that the incident of the 150 kina would be the cause of Gara's death. The suspects could, therefore, do little to defend themselves. Such behavior was a form of covert attack. A buzz of rumor seemed to implicate the new business group, Hilanda, and Nakukwiya. Moreover, Gara had ensured that they would be accused if he died. But it was hard to find the source of the rumor since Gara and Apsambwai did not name their suspects and did not want a public discussion of the issue when Mwanchambor suggested it.

In this case, as in those discussed in previous chapters, it is not hard to understand why Gara and the others preferred to drop hints and spread rumors and to avoid public confrontation. Those who took more open measures to satisfy grievances suffered reprisals. Small incidents were distorted in gossip and had serious consequences. When Haumele said she wanted to marry Gara, Apsambwai and Bemba were outraged. When the new board of the business group refused to return Gara's fifty kina, they were suspected of plotting to ensorcel him. Gara's incompetent leadership of the business group prompted suspicions of theft, which led to the replacement of the board, which led to sorcery accusations. Tunumu's gifts of meat to Haumele led to speculation that he was trying to seduce her and that she wanted to marry him. And this created gossip about her remarriage which angered Gara and caused my informant and perhaps others as well to speculate that he wanted to marry her and that he was using his Ta'uanangas kin to oppose her marriage to Ambwambuli. Similarly, in the case of rain (chap. 1), Mary's prediction that someone might die soon led to rumors about the Christians and rain. Karalanda's attack on Hapandi also aroused many suspicions. Apparently almost anything that happens, trivial or serious, leads to speculation about what remains hidden and to rumors that distort the truth and escalate conflict.

These cases followed a, by now, familiar pattern. First, people suspected each other of concealing their desires and pursuing them in secret ways. Second, people were worried that others suspected them of the very same thing. They were concerned about their reputations—justifiably so since there were many nasty rumors—and tried to stop suspicions by publicly denying covert maneuvering. Third, people were, indeed, not being totally honest in public. Fourth, people were reluctant to do things that might offend others realizing that this could lead to sorcery attack or sorcery accusations. Fifth, when people did act assertively this did, in fact, often cause trouble.

As was evident in previous chapters, these things are all related. Because visible actions can have serious repercussions, people hide their opinions and, if they act, do so covertly. But knowledge that people behave this way leads people to read deeper and darker meaning into apparently trivial words and incidents. This in turn creates rumors. People are worried about others' intentions and also worried that they themselves are suspected of nefarious hidden deeds. Being suspected of covert attack is dangerous because it can lead to equally secret retaliation through sorcery, or to accusations of sorcery. This self-reinforcing web of suspicion and counter-suspicion seems to concern the participants more than disputes over women (case 1), money (case 2), or rain (introduction). Community meetings address both rumor and conflict and ease people's fears of attack by allowing them to deny charges and warn others that attack will bring reprisals.

In the two discussions, and the meeting about rain, people also feared that conflict and rumor would harm the community. In the case of the rain, bad feelings between the Christians and Hapandi were suspected of causing the rain. Hilanda, who was not directly involved, brought the case of Haumele to the community meeting, saying that it should be resolved before it caused problems. The rumors started by Apsambwai's dreams in the third case similarly cast suspicion of sorcery on a large number of people. There seem to be two underlying premises: first, that public discussion prevents conflict from spreading, and second, that private problems can cause rumors that draw more and more people into the dispute and can have harmful effects on the whole community through natural disaster (such as rain), sorcery deaths, or sorcery accusations.

Things that are hidden are potentially dangerous. Bringing them out into the open neutralizes the danger. These themes crop up again and again in Kwanga meetings and examining a few more cases will show why "hidden talk" is dangerous and how publicity neutralizes it.

The Destructive Potential of Rumor

When two-year-old Katherine died, Fembor, her father's father, opened a meeting to discuss her death by suggesting Hapandi had killed her. Hapandi's stepson Samwa had died a few months earlier and Fembor had been among those suspected of killing him. Now he believed that Hapandi had ensorceled Katherine in retaliation. But Fembor said he had had no hand in Samwa's death and that he had only been accused because of a groundless rumor that he was angry about a pig.

He described what he believed to be the origin of this rumor. Samwa and his wife's brother, Ainumu, killed a pig in the bush but instead of bringing it to the village and presenting it to Fembor and Hapandi, the lineage headmen in charge of the bush, the young men cooked and ate it on the spot.[3] Afterward rumors began to fly around the community that either Fembor or Hapandi (or perhaps both) were angry. In the inquest, Fembor's daughter's husband Kewangu claimed that Fembor had had a more active role in creating the suspicions about Samwa's death than he was willing to own up to. Kewangu said that Fembor had told him that Hapandi would kill Ainumu "on Saturday or Sunday." Kewangu said that he had gone to warn Ainumu, who was a close classificatory brother, and that, as a result, Ainumu's classificatory father Henry took compensation money to Hapandi and Fembor. But both refused the money and denied that they were angry about the pig and said that, in fact, they did not even know that the young men had killed it. Both men repeated these denials in the inquest.

At the meeting, they tried unsuccessfully to find the truth behind this rumor. Finally Kwaru, a man of Fembor's lineage, made a general comment about gossip, which he felt was the true problem in this situation. He felt that both Fembor and Hapandi had been victimized by rumors that exaggerated the extent of the hostility between them:

I think it goes like this: Fembor sits down and he says some little thing about Hapandi. But all of Hapandi's kin hear it and they go and report to Hapandi. They carry this talk around and they themselves talk about it and talk about it and talk about it and the talk becomes a big thing now. Then later Hapandi says something angry about Fembor. All of Fembor's kin hear it and carry it down to Fembor. They carry it along: one man hears it and goes and reports to another man and so on. Then this talk gets really big. Both talks are big now. Then if someone dies on either side people say: "Oh yes, that's it. Look we heard this angry talk from Fembor and now someone on Hapandi's side has died. We heard it, this talk of Fembor's." Then when someone from Fembor's side dies it will be the same way. They say: "Look, this angry talk we heard from Hapandi, now it has come true and someone has died."

According to Kwaru "talk" is a problem in its own right. In this case there seems to be a lot of truth in Kwaru's interpretation. People drop hints in private conversations but in public they deny their words. This allows people to influence events without cost (chapter 3), but it can also backfire and cause problems. Thus, when Kewangu carried Fembor's warning to Ainumu and Henry, it was distorted so that Henry felt that Fembor himself might be annoyed over the affair of the pig. Later when Samwa died, Fembor was implicated. Then when Fembor's granddaughter died he felt that this web of rumors caused Hapandi to believe that Fembor killed Samwa and retaliate by killing Katherine.

Rumor spreads unchecked among kin and causes unforeseen problems for those who start it. Kwaru eloquently described this process when he told how Fembor made some little remark but it was picked up and passed along by his kin and soon many people were talking about it and what started as a trivial comment became "a big talk" that resulted in Katherine's death.

The Asanakor Schoolgirl

Hidden talk also threatens the whole community. While returning from school one day, an Asanakor girl remarked to her friends: "In Inakor when they finish Grade Six they come to the village and get married right away. People who have graduated from high school, too, just come to the village and get married and plant yams." This remark (which was felt to point up the "bushiness" of Inakor people who were unable to get good jobs in town and had to stay in the village and plant yams) caused an uproar among the teenagers and young adults of Inakor and a large group stormed down to Asanakor that evening and demanded that the schoolgirl come out so that they could respond to her comments. I joined the Inakor crowd to see what would happen in Asanakor. Some Asanakor men met the group and told them to go home, saying they could discuss the matter in court. A brawl seemed imminent but the Inakor youths eventually left, although they engaged in some minor vandalism along the road.

The next morning a police car came to Inakor. The police claimed that someone had gone to the local mission station, Brugam, and radioed to the police in Dreikikir, saying that a group from Inakor had attacked Asanakor with spears and knives the night before. The assembled Inakor people (myself included) denied this charge describing (reasonably accurately) the events of the previous night. A group of men from Asanakor then appeared. They said that the Inakor version understated the seriousness of the event, but admitted that there had been no spears and knives. The police set a date for a hearing in Dreikikir court and left.

I did not go to Dreikikir but witnesses told me that the Dreikikir magistrate said that the village court should handle the matter since it was not serious. A month later the village court magistrates tried to reconstruct the events that had resulted in an Asanakor man calling in the police. The Asanakor people said that they had heard a rumor that some Inakor people were about to attack Asanakor. After much discussion it became apparent that after the young people returned from Asanakor on the night of the fight, several of them had told the story to a group of older men who were also enraged by the Asanakor schoolgirl's remarks and boasted that they would attack Asanakor that night. Ainumu, a young Inakor man, overheard this conversation and went to Asanakor to warn his wife's family. The rumor spread quickly through Asanakor, and a man was dispatched to call the police. The magistrates reprimanded Ainumu for spreading the rumor. They said he should have realized that when people boast at their own doorstep they do not necessarily intend to act. People who "carried talk" caused trouble.

A remarkably efficient gossip network spread two chance remarks through the villages and created a serious incident. When the gossip crossed between the two villages, whose relationship tended to be competitive and slightly hostile, careless words were taken seriously and became "a big thing." This is similar to the suspicions that arose when Kewangu "carried the talk" from Fembor to Ainumu and Henry in another lineage.

People are careless when they gossip because they know they will not have to take responsibility for their words. This means that rumor spreads easily and the truth is distorted. Public discussion of rumors imposes accountability and checks the destructive potential of rumor.

Kichambwai's Inquest

People stressed the difference between public and private talk. When Kichambwai, a ten-year-old Asanakor girl, died, many people immediately suggested that she had been ensorceled to punish her father George for revealing tambaran secrets during the Christian revival. Several suspicious statements made by Inakor men which indicated that they might be angry about the revelations were discussed in the inquest. George was particularly concerned about a rumor that Henry, an Inakor man, had said in a Monday meeting that "the ground is a big thing." "The ground" is a figure of speech commonly used to denote the ways of the ancestors, particularly the tambaran cult, and so George thought that Henry, by pointing to the strength and importance of the institution ("a big thing") was threatening those who challenged it. Henry said that all he had meant was that the Christians should not throw away hunting and gardening magic associated with the cult because it was necessary for survival. He privately told me that he thought that his classificatory brother Bwalaka, an Inakor Christian, had reported the remark to George.

Henry did not attend the funeral discussion but went, instead, to a parent and teacher association meeting in another village. His classificatory son Walafuku defended him at the gathering:

This father of mine, he isn't a big-man like Hilanda. He is truly a rubbish man. What he says is that to throw away all of our things is not good. Things for finding meat, for planting yams. So every Monday [in the Inakor community meeting] he gets up and talks about this. He doesn't hide away and say this. He comes out into the open and talks about this every Monday. It's true that he said: "The ground is a big thing. Why have you thrown everything away? Now we have nothing." This is the story of Henry. But you can't worry about him. I am his child. I live near him and see him. He doesn't go around and talk about sorcery. All he is interested in is [cash cropping and making money]. If he hears you talking about this he'll sit down and talk with you. This man, if he hears you talking about women or planting yams or whatever he won't sit and talk with you. This kind of talk is like a spear shooting him in the stomach and he runs away. He doesn't sit around and talk with big-men either. He just meets with the youth group and talks with them about business.

But George was unconvinced and replied, "If you've made some talk and then the man dies do you think you can get away with it? Hah hah! It doesn't matter what kind of man you are. You said it: 'The ground is a big thing.'"

In his defense of Henry, Walafuku did not question George's interpretation of the statement but said that since Henry said it in public, he would not have hired a sorcerer. Moreover, Walafuku said that Henry did not gossip about sorcery, or indeed anything but business, and did not talk with big-men (who would be likely to hire sorcerers) but only with young men. What is implied is that people with intentions of hiring sorcerers hide their feelings in public and speak of them only in private. Since Henry's behavior was just the opposite—he made his grievance public and he did not gossip—he could not have hired the sorcerer to kill George's daughter.

George's reply, in fact, confirmed the logic of Walafuku's argument. If you have made a statement in public, George said, and then afterwards someone dies, how can you get away with it? You have gone on record as having a grievance and will not be able to deny it later. It is precisely for this reason that someone who had thoughts of hiring a sorcerer would not state his grievance openly, because then if someone died, everyone would know who was responsible. Following the same logic, if you want to stop someone from attacking covertly through sorcery or other means, you should publicize his grievance. Then he will know that it is unwise to hire a sorcerer since he will be suspected and may face reprisals.

Talk is a problem in its own right, but, by the same logic, "just talking" can resolve situations.

Kimbasumwa's Death

The idea that people often hide grievances in order to attack covertly and can be stopped if these grievances are publicized was also present in another inquest. In September of 1985 a new medical aid post was built to serve Inakor and Asanakor. A large celebration was planned for the opening and both villages spent the previous week hunting pigs. Traditional communal net hunting methods, the success of which were thought to be dependent on magic, were used. Hunting magic was distributed among several initiated men in a village and all of them had to cooperate to insure the success of the hunt.

As the week of hunting progressed one moiety of Inakor captured five pigs whereas the other moiety had no success. A fight broke out among the members of the unsuccessful moiety. Some young men outraged the initiated men by accusing them of using their magic to sabotage the hunt. The very existence of hunting magic is an open secret theoretically known only to initiated men, so young uninitiated men are not supposed to talk about it let alone criticize those who control it. A meeting was held to discuss the matter. Henry described this meeting when I interviewed him after a woman's death was linked to the incident: "In the middle of the argument, Hapandi [the Inakor sorcerer] came up to me and said, 'Don't argue, Henry, we are all from the same village here.' I continued to scold the young men and Hapandi came up again and said, 'It's our own village here.'"

According to Henry, Hapandi meant that Henry should not bother to scold the young men because Hapandi wanted to deal with them. If the young men wanted to challenge the initiated men then Hapandi would accept their dare and pit his strength against theirs. Implicit, of course, is the idea that Hapandi, a sorcerer, would surely win.

A middle-aged Inakor woman, Kimbasumwa, died about a month after the fight over the hunting magic. Henry, Ronald, and Gwarambu were all delayed in Maprik and missed the first inquest. That night, Henry listened to tape recordings that I had made of the meeting. He was disgusted with what he heard, considering that the "truth" (that Hapandi had killed Kimbasumwa because of the fight about hunting magic) had been "covered up." If people acted like that, Henry maintained, sorcery would never stop in Inakor. The right way was for the community to make clear that they all knew what Hapandi had done and that they disapproved. Faced with this consensus, Hapandi would be afraid to practice sorcery again. Having heard from many people in the past that it was imprudent to expose sorcerers, I was surprised. But Henry explained that if the whole community agreed on the issue it was safe to accuse Hapandi because he could not kill them all.

The next day Henry chastised his fellow villagers for failing to follow the lead he had given them. He said that bird familiars of sorcerers had started to cry out after the fight over hunting magic and had not stopped until Kimbasumwa died, implying that the fight had activated sorcerers. He told them that they should have brought this up in the inquest and accused Hapandi:

You don't know how to hold a proper discussion. When we all met you didn't follow up on the point I made. . . . If you had followed my lead it would have been easy but you talked of other things. . . . You didn't discuss things properly. You talked and you talked and you told plenty of lies. You should have made the discussion short, accused Hapandi of doing it, and told him to throw out his spears.

Henry also claimed that the death could have been prevented if the Councillor had addressed the issue a few weeks earlier in a Monday meeting. There had been no meetings for two or three weeks prior to the death. He chastised the Councillor in the inquest: "There is sorcery all over the village now. It's the fault of the Councillor. He didn't warn us when the birds started to cry out. If he had done that, the sorcerer would have heard it and been ashamed and stopped it."

Later Henry continued:

It's out in the open now. For two weeks I heard the birds cry but the Councillor didn't call any meetings. He just sent us out to cut grass [along the road as government labor]. I warned the young men when I saw them sitting around. I told Feambu that if we had a meeting I was going to introduce the issue that sorcery had started up. . . . If we had met I would have talked and sorcery wouldn't have killed Kimbasumwa. But for two weeks we didn't meet and now look, it's happened. We fought over hunting magic; the birds started to cry out, and sorcery came up.

Two other men, Suroho and Nakumini, echoed Henry's remarks. Suroho said:

If there were any leaders in this village we'd meet and talk about this. We'd put it all out into the open and tell [Hapandi] to get rid of his stuff. . . . If you had brought the matter to court, [Hapandi] would have thought: "They know about me now. They know about me." He would have thought that and he wouldn't have done it.

Nakumini expressed similar sentiments: "If we accuse him in strong terms then he will be afraid and throw [his sorcery spears] out. If we don't speak up then he'll say: 'They're just talking on the side.' And he will leave his sorcery spears."

Evidently Inakor and Asanakor villagers believe that warning culprits that the community suspects them is often enough to check them. When people cannot count on protective ambiguity, they know they may be held accountable for their acts and are unlikely to take controversial actions.

Getting It All Out into the Open

Like many other Melanesians, even though the Kwanga have village courts, they also hold long community meetings to look into conflict and other problems. These meetings often reach no decision about how to resolve the dispute, and even when they do it is generally not implemented. Instead, the Kwanga and many other Pacific peoples stress the value of bringing hidden things "out into the open." Why is this necessary and why is this goal accomplished more effectively in community meetings than in courts?

The cases in this chapter reveal that behavior in meetings is shaped by an elaborate set of beliefs about human behavior and its often unintended consequences. First, the Kwanga say that people hide grievances and attack in covert ways. If they think the public knows what they are up to they will do nothing, and so in meetings, people try to prevent covert attack by publicizing secret plots. People use circumstantial evidence and rumors to construct theories about what others might be up to. Many of these theories (such as the suspicion that Gara had put his Ta'uanangas kin up to demanding compensation) are probably untrue, but in some cases there really is something going on and telling of covert plots in public warns people that the community is aware. Issues are brought out of the ambiguous realm of gossip and veiled speech into an open forum where people can be held responsible and fear reprisals through sorcery, court action, or embroilment in long, expensive competitive exchanges.

Second, the Kwanga evidently believe that hidden suspicions are dangerous. People who suspect others of treacherous misdeeds may plot secret revenge, even if their potential victim's guilt is not proven. Fembor, for instance, believed that his granddaughter died because Hapandi erroneously believed that Fembor had killed Samwa. Consequently, the Inakorians believe that when people harbor secret suspicions about you, it is important to try to convince them that they are wrong by presenting yourself as a good and moral person in public meetings or by trying to show the audience how they could have reached mistaken conclusions. Thus, Fembor tried to show how rumor and miscommunication could have created the false impression that he was angry at Samwa.

The Kwanga also say that "talk" is a problem particularly when irresponsible young men and Christians "carry it around" so that it becomes a "big thing" and takes on an appearance of reality. Speakers in the meetings said that when people get together and talk they start rumors and these can be dangerous because they can make trivial incidents seem much more ominous and, thus, can draw the whole community into a conflict (as happened in the case of the Asanakor schoolgirl). Rumors also can have serious repercussions for individuals like Fembor. Such hidden talk should be checked by "getting it all out into the open," that is, by discussing rumors in public. In the meetings, people brought rumors before the public eye and then tried to show the audience that they were false. For instance, the Inakorians tried to show the Asanakor people how empty boasts might have led them to the mistaken conclusion that Inakor would attack Asanakor. These strategies allowed people to raise doubts in the audience's mind about the accuracy of the rumors and, thus, hopefully, helped to calm everyone's fears.

In each of these instances, in the local view, it is not necessary that a solution be found or even that the truth come to light. When people present accounts of what might have happened, what might have been said, or what others might suspect before an audience, they can check rumors, perhaps clear their own names, and prevent conflict from escalating.

Such a discussion would be difficult in court. Magistrates seek solutions to specific problems and try to restrict the discussion to matters that are immediately relevant. They discourage people from discussing tangential issues. But that kind of debate would do little to check the rumors and covert plots that are often the participants' central concern. Magistrates also often try to stop people from speculating on the basis of circumstantial evidence and rumor. In community meetings, however, people want to discuss possibilities that they cannot prove. They suspect that others may be hiding things from them and want to address this secret maneuvering even though they cannot provide conclusive proof of their suspicions. A court discussion that discourages speculation (though we have seen in chapter 4 that the magistrates do not always adhere strictly to this rule), would do little to ease people's fears of covert plots. Finally, magistrates discourage idle bystanders from watching court hearings. In community meetings, however, the audience is essential because it is the knowledge that everyone suspects him that is supposed to check the culprit, and, conversely, proving a rumor to be untrue would have little benefit if those who had doubts about your motives were not there to hear your argument. Perhaps, in short, the neighboring Abelam prefer unstructured community discussions to more narrowly focused mediation sessions (Scaglion 1983*a*), and people in many areas of Melanesia prefer public debates to courts, because unstructured public discussions are a more effective way of checking the rumors and covert aggression that seem to be such a central preoccupation of the local people.

The concern with rumors and covert aggression which prompts people to try to get things "out into the open" seems to be part of a more pervasive spirit of distrust[4] that is common in Melanesian societies. When the Kwanga discuss disputes, deaths, and matters of common concern they also make general comments about human behavior and about social life. In such rhetoric a dichotomy between things that are visible, or "out in the open," and things that are hidden or "covered up," is often prominent. Appearances are deceptive. People often conceal the truth. The Kwanga say you can never know what anyone is thinking, and they speak of "talking on the surface," "making houses to cover up sorcerers," "head talk," and "talk on top." Things, like sorcery and grievances, which lie hidden beneath misleading surfaces, are dangerous (see also Goldman 1983; M. Strathern 1972).

Comments by ethnographers about other Melanesian societies indicate that the Kwanga's pervasive spirit of distrust is not unique. Hau'ofa (1981: 82) says the Mekeo have a dualistic view of the world. Everything has a visible side characterized by "surface amity and harmony, like the beautifully decorated head of a Mekeo dancer" but this masks "the underlying tensions and hostilities among kinsmen." Visible things are safe and controllable, just as the person who walks through the center of the village can be seen by everyone and controlled by gossip and other measures if he deviates from norms of expected behavior. But each visible surface conceals a hidden, and more dangerous and uncontrollable, inside. This dichotomy is apparent in ideas about leaders. Chiefs live in the center of the village where everyone can see them and this checks their power. Their counterpart, sorcerers, live on the edges of the village or in the bush, are invisible to the public eye, and are thus uncontrollable, powerful, and dangerous. Secrecy and danger are closely related.

Young describes a similar situation among Goodenough Islanders. Villagers experience (1971: 135) "a superficial cordiality masking private fears and hatreds, and an almost unrelieved state of subconscious

stress. Most men cope, helped perhaps by seeking release in the practice
of sorcery themselves, or in *veyaina*, malicious gossip, which is thought
to be almost as damaging."

White (1985: 363) also argues that among the A'ara hidden "bad
talk" is the most negatively evaluated form of interpersonal conflict.
Villagers distrust surface impressions and they often suspect each other
of lying (1985: 359). People believe others attack covertly while preserving a face of goodwill.

I have argued that "getting it all out into the open" is a process that
makes sense in terms of a set of cultural beliefs about hidden danger.
Moreover, these concerns are not entirely delusional. Worries about
rumors and covert aggression, at least in part, reflect an experience that
lies beyond them. This seemed to be the case among the Kwanga. For
instance, when Ainumu carried rumors of imminent attack to Asanakor, a serious fight almost erupted between the two villages. The dense
web of kin ties provided an efficient gossip network and when rumors
traveled between villages, the distrust inherent in people's attitudes toward other villages guaranteed that they were prepared to believe the
worst, and, as a result, they were so alarmed that they called in the
police. In this way, the rumors aggravated conflict and drew in more
and more people. But public discussion of how the rumors began
showed people how they could have been mistakenly alarmed and,
thus, restored the peace. Evidently, it is true that rumors can cause
problems and public discussion can check their destructive potential.

Likewise, the pervasive fear of hidden malice and the suspicion that
people are lying in public reflect a situation in which people constantly
cast aspersion on each other in gossip and then deny it in public. Gara,
for instance, told Mwanchambor that he suspected Apwelaka of hiring
a sorcerer, but then Gara was reluctant to discuss his fears in public.
There were also cases in chapter 3 of people dropping hints about
sorcery but publicly denying their words. Furthermore, rumors and
hidden grievances do have serious consequences. Whispered attacks
on reputations can have serious consequences (real and imagined), but
when rumors are discussed in public people can deny charges and show
how trivial statements have been misinterpreted.

Perhaps there is something about small communities which generates the concern with hidden aggression and rumors. First, in small
villages with a high rate of local marriage, everyone is related to everyone else and many people have a legitimate concern in any decision or
conflict. People are bound to have conflicting interests and so almost
anything anybody decides is bound to displease someone. This prompts

people to avoid public action and pursue their goals in less visible ways. Consequently, people have a legitimate reason to fear that others are involved in covert plots. Second, small communities generate gossip since people share many common acquaintances whom they can talk about (Merry 1984). Furthermore, rumors can be damaging. Gossip, by its very nature, distorts its subject matter; people speculate irresponsibly because they know that they cannot be held accountable for their words since no one can be sure who said what to whom. The resultant rumors, therefore, often make trivial matters seem more ominous and thus draw neutral people into the conflict (Brenneis 1984; White 1985). Rumors can also seriously damage people's reputations. In fact, in some small communities, people are so afraid of malicious gossip and rumor that they avoid participating in public affairs.[5] Merry (1984) argues that in small close-knit villages, people are unusually sensitive to backbiting because it can damage their reputations, and this is serious since villagers are dependent on each other for companionship and aid. People who have contacts outside the local community will, conversely, be relatively unconcerned about slurs on their reputations because they can turn elsewhere if relationships in their own village go sour (see also S. Hutson 1971: 60). Third, and related to the first point, because people are so dependent on their fellow community members, they avoid acting in ways that will offend them. They may, however, pursue their goals or express their anger in covert ways since there is little cost as long as no one knows what is going on. But, again, this preference for secret maneuvering creates a pervasive fear of what is hidden from view. People fear gossip, rumors, and covert plots in small communities because they have reason to.

Meetings to address rumors, in short, seem in many ways to be the logical consequence of the processes discussed in chapters 3 and 4. Where people try to avoid accountability, rumors and suspicions can be dangerous, and so individuals try to neutralize hidden and diffuse danger by bringing it all out into the open. Publicity imposes the very accountability that people usually try to avoid.

"Getting it all out into the open" is a process that checks the fear of hidden danger which small communities create. In societies where people attempt to influence events by presenting themselves as knowledgeable, by whispering charges against others, and by advancing interpretations of natural events, "talk" is a problem, but talk can also be a solution.

CHAPTER SIX

Rivalry and Institutionalized Duplicity: The Sociology of Rumor

The Inakor and Asanakor people are so concerned about rumors that they hold long meetings just to look into them. They believe that rumors can have serious consequences and the evidence shows that, at least sometimes, they are right. When people gossip about things they speculate about secret plots and hidden malice. They start rumors that, over time, are often viewed as factual accounts. These can seriously damage reputations and can lead to undesirable repercussions, real or imagined, such as sorcery attacks or accusations of practicing sorcery. Furthermore, rumors can frighten everyone by making insignificant incidents seem much more ominous and can draw much of the community into even the most trivial of quarrels.

In this chapter I will examine the set of relationships in Kwanga villages which are so effective in generating rumors and ensuring that they have serious consequences. First, villages are comprised of many groups such as lineages, initiation classes, and moieties, which are predisposed to distrust each other and to resent outside interference. There seems to be something of a segmentary ideology among the Kwanga. Thus, the whole village of Inakor formed a united front in face of an insult from Asanakor, but as the case in this chapter will demonstrate, the two moieties of Inakor who stood united against Asanakor may separate on other occasions into antagonistic groups in response to perceived or real insults from each other. People are prepared to think the worst of members of other groups and tend to find dark meaning in apparently trivial remarks. Consequently, when gossip concerns other groups, people take the darkest possible view of what they hear and are sure that their group has been insulted or is about to be attacked. Then each social segment coalesces into a fiercely loyal unit in response to the perceived challenge. Thus, trivial quarrels between members of different groups often escalate until they involve all of the members of both groups.

Second, a dense web of kin and affinal ties cuts across lineage, moiety, initiation class, and village divisions. Consequently, many people do gossip with friends and relatives in other groups and so there are plenty of opportunities for rumors to start and conflict to escalate.

Third, the tendency to look for a hidden meaning in apparently innocuous remarks is exacerbated by the fact that less than honest communication is expected among certain categories of people. Individuals are supposed to preserve a public face of goodwill at all times toward cross-nepotic kin, distant kin, and exchange partners. But they are allowed to, and even sometimes supposed to, attack these people secretly by cursing them, by making veiled insults, or by spreading malicious rumors. Consequently, in many situations people have good reason to suspect that remarks have a deeper meaning. But this fosters a pervasive spirit of fear and distrust in which everyone looks for hidden attack in trivial words and actions. Sometimes they read a deeper meaning into incidents that should, in fact, be taken at face value. This results in rumors that distort the truth.

In short, the social structure of Kwanga villages ensures in various ways that rumors will rapidly depart from fact, and that they will have serious consequences unless someone manages to stop them in public meetings. Below I will examine these social structures in more detail.

The Dual Structure: Crosscutting Moieties and Initiation Classes

Lineages will be examined in chapter 10. Here I will investigate the institutionalized duplicitous behavior and rivalry between moieties, initiation classes, and exchange partners. I will first describe the social structure and then will show, with a case as illustration, how these structures create rumors.

Inakor is bisected by crosscutting moieties and initiation classes (see map 2). Moieties are localized and totemic. They comprise several

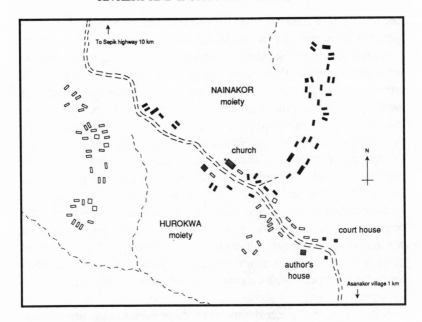

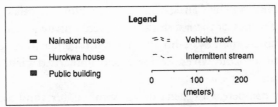

Map 2. The moieties of Inakor Village

lineages that have a vague notion of patrilineal connection. Genealogical relationships between the component lineages are, however, unknown, and people do not remember the names of, nor do they seem to find important, the apical ancestors who mark the connection between lineages. Nor do people rank lineages within a moiety according to genealogical seniority. Moieties are not exogamous.

The village is built along the tops of three adjoining ridges. The moiety variously called "Hurokwa," "Inakor," and "on top" (a literal translation of the Neo-Melanesian label for this moiety which refers to the fact that the ridge where they live is higher than that inhabited by the other moiety) lives on the western ridge. I will refer to this moiety as Hurokwa to avoid confusion. The other moiety, Nainakor, or "down below," lives on the central ridge and on a third, lower ridge to the east.

The hamlet of Waramemu is on the central ridge, physically contiguous with Nainakor, but part of Hurokwa.

Each moiety is further divided into localized subgroups. The Hurokwa moiety comprises three groups: *apwe umwe* (literally: bird meat, this refers to cassowary meat) on the northern half of the upper ridge; *fe umwe* (pig meat) on the southern half of the upper ridge; and finally, *kini che* (literally: tail child, this means last child) in Waramemu, the Hurokwa hamlet adjoining Nainakor.[1] Similarly, Nainakor is further divided into Nainakor or *ki tokwe*, living on the northern tip of the lowest ridge, and Umwanjimbi or *howe tokwe* living on the central ridge and on part of the lower ridge. These subgroups seldom act autonomously and their main purpose seems to be facilitating the distribution of prestations. For example, a man from *kini che* who receives a small pig may distribute meat only to *kini che* members (of both initiation classes), but a larger prestation will be shared with *fe umwe* and *apwe umwe*. Each of these localized subgroups are internally divided into two initiation classes.

Initiation classes bisect the moieties. They initiate each others' sons into the tambaran cult. The two classes are currently called *gwar* and *ambwa*, the names of the last grade they were initiated into. Initiation classes comprise the boys who are initiated together, their elders and juniors, and also the wives, widows, and unmarried girls associated with the men.

Moieties compete with each other in some contexts and cooperate in others, but there is a persistent competitive sentiment between them. The relationship between the two initiation classes is similar, but less highly charged. Traditionally, most of the competition between moieties, and between initiation classes, was related to the tambaran cult. Tambaran initiations involved competition between initiation classes, each claiming that their staging of the event was far superior to that performed for them by the other. But each initiation class was internally divided into two moieties that competed with each other (so for instance, the Nainakor half of the ambwa class competed with the Hurokwa half of ambwa). The facade of the tambaran house was divided down the middle; the paintings of the Nainakor artists were displayed on one-half and those of the Hurokwa artists on the other. Likewise, when the decorated initiates emerged for the first time into public view they did so in alternate pairs of Nainakor and Hurokwa men. As each pair emerged, people from the audience ran forward to mark with lime those whose decorations they considered to be particularly fine, and at the end of the day, the initiates of one moiety were voted superior to the other. Similarly, Nainakor and Hurokwa initiators displayed their yam harvest inside the tambaran house and tried to outdo each other.

Although the last tambaran initiation was performed in Inakor around 1978 and there was doubt about whether there would ever be another one, both moieties and initiation classes continue to compete in other contexts. This rivalry is particularly marked between moieties. For instance, when two young Hurokwa women announced their intentions of marrying Nainakor men, Hurokwa people objected at the next Monday meeting that although many of their women married Nainakor men, the Nainakor men always "kept their women for themselves." (But no one seriously attempted to prevent the marriages.) The young men of the two moieties also formed separate youth work groups.[2]

The persistent competitive sentiment between the moieties is most obviously linked to their physical separation. Although many people have kin and affines in the other moiety and they work in the gardens regularly with them, in everyday life the moieties are, in many ways, like separate villages. News, such as the birth of babies, is slow to travel between moieties and at night, the primary visiting time, people are often reluctant to go to the other moiety unless the moon is bright because they fear sorcery attacks.

Interviews with children and with adults about their childhood revealed that the moieties are prominent in a child's view of the village. When asked who she disliked, a Hurokwa girl said that she did not like the people in Nainakor. She later went on to say that at school the Hurokwa girls fought with the Nainakor girls. Another woman said that when she was a child in Hurokwa she did not like all the adult men and women in Nainakor because she did not know them and was afraid they would yell at her. Because she knew all the people in Hurokwa she was not afraid of them. When I asked children to list their kin they would often start with their own moiety and, after exhausting this, would go on to the other one.

The salience of the moieties in the child's view seems primarily to be based on the physical separation of the groups but the association of the opposite moiety with marriageable people serves to increase the importance of moiety divisions in adolescence. It was, in fact, a group of "eligible bachelors" who told me (on several different occasions) that people should choose marriage partners from the other moiety. The schoolgirl who said she did not like Nainakor people also said this was because "they are no good; they are always flirting. They like the girls [in Hurokwa]." Her father once got angry at his adolescent classificatory daughter for going to Nainakor. He said it was dangerous for a young eligible female to go alone to the other moiety unless she went straight to the door of her kin there. In short, there is a pervasive spirit of distrust between moieties.

Rivalry between moieties, and between initiation classes, is never very deeply buried and there is a tendency for apparently trivial events and actions to activate and intensify these feelings. But although the two moieties compete with each other, as do the two initiation classes, neither moieties nor initiation classes are likely to become permanently opposed factions. This is because, as we have seen, the two moieties cooperate with each other in some contexts, as do the two initiation classes.

The overlapping patterns of cooperation and competition are further complicated by kin and marriage ties that cut across moieties and initiation classes—and the tendency to marry within the village and across moieties ensures that everybody has such ties. In this situation, a person who is in some contexts looked on as a kin or affine is, in others, a rival. For instance, when a woman from the gwar class is married to a man from the ambwa class, she and her husband will be aided in making prestations to their exchange partner by her kin, many of whom will be members of the ambwa (receiving) side. And these contributors will receive a share of the return prestation. In short, institutionalized rivalry between moieties, between initiation classes and between exchange partners does not lead to permanent enmities within the village because everyone who is in some contexts an enemy is in other contexts an ally.

Moreover, rivalry and antagonism is not expressed through violence or splitting of the village but in competitive food exchanges and, in the past, tambaran initiations (Tuzin 1976). Interestingly, moieties compete in food exchanges, but tambaran initiations involved cooperation within an initiation class which cuts across the moieties. Thus many of the people who competed in the initial food exchange cooperated in the tambaran initiation, and so rivalry did not result in permanent factional divisions within the village.

Exchange Partners: How Conflict and Competition Escalate

Each man inherits two exchange partners.[3] The individual's primary exchange partner, called *anumbo* in Kwanga (and *gawas* in Neo-Melanesian), is from the opposite initiation class and the same moiety.[4] Anumbo initiate each other into the tambaran cult and also bury each others' dead. Both activities are associated with a series of food exchanges. In some cases lineages are paired as anumbo.[5] Anumbo live in the same or adjacent hamlets, have gardening land near each other, and share hunting bush and magic.

There is a general notion that anumbo are brothers. But this seems to be a metaphorical rather than a literal description of the relationship since people are unable to trace their genealogical relationship to their anumbo and, indeed, seemed somewhat puzzled when questioned about it, claiming not to know even if there is a common ancestor, let alone who it was. One anumbo is considered to be the older brother and the other the younger but this is not consistent across initiation classes, that is, one class is not considered to be the "older brothers" of the other.[6] Marriages between members of anumbo groups are not in principle proscribed even when they belong to lineages that are believed to be patrilineally related. But because of a rule that proscribes marriage between blood relations, (reckoned bilaterally through three or four generations from the last marriage), many anumbo are, in fact, considered to be too closely related to marry each other.

The second exchange partner, called *umweminga* or *nau* in Kwanga (and *pren* in Neo-Melanesian; literally: friend), is in the same initiation class and opposite moiety. During the ambwa mwe tambaran, initiates consume hair of pigs and feathers of cassowaries caught in their moiety's bush. This is believed to give them the power to attract game to hunting nets but it also means that eating this game would make them ill. Rhetorically, this is the basis for the competitive exchange of game between the two moieties as a man, unable to consume his own catch, presents it to his "friend" in the opposite moiety.[7] This is a gesture of competition since the recipient risks the shame of being proven an inferior hunter if he fails to return a similar gift. Umweminga also exchange domestic pigs and participate in competitive yam exchanges associated with the tambaran cult.

Umweminga are described as eligible marriage partners. But, again the rule proscribing marriage between blood relations may mean that many umweminga cannot, in fact, marry each other. Even in these cases, however, the two umweminga will continue to call each other "nau," a term that captures the ambiguity of the situation since it is used to refer to: (1) people who are both umweminga and eligible marriage partners; (2) people who are eligible marriage partners but not umweminga; and (3) people who are umweminga but not eligible marriage partners. (To further the confusion, the word "nau" is also used to describe the relationship between villages allied in warfare.) There is also a general view that people should choose marriage partners from the opposite moiety. But in a community with a population of less than four hundred, a high rate of marriage within the village, and a fairly wide proscription of marriage to blood kin, people often do not have many eligible marriage partners, and this may be the reason why there is only a slight statistical preference for marriages between moieties.

Individual pairs of anumbo and umweminga cooperate in some contexts and compete in others. The Kwanga gloss both types of exchange partners sometimes as "friends" and in other situations as "enemies." In fact, cooperation with an anumbo or umweminga almost always has a competitive tinge. For instance, when making a prestation to his anumbo, a man is usually helped by contributions from his umweminga who is then given part of the return prestation. But this "gift" is also a challenge to the recipient to make a return.

A community-wide food exchange between the initiation classes which occurred in fall 1984 illustrates the overlapping patterns of cooperation and competition between anumbo, between umweminga, and between both moieties and initiation classes. The two initiation classes of Hurokwa exchanged pigs and yams. During the Hurokwa exchange people debated whether, on receiving a prestation from their anumbo, they should share it with their umweminga in Nainakor. Some people said that since your umweminga is a "friend" you should follow Christian principles of generosity and "help each other" by sharing food. Others maintained that giving part of the prestation to an umweminga was a competitive gesture, since the recipient is obligated to return the prestation. Furthermore, this would start competition between the moieties since when the two initiation classes of Hurokwa had a food exchange and each man shared his prestation with his umweminga in Nainakor, this was a challenge for the two initiation classes of Nainakor to have a food exchange so they could return the gifts to their umweminga in Hurokwa. In fact, Hurokwa's food exchange did prompt an exchange in Nainakor a few months later. Thus "cooperation" between umweminga in competition between anumbo prompts a further round of competition between umweminga.

Groups as well as individuals are paired in anumbo and umweminga relationships. Apwe umwe and kini che from Hurokwa are umweminga to the Nainakor subgroup of Nainakor; fe umwe from Hurokwa is umweminga to the Umwanjimbi subgroup of Nainakor. Usually individual pairs of umweminga and anumbo compete in the context of exchanges that involve larger groups. For instance, tambaran initiations involve a series of yam and pig exchanges between individual exchange partners but there is also a notion that the whole of one moiety/ initiation class is competing with the other.

When individual pairs of anumbo and of umweminga compete with each other, the affair usually escalates to involve most of the community. The success or failure of a particular individual in a competitive exchange is thought to reflect on his whole moiety or initiation class (depending on the type of exchange). Consequently, he is almost always helped out by contributions from his fellow moiety or initiation class members and he, in return, divides the prestation he receives back among them. Rivalrous sentiments between moieties and between initiation classes mean that the entire group is likely to take it personally when they feel that one of their number has been insulted by a member of another group. Thus, private quarrels between members of opposite moieties can easily result in exchanges involving the whole village.

To make matters worse, people have reason to suspect that their umweminga will avoid public challenges and attack in indirect ways. Umweminga should maintain a "face" of cooperation and mutual support although true feelings are often thought to be (and are) rivalrous. The conventional way to challenge one's umweminga to a competitive food exchange is to imply that he is a poor hunter or a poor gardener when gossiping with kin in the other moiety, who can be relied upon to pass the message along to the intended recipient.[8] Consequently, people pay close attention to gossip and are inclined to suspect that remarks made by members of the opposite moiety contain veiled insults. So almost anything anybody says could be interpreted as a challenge and could eventually involve the whole community in a competitive exchange. These processes will be illustrated in the following case.

A Quarrel over House-Thatching

Many forms of competitive exchange between moieties, between initiation classes, and between exchange partners have disappeared with the tambaran cult. But the impulse to competition, particularly between moieties, has survived the cult and is often expressed in the unlikely context of house-thatching.

Traditionally, houses were thatched with sago palm fronds split lengthwise and lashed to the frame of the house. Europeans introduced a new style of thatch produced by a labor-intensive process of securing individual sago leaves to a central bamboo pole about four feet long. Making enough thatch to roof a large house (which would require about three hundred panels of thatch) would be almost impossible for a single family and so when a large "European style" house is built, the owner usually recruits his kin and affines to help him and in return prepares a meal for them and returns the labor when they need help. This is an unremarkable extension of a general pattern of mutual aid among kin and affines.

But sometimes the opposite moiety is invited to help thatch the house and is given a large prestation (usually including a pig) in return. Since the Kwanga believe in the exchange of equivalents (see also Forge 1972), the affair is not finished until the host moiety has been invited to thatch one of the recipient's houses and is given a food prestation in return. Exchanges continue until each side has given and received precise equivalents in labor and food.

People are often willing to overlook discrepancies between what they gave and received back, since complaining will shame the other side and will prompt them to prove their honor by seriously escalating the scale of the exchange, which will involve both sides in considerable expense and labor. But all it takes to involve the whole community in an expensive and time-consuming exchange is for one person to whisper a complaint to kin in the opposite moiety. So competitive exchanges have a tendency to grow in spite of the expressed wishes of most of the participants. This was the case in a series of exchanges linked to house-thatching which occurred in the spring of 1986.

ROUND ONE: THE TALK OF THE CHICKENS

When Hilanda, an elderly Nainakor man, decided to build a large new house to accommodate himself and his two wives, the Inakor Councillor (also from Nainakor and a classificatory sister's son of Hilanda) assigned the villagers to thatch the house as Monday government labor. Since the Councillor had asked both Hurokwa and Nainakor to help Hilanda as public aid for the elderly and also to express appreciation for the fact that Hilanda had served the village in his younger days, first as headman under the Australian colonial administration and later as village Councillor, Nainakor did not give Hurokwa a pig in return for their help. Instead the two moieties just exchanged food on the day of the thatching, as an expression of goodwill and as a small community celebration.

From the beginning, however, the status of the affair was ambiguous. Some people took the already stated view that they felt this was not a case of Hurokwa helping Nainakor. Instead, everyone had been doing public service. In this view, if the two moieties exchanged food at all, the exchange should have been balanced since neither was paying the other; they were just celebrating a festive day of community service. Others, however, did not share this view. They felt that Hurokwa had helped a Nainakor man and should, therefore, have received more food than they had given to compensate them for their labor. These differences of opinion surfaced when, a few weeks later, Kenamini, a Hurokwa man, started to build a large house for himself and his family. Seeing this as an opportunity for another exchange of food and labor, some young Nainakor men began to complain loudly that they had cooked some chickens for their exchange partners in Hurokwa on the day of Hilanda's house-thatching, and had received back only soup (with no meat). These young men seemed to view the roofing of Hilanda's house as community labor and, in this light, their complaint was somewhat justified since they felt that they had given more than they had received in an exchange that should have been balanced. They felt that this imbalance could be corrected if the whole community thatched a Hurokwa house and then when the two moieties exchanged food afterwards, Hurokwa cooked some chickens and gave them to Nainakor to pay them back for the ones Nainakor had given Hurokwa during the exchanges after thatching Hilanda's house. But many Hurokwa residents felt that thatching Hilanda's house had not been community service at all but had been an exchange between moieities. They felt that they should have been given a pig since they had helped a Nainakor man thatch his house (at the request of another Nainakor man, the Councillor) and so they were irritated by the Nainakor boys' complaints about a trivial thing like chickens. It later became apparent that there was also something else involved. Exchanges between moieties can drag on for years. Moieties may take years to return prestations and so at any given time there may be several outstanding debts on either side. This situation is further complicated by the fact that there are always disagreements about what exactly are the debts owed by each side. Who owes what is always ambiguous because prestations can be interpreted in various ways. For instance, if Hurokwa gives a pig to

Nainakor and Nainakor returns a cassowary some people will feel that the pig and the cassowary cancel each other out and the affair is finished. But others will say that since the two are not equivalent, Nainakor owes Hurokwa a pig, and is owed a cassowary in return. In subsequent discussions, it seemed that at least some Nainakor people felt that Hurokwa was still in their debt from some (unspecified) past exchange and that they, therefore, should either have given Nainakor extra food in the exchange over Hilanda's house or should, at least, have foregone their payment for helping with the thatching.

I first heard about the issue when it was discussed at length at the next Monday meeting. (I pieced together the background to the case from discussions with translators and interviews with others who had been involved.) In the meeting, some Christians scolded the young Nainakor men for complaining about their chickens, saying that this would surely provoke a competitive exchange between the moieties which was a bad custom of the ancestors and should be abandoned. The young Nainakor men tried to explain by saying that they were angry because they had been tricked into giving the chickens by some Huro-kwa boys who had boasted to their Nainakor kin that Hurokwa was going to include a pig in its prestation. Fearing that they would be shamed by receiving meat without giving any in return, the Nainakor men quickly killed the chickens. But the talk of the Hurokwa pig turned out to be an empty boast, and now the Nainakor men wanted some chickens in exchange for the ones they had given Hurokwa.

This discussion roused the ire of two Nainakor men, Wange and Feambu, who called out: "Go ahead, Hurokwa, you tell us how many pigs are on each side!" This challenged Hurokwa to provide a reckon-ing of the state of exchange debts between the moieties going back over several years and almost certainly implied that the Nainakor men felt that Hurokwa was in their debt from some past exchange.

Feambu and Wange's remarks enraged Numu, an elderly Hurokwa man. He screamed: "We are Christian now; we don't do this anymore." And in contradiction to his first remark: "Wange, you don't have any bush land to go and kill a pig and give it to me so you sit down and shut up!" This was a clear challenge in local eyes since Numu was publicly shaming Wange by suggesting that he would surely lose in a competi-tive exchange because he had no bush in which to hunt pigs. The only honorable response to such a remark is to prove your opponent wrong by giving him an impressive prestation.

Numu's remarks were met by tittering from the audience and calls for him to sit down and shut up. People were embarrassed by Numu's words since he was Wange's umweminga. Umweminga should maintain a public face of mutual respect and should challenge each other only indirectly through kinsmen in the opposite moiety. Someone suggested to me later that Numu should have gone to one of his many classificatory brothers in Nainakor and suggested that Wange had little bush land and was unable to catch pigs and should have let the message reach Wange's ears through gossip. This would have been proper behavior; shaming Wange publicly was embarrassing to everyone and probably indicated that Numu, an old man, was getting a little senile.

By the end of the meeting, Hurokwa had invited Nainakor to assist in the thatching of Kenamini's house, saying they would return the "chickens" on this occasion. "Chicken" is often used as a euphemism for pig and almost certainly had this meaning on this occasion since Nainakor's blatant complaints could only be honorably met by a large prestation, including at least one pig, which would demonstrate Hurokwa's productive powers and allow them to shame Nainakor by pointing to the new debt. This move unambiguously established the thatching of Hilanda's house as the first round of an exchange of labor and food between the moieties which would be completed with the thatching of Kenamini's house. By doing so, however, the Hurokwa men implied that they had not been adequately compensated for helping Hilanda, since that work could no longer be viewed as community service.

A few weeks later, a group of Nainakor men helped thatch Kenamini's house and received two wild pigs and a domestic pig in return for their efforts. These pigs went officially to Kenamini's umweminga Wangembor. Later that night, a group of Hurokwa men purchased a pig in another village, Yubanakor, and carried it to Numu's house in "the dead of the night." The next day Numu presented the pig to his umweminga and adversary of the previous Monday, Wange. Wange and Wangembor both distributed their pigs among all of Nainakor. This was a large prestation by local standards.

ROUND TWO: HUROKWA DEMANDS A RETURN

Hilanda (the Nainakor man whose house had started the affair) opened the next Monday meeting by saying that he was ashamed because he had heard that Hurokwa had been complaining that they had been inadequately compensated for thatching his house (which was now established as an act of aid to the Nainakor). He had wanted to give Hurokwa a pig on this occasion, but when he asked his family and fellow moiety members to help him, they had refused, saying that they had contributed to prestations to Hurokwa for two other houses for Hilanda and that was enough. This statement can in part be taken at face value as an excuse for Hilanda's failure to give Hurokwa a pig in thanks for thatching his house, but was also possibly a veiled reminder to Hurokwa that they had not yet returned these previous prestations.

Hilanda said that he was going to give a pig to Kenamini's family and their anumbo[9] (the kini che subgroup of Hurokwa), since they had taken the lead in thatching his roof. In fact, Hilanda told me later that he was giving the pig to Kenamini's group because he believed that most of the complaints about the inadequate compensation had come from them. This would not have been surprising since this group had carried a disproportionate share of the burden of contributing to the prestation to Nainakor for thatching Kenamini's house, and so they were most likely to resent not having received a pig from Hilanda. But Kenamini's group told me privately that they had not complained about Hilanda's stinginess; they said that it was Hilanda's own son's wife Mwandipi, a Hurokwa woman married into Nainakor, who had been complaining that Hilanda had shown disrespect for her brothers in Hurokwa when he had not given them a pig.

The pig Numu had given to Wange was also discussed. Some Nainakor men claimed that Numu's prestation was blatantly aggressive and would provoke a large-scale competition between the two moieties that no one wanted. Numu's pig should have gone with the other pigs as return for the thatching of Kenamini's house. For Nainakor to "help out" their "friends" in Hurokwa by thatching Kenamini's house, and Hurokwa to, similarly, express their appreciation with a gift of pigs and yams, was in accordance with Christian principles of generosity. But Numu's gift was entirely aggressive, following as it did on a blunt disparaging of Wange's ability to return the gift, and so marked a return to the bad old ways of competition. Furthermore, by both traditional and modern standards, Numu's initial criticism of Wange had been rude, and the secretive way he had gone about obtaining a pig at night, so that the gift caught Wange totally unaware and he could not lessen the disgrace by making a small return gift immediately, continued this pattern of bad manners. Numu, however, claimed that the pig was just a peace offering to "shake hands" with his umweminga Wange after their quarrel and that he had meant to give his pig along with the others, but when the men had gone to Yubanakor to pick it up, the pig had run away into the bush and had only reappeared when it expected to be fed in the evening. It was already night before the men got it back to Inakor.

After the meeting, the Nainakor people pooled their money and purchased four pigs. Wangembor quietly gave one of these pigs to Kenamini in return for the one he had received.[10] In a large communal exchange, Wange gave one of the pigs to Numu, Hilanda gave one to Kenamini's family and anumbo, and Fuku'asa gave one to his umweminga Henry, the senior man of Kenamini's lineage.

The first three pigs were expected in return for the pigs given by Hurokwa, but the fourth pig caused general confusion in Hurokwa. The intended recipient, Henry, claimed to be mystified. But others said they had heard Henry complain that the pig Wangembor had given Kenamini was too small and should have been cooked since Kenamini had given Wangembor a large cooked pig. (Cooking a pig involves a lot of work and so if someone shows enough consideration to present their anumbo or umweminga with a cooked pig, the recipient should show similar consideration when making the return gift.) Nainakor was insulted by these complaints and wished to shame Henry by giving him a pig.

I volunteered this explanation to Henry's wife Kwahapa who denied that she and Henry had complained about Wangembor's pig (although she told me privately that she thought the complaints were justified). She said that it was Kenamini's brother's wife Chalimbwai who had been enraged at receiving a small uncooked pig and had gone to the door of some of her classificatory brothers in Nainakor and shouted: "Does Wangembor think that we are his rubbish that he should give us an uncooked pig! The pig we gave him was cooked." I asked Kwahapa if she was going to tell Nainakor that they had given the pig to the wrong person, but she said that only someone who was "rubbish" and could not make a return prestation would not welcome a "gift" from their umweminga. In other words, if she had publicly complained about the pig it would have looked as if she did not want to receive it because she was poor and lazy and so could not make the required return gift of another pig. Later in the day, however, Kwahapa and I were sitting together when Kwahapa's classificatory brother Apwelaka, a Nainakor man, walked by. Kwahapa called him over and explained to him that it was not her but Chalimbwai who had complained about Wangembor's pig and who was the appropriate recipient of the retaliatory prestation.

That evening, Nainakor officially presented the four (cooked) pigs to Hurokwa. Henry graciously received his pig with a speech denying that he had criticized Wangembor but saying that he was happy to act as spokesman for his group (which included Chalimbwai) and accept responsibility for their actions. He continued with a general comment on the nature of relations between moieties: "We'd like to finish with this custom. But like I said before, it's not just us [big-men] who do the talking: it's all the men, women, children, coconut and betel palms, pigs, and dogs. We'd like to finish with this but they all talk." In other words, as Kwahapa later explained, it is not the big-men but the women, young men, and children who start food exchanges by complaining. This seemed to be largely true in this case.

ROUND THREE: HUROKWA GIVES A FINAL PRESTATION TO NAINAKOR

Each side had given and received four pigs. But an informant explained that the local people reckoned that since two of the pigs Hurokwa had given Nainakor were wild, and all four of the pigs returned had been domestic, Hurokwa now owed Nainakor two domestic pigs, since wild and domestic pigs are not equivalent. No one demanded two wild pigs from Nainakor (the logical concomitant) because people realized that Nainakor could not control when they would be able to capture two wild pigs.

The affair was brought to a close when Hurokwa pooled their money and bought two pigs, which were presented to Nainakor (specifically to Hilanda and Fuku'asa). The exchange and the events that led up to it were discussed at the next Monday meeting. Ainumu and Rambuli, two classificatory brothers, one from Hurokwa and the other from Nainakor, were scolded for precipitating the exchange by passing on inflammatory rumors between the moieties. But the two men (predictably) claimed that they had said nothing serious; their words had been distorted. Rambuli claimed that all he had said was that if Hurokwa did not return Nainakor's prestation before the next yam harvest, the whole exchange would start over again. My translator explained that Rambuli meant that since Nainakor had made its prestation when they were short of yams just before the harvest, waiting to make their return until after the harvest would give Hurokwa an unfair advantage and would prompt Nainakor to retaliate with a new prestation.

The discussion soon drifted to the more general issue of competitive exchanges. Most people agreed they should be stopped. Wange said bitterly that Nainakor would like to stop the custom but was always provoked by complaints from Hurokwa. Henry tried to defend his moiety:

We [Hurokwa] didn't say anything. What happens is that we meet and discuss things. We are just finding ways [that is, just discussing what could be done rather than necessarily stating what they will do]. Then someone hears it and says: "This is what they are going to do now. We are going to beat you guys [Nainakor] now." You [Nainakor] hear this talk and are afraid.

This was an interesting analysis of the genesis of exchanges. Henry claimed that competitions resulted when people misinterpreted empty boasts and carried them as challenges to the opposite moiety. No one wanted to participate in exchanges; they resulted from uncontrollable rumors.

Fembor, another Hurokwa man, picked up this theme trying to explain away a rumor that Ainumu had told Rambuli that Hurokwa was going to give six pigs to Nainakor (a serious escalation of the exchange). Fembor claimed that Ainumu had overheard a conversation between two men, had misunderstood their words, and had passed on this misinformation to Rambuli. Once again rumors and misunderstandings were the culprits.

Later in the meeting Wange returned to the subject of rumors saying, "You people who carry the talk back and forth must stop. This is forbidden. If we down below [that is, Nainakor] or you on top [that is, Hurokwa] sit down and agree to make a prestation, then no one can go carry the talk around. We are just talking. We aren't really going to do it. So you can't carry this kind of talk around."

Wange's remarks were greeted with a chorus of agreement.

After more general discussion of food exchanges, two umweminga, Fembor, from Hurokwa, and Ambwambuli, from Nainakor, ended the discussion by once again chastising those who "carry the talk back and forth." Fembor said, "If I say something [in Hurokwa], you can't carry this talk down to Ambwambuli. This is the custom from before. We used to do that, carry the talk."

Ambwambuli replied, "Before when we wanted to do a tambaran initiation, if a man [in Hurokwa] said some insult [about Nainakor] then we would hear it and worry. Then I'd say: 'We'll have a competitive yam exchange now.' So we harvested our yams and competed. Then it would go and go and become a big thing and then we'd start a tambaran."

In short, "carrying the talk back and forth" leads to competitive exchanges and tambaran initiations. Umweminga should challenge each other indirectly by leaking their complaints to kin in the opposite moiety. But this institutionalized indirection leads people to take gossip seriously and so they often end up attributing inappropriate weight to empty boasts. Rumor becomes a "big thing" and results in food exchanges that no one wants. Once again, hint and gossip may be tempting strategies but they come back to haunt people. As with sorcery, gossip and innuendo lie at the heart of the system of exchange and initiation. Exchanges cannot be stopped as long as there are rumors.

Moieties, Kin, and Competition

Rivalry between moieties is never very deeply buried, and there is a tendency for apparently trivial events and actions to activate and then aggravate these feelings. In the case of Kenamini's house the Nainakor boys' complaint about their chickens started an exchange between Hurokwa and Nainakor which soon involved everybody in the village and lasted for several months, despite the expressed desire of many of the participants to stop competition between moieties. Men, women, and children were deeply involved in the affair and instigated the exchanges through their complaints.

Kin ties cutting across moiety divisions aggravated the situation. In some cases, as when Rambuli told Ainumu that Nainakor might escalate the exchange, people warned their kin in the opposite moiety about complaints and threats they had overheard in their own moiety. In other cases, people purposely sought out their kin in the opposite moiety to complain of ill treatment by that moiety, as when Chalimbwai went to her Nainakor brothers to complain about Wangembor's pig.

But the rivalry and antagonism created by these processes culminated not in violence or splitting of the village but in a competitive food exchange. Traditionally, the cycle would have been completed by a tambaran initiation, as Ambwambuli indicated in his speech in the last meeting about the exchanges associated with house-thatching. An informant, Kwahapa, made a connection between gossip, food exchanges, and initiations. When I asked her whether the apparent cause of a Hurokwa-Nainakor exchange, complaints over food, concealed some more significant problem, she replied:

I don't think so. This is really a fight over food. When down below [that is, Nainakor] cooks some food for on top [that is, Hurokwa] and then they wait and wait and don't get it back, then they complain. Then we [Hurokwa] hear that and worry and give them back some food. Then all down below [Nainakor] looks at it and says: "This isn't the same as the food we gave you. This is different. This is a new debt." Then down below [Nainakor] gives another prestation to us [Hurokwa]. It's always been like that. Before we did that and they started up an initiation festival and we competed with that.

In other words, in the past gossip led to inter-moiety food exchanges that eventually resulted in tambaran initiations. In short, although latent rivalrous sentiments are easily activated and conflict quickly escalates, this rivalry does not result in violence or community fission. Gossip leads to inter-moiety food exchanges that could very well have resulted in a tambaran initiation if Christian opposition to the cult had not been so strong.

Rumors and Institutionalized Duplicity

Speeches by Fembor, Henry, and Wange in the final Monday meeting show that the Kwanga recognize the close connection between gossip and competitive exchanges. Henry displayed considerable insight into his own social system when he complained about the way idle boasts seem much more serious when people carry them to kin in the opposite moiety. Kin ties facilitate the transmission of information and institutionalized distrust between members of opposite moieties means that people have a tendency to place undue weight on innocuous boasts. Rumors get out of control and seem almost to take on a life of their own, involving people in exchanges they do not want. Fembor and Ambwambuli, two umweminga, picked up this theme by warning the young men not to carry inflammatory remarks to exchange partners in the opposite moiety.

But, ironically, this points to another key element of the pattern, that is, "carrying talk back and forth" to kin in the other moiety is not always irresponsible behavior on the part of young men. Quietly complaining to your kin about your umweminga is actually the prescribed way to attack him, as Fembor indicates in his speech and as was also apparent in comments on Numu's behavior. People cast their complaints in veiled ways and communicate indirectly through gossip networks, partly because they want to avoid being held responsible for food exchanges that will involve the whole community, but also because hypocrisy and covert attack are institutionalized in relations between umweminga. In public they must appear friendly, helpful, and supportive but in private they are allowed, and in some contexts even supposed, to attack by spreading malicious rumors. People take rumors seriously because they have reason to believe that they will be challenged indirectly through gossip by umweminga who preserve an innocent public face of goodwill.

Kwanga social structure creates a situation in which people always have reason to suspect a hidden meaning behind every remark or action. But when everyone is always trying to read between the lines, this creates rumors that, because of the segmental structure of Kwanga villages, are bound to have serious consequences.

Clearly, the kin network that crosscuts moieties and initiation classes is an important part of the system. Kinsmen are supposed to convey insults between exchange partners. They also sometimes start exchanges inadvertently when they talk with relatives in the other moiety and their words are given greater weight than the speaker originally intended. In the following section I will examine the role of the kin network in spreading rumors.

The Kindred

Kwanga genealogies are shallow. Most people cannot name relatives who died before they were born, even within their patrilineage. Apical ancestors who mark the point of fission between two groups are also usually forgotten. The lateral extent of kinship reckoning is, however, much more impressive. People know the appropriate kin term for someone with whom they have no more in common than a great-great-grandparent, even if they cannot trace the precise relationship. A common Kwanga explanation of a relationship, for instance, goes something like: "Oh yes, she is my sister. No, not my true sister. Her mother and my father came on the same road [that is, they called each other sibling]. No, they were not true siblings either. Her mother and his mother were of one blood. No, their mothers did not have the same parents. They were just sisters." The reckoning of kin ties is bilateral and genealogical memory is as great for links through women as for those through men.

The Kwanga kin term system does little to differentiate patrilateral and matrilateral relatives or to distinguish the patrilineage. One can have mothers, fathers, sisters, brothers, and children both inside and outside one's own patrilineage. Furthermore, the kin terms that specifically take into account cross-sex links (*mango* for mother's brother, *wabuko* for mother's brother's wife, *hinoko* for father's sister and also for father's sister's husband, *ruwache* for a man to his sister's child, and *naruche* for a woman to her brother's child) are not restricted to particular patrilineages. For example, men of ego's mother's generation and patrilineage are mango, but so are ego's mother's classificatory brothers from outside her patrilineage.

The result is a broad, bilateral network of kin which cuts across other social divisions.[11] People are not only members of particular lineages, moieties, and initiation classes but are also the centers of idiosyncratic kindreds to which they owe affection and support. These links facilitate the transmission of gossip between groups and also ensure that many people from different groups will be involved in the same affairs.

There is another way that kin relations generate rumors. Certain kin relations also involve an institutionalized duplicity similar to that found in relations between umweminga which leads people to suspect a concealed meaning behind any statement. It is received wisdom that kin terms do not always accurately reflect the nature of relationships and, among the Kwanga, two criteria that are not readily apparent in terminology distinguish among kin. First, people distinguish close from distant kin. Distant kin are called *hima wa'i* in Kwanga (which roughly translates as domestic people) and *bisnis* or *hap lain* in Neo-Melanesian. Close relatives are marked by adding *umwe* (literally: real) to the term; a man might emphasize his close tie to a child, for example, by calling himself, *yapai umwe* (literally: real father; Neo-Melanesian: *papa tru*). People also distinguish parents, children, and siblings, on the one hand, from affines and cross-nepotic relatives, on the other hand. Distant and cross-nepotic kin, like umweminga, must be treated with respect and friendliness in public but should secretly attack each other in a variety of contexts; close kin, on the other hand, can be criticized directly but can usually be counted on for support.

This set of relationships also patterns communication in the village. In public people are duplicitous, since straightforward speech in front of an audience that includes the first category of kin often involves violating the etiquette of these relationships, and, moreover, these people can curse if displeased. Privately, people speak freely, and information disseminates rapidly through networks comprising people of the second category of kin.

Cross-Nepotic Relatives: *Kandere*

The relationship between mother's brothers and father's sisters and their cross-sex siblings' children is a culturally elaborated one of mutual support and aid. For convenience, I will use the Neo-Melanesian term *kandere* to refer to these four relationships. Although parents and children can and often do fight, argue, and scold one another, kandere should do none of these things. For instance, Satapi, a young newly married woman, ran away from her husband and went to stay with her father's sister and her husband Gwarambu. Satapi's husband's family asked that Gwarambu scold Satapi and send her back. But he responded that, as her kandere, he was obliged to give her refuge and he could not reprimand her. People are obligated to help their kandere and also to give them anything they want.[12]

The close relationship between kandere is particularly emphasized in funerals. The death of a parent is also one of the few contexts in which cross-cousins are distinguished from parallel cousins. When a man dies he is buried by his anumbo and by his true and classificatory sisters' children. Similarly, a woman is buried by her anumbo and her brothers' children.[13] A pig and yams are given to both kandere and anumbo to "wash the dirt" of the burial from their hands. Both the labor and the food will be reciprocated at future funerals of members of the recipient side.

The prestation is almost always described as compensation for the labor and risk of pollution involved in the burial. But this rhetoric masks a more complicated set of beliefs. True kandere never take part in the burial because it is said that they, like the nuclear family of the dead person, are too grief-stricken to perform this labor. But the payment always "goes in their name." When a woman dies, for instance, her classificatory brothers' children will bury her but the payment is given

A yam garden

A man and his two wives spreading coffee to dry in the sun in an Inakor hamlet

A Monday community meeting in Namingawa (Inakor)

Inakor and Asanakor men listen to a discussion about land in Yubanakor

A meeting breaks up in Namingawa

An Inakor man making a speech in a
community meeting

A woman makes a net bag as she sits with her young son listening to a meeting in the shade underneath a house

to her true brothers' children who then distribute the food to all of her classificatory and true kandere, making sure that those who buried her receive handsome shares.[14] So it is clear that the payment is not just a compensation for the labor involved in the burial but it also recognizes the loss of an important relative.

Indeed, the food payment is also said to "cool the anger" of the kandere over the loss of their mother's brother or father's sister. Traditionally when a man died, his sister's children would destroy his garden, cut down his coconut palms, sago palms, and other things created by his labor to punish his children for hastening his death with neglect and abuse.[15] An informant explained this custom in words to the effect of: "When our kandere is alive, he looks after us and gives us things. We see all the time that his children disobey him and abuse him. Later when he dies, we think of how his children have disobeyed and abused him and we go and cut down his coconut palms and destroy his garden." This attack appropriately prevents the unworthy children from enjoying the fruits of their dead parent's labor. True kandere almost always say that they have too much affection for their cross-cousins to destroy their father's possessions, and so it is classificatory kandere who make the punitive raid. The attack can be forestalled by a handsome prestation from the dead man's children.[16]

Interviews indicated that the ideological emphasis on the warm supportive relationship between kandere is not borne out in practice. I asked some children about their relationships with their kandere. To most their kandere were distant figures. Most said they never went to stay with their kandere or were given food by them. Children under the age of ten, moreover, did not even know the word (in Kwanga or in Neo-Melanesian) for "kandere" and called relatives in this category "father" or "mother."

Furthermore, although the Kwanga usually describe the relationship between kandere in positive terms, it also has a negative aspect. Mother's brothers and father's sisters possess a cursing power that they can use to make their kandere ill or even to kill them in infancy. They are said to do this when children abuse their parents. A woman may ask her brothers to curse her disobedient children. A breach in the behavioral norms between kandere can also lead to cursing. Mother's brothers and father's sisters who feel that they have not received an adequate portion of their female kandere's brideprice can also kill her children in infancy.

The mother's brother's curse has three variants. The less serious form is performed by saying the victim's name while spitting. This makes the victim ill but the sickness is usually not fatal. A more serious curse is effected by doing this over a leftover portion of the victim's food. Finally, the mother's brother can curse his kandere by calling the names of his lineal ancestors. These second two curses cause illnesses that may be fatal unless the victim or his family takes steps to identify the culprit and get him to reverse his curse. The father's sister's curse is believed to cause poor garden harvests and inability to catch game.

The mother's brother's curse can be reversed by asking him to blow on a leaf that is put in a bowl with water and hot stones. This process is believed to first imbue the leaf with the spirit of the attacker (Kwanga: *himamwale*; Neo-Melanesian: *win*) and then to release the hold of this spirit as the vapors are released by the hot stones and boiling water. When people are ill, their mother's brothers are often asked to blow on a leaf just in case they are responsible.[17]

It is also interesting to note that almost all of the practices described above apply to classificatory rather than true kandere. People say that the relationship between a man and his true sister's child (or a woman and her true brother's child) is like that between parent and child. One woman told me that she could scold her true brothers' children but not those of her classificatory brothers. Similarly, it is believed that classificatory rather than true kandere perform curses, and funerary behavior also involves classificatory rather than true kandere. "Sentiment" is seen to be stronger between true kandere, as shown by the facts that a close kandere is thought to be too grief-stricken to bury a dead relative whereas a classificatory kandere is not similarly incapacitated by emotion, and that true kandere are too concerned about their relatives to curse them whereas classificatory kandere are not. But institutionalized, culturally elaborated expressions of "sentiment," such as the prohibition of criticism and fighting, are characteristic of classificatory rather than true kandere. Ironically, it is real sentiment that prevents the close cross-nepotic relatives from acting as kandere, and, for this reason, they are considered more like parents than kandere. Cultural elaboration of support and positive feelings seems to be greatest where, in fact, mutual aid and affection are not great and there is even a fear of covert aggression through cursing. In short, between kandere, people have good reason to suspect that a benign public face might conceal a much more dangerous reality.

Affinal relations are in some ways similar to those between kandere. A man should not fight with or otherwise abuse his wife's parents and brothers (and vice versa) and is obligated to give them anything they want. A woman's husband's mother is believed to possess the power to curse the garden of a neglectful or abusive daughter-in-law.

Close and Distant Kin

Relations with siblings and parents are in many ways thought of in opposite ways to those with affines and classificatory cross-nepotic relatives. Siblings and parents can be relied on to help in times of need. In a community meeting Hilanda, for instance, chastised a man and his brother's son for fighting:

Families should not break up like this. Families should get along with one another and watch out for [attack from] other families. If another family wants to fight with you, you must all band together against this other family. . . . So I am telling you clearly. You must know this. A family is a good thing. They will support you when you fight with other people.

Funerary behavior also recognizes a person's dependence on siblings, children, and parents since, if cross-nepotic relatives were usually an important source of support, presumably they, too, would be suspected of hastening a relative's death by failing to give him or her the expected attention.

But whereas cross-nepotic relatives must always maintain a face of goodwill, the basic harmony between close kin is not thought to be threatened by a certain amount of criticism and fighting. Techambu, for instance, said of his brother's son at an inquest: "If you want to scold Apwelaka about this go ahead. I scold him too all the time. He is not my kandere that I should be silent. He is my son so I scold him."

Distant kin, however, are treated similarly to cross-nepotic relatives and affines. Goodwill and obligation to help each other are ideologically elaborated but not borne out in practice. A young woman, Kenuku, for instance, told me in an interview that she had expected to have to drop out of school after her father's death. She said, "We thought that only our parents would look after us and give us food while we were in school, not other people. Only our true parents. . . . We thought that we should stay home and grow the food that we needed for ourselves. If we went to school who would there be to do it for us?"

In adulthood, siblings replace parents as those who will help in times of need. But only true siblings are considered reliable. After a little girl died, Mwachambor chastised the child's mother's brother for mistreating his sister:

I hear him yelling at his sister all the time. So I scolded him once. I told him he shouldn't fight with his sister all the time and then later go and ask her to give him some food. That's not right. You should have helped her when her child was sick but you are no good. You always fight with your siblings. You shouldn't fight with your sisters; when you are short of something they will help you out. And when they are short you will help them out. We only children find it hard. Who is there to help us when we are short? You people with lots of brothers and sisters, you can ask them for help. We only children, it is hard for us: with classificatory brothers and sisters we will think: "I can't ask them for help, they might rebuff me." But with people who are the same blood as you, you can take whatever they have and you will give them whatever they want.

As blood links become attenuated, the ideal of mutual aid and generalized reciprocity is retained. But in reality, the generalized reciprocity of close kin gives way to a carefully balanced reciprocity between distant kin. For instance, when a married couple makes a food prestation, the woman's brothers, true and classificatory, contribute yams and money. But true brothers often wait and help only if the classificatory brothers fail to do so.[18] Thus the food exchange symbolically elaborates mutual aid among classificatory kin. But unlike the generalized reciprocity between true siblings in day-to-day life, mutual aid between classificatory siblings in food exchanges must be carefully balanced. In theory, if the woman fails to give a small feast of small game or tinned fish and rice for her classificatory brothers in recognition for their help, they may curse her pigs causing them all to die in infancy.[19] True brothers also have this power but will not use it because of their affection for their sister. Here again, where the ideal of mutual aid is culturally elaborated, in reality, it is limited.

Two Categories of People

Evidently, the Kwanga make two main distinctions among kin. The first distinguishes cross-nepotic relatives and affines from others. The second distinguishes close from distant kin. These distinctions overlap since close kandere fall into the same category as close nuclear relatives. Relationships with classificatory kandere, affines, and distant kin are marked by an obligatory attitude of support and generosity, a proscription on overt fighting and criticism, and the possibility of covert attack through cursing. In other relationships mutual aid and support is less emphasized in ideology but greater in practice and negative feelings are expressed more freely.

The Kwanga usually describe the ban on quarrelling and criticism among kandere, distant kin, and umweminga in positive terms but the same set of rules can be seen to prescribe covert attack at least in some circumstances. Close kin can be criticized directly. This criticism may be unpleasant but it is relatively harmless.[20] Distant kin and kandere must hide bad feelings behind a deceptive face of goodwill. But, as long as this "face" is preserved, kandere and distant kin are free to attack by cursing or by leaking criticism through gossip networks. In fact, such behavior is considered proper in some situations as when a mother's brother curses a sister's child who is abusing his or her mother. Thus, as in many of the cases in previous chapters, it is what is hidden that is most fearful.

This set of relationships patterns communication in the village. In public people are duplicitous but privately information disseminates rapidly through kin networks. Close kin demonstrate their concern about each other's welfare by passing on any criticism or threat that they hear in gossip so that the object of the rumors can take steps to defend themselves against possible challenges, slurs to their reputations, or sorcery plots. For instance, Annie, a little girl who often stayed with me, would drive me to distraction by faithfully telling me about any complaint about me that she heard. In a weak moment I complained about this to her mother. Later when some tinned fish disappeared from my house, some people suggested that Annie might have taken it since she was often inside the house. Her mother responded that this could not possibly be because Annie was very loyal to me as shown by the fact that whenever anyone complained about me, Annie would tell me about it.

Everyone monitors gossip closely, believing that public speech often hides more than it reveals, because distant kin, classificatory kandere, and umweminga could easily be concealing intent to harm behind an obligatory face of goodwill. But this creates a situation in which everyone looks for the concealed truth in apparently trivial words. Furthermore, sometimes statements are genuinely innocuous and when people read some darker meaning into them they start unnecessary rumors.

Thus, the combined effect of moiety and kin relations is not only to facilitate and encourage indirect action but also to make inevitable the problems associated with such strategies, that is, rumors that are damaging to individuals and to the community at large.

Clearly the etiquette of social relations involves a prescribed duplicity that shapes political strategies and can also cause unforeseen problems. People are expected to treat umweminga, kandere, and distant kin one way in public and to reserve other sorts of behavior, such as challenges and cursing, for private contexts. The distinction between public and private behavior also involves a complex code of communication. In the following section I will reexamine the rationale behind the etiquette governing relations between exchange partners, between moieties, and between initiation classes by going back to a few incidents in the case of Kenamini's house and also bringing in some new material on the tambaran cult.

Stage Culture

In his description of the Mehinaku Indians of Brazil, Gregor evokes an extended dramaturgical metaphor, saying that social life everywhere can be understood as drama:

Like their theatrical counterparts, the real-life performers act out their parts in a spatial setting whose physical characteristics mold the course of the action. Preparing their performance backstage with the help of teammates and presenting it to an audience whose response further affects their conduct, they do not simply repeat their lines, but dramatize or overcommunicate them so that the audience will be sure to know who they are in the drama. [Gregor 1977: 7]

On the quite different subject of academic politics, Bailey (1977) evokes a similar stage metaphor distinguishing the "front stage": "what is said out in the open where anyone can listen" from the "backstage": "what must be communicated to a more restricted audience" (1977: 10).

Such stage metaphors (which are, of course, common in social science models since the publication of Goffman 1959) differentiate public and private behavior. What occurs in public is often symbolic. People attempt to convey certain messages about the "roles" they are playing, that is about their own character and status, and they also make claims about the relative position of individuals and of groups.

"Backstage" in more private conversations they can communicate more freely since no one can later be sure who said what to whom.

The stage metaphor sheds light on the etiquette of exchange relations. Public and private actions and words have quite different implications. If Numu had challenged Wange privately, for instance, he would have signaled recognition of Wange's (and his whole moiety's) fundamental equality. But his inappropriate public challenge showed profound disrespect for the whole Nainakor moiety. It seems that when relationships, as between umweminga, distant kin, and classificatory kandere, cease to be principally personal (that is, involving two individuals) but also implicate the relative positions of groups such as lineages, moieties, or initiation classes, then public interactions are taken as symbolic claims about status. The tambaran cult and the system of social statuses associated with it are full of similar dramaturgical devices.

KWAHAPA AND HENRY RESPOND TO THE "MYSTERY PIG"

When the "mystery pig" was given to Henry (the senior man of Kenamini's lineage) by his umweminga, Fuku'asa, Henry and his wife Kwahapa graciously accepted the pig in public but Kwahapa privately told her classificatory brother in Nainakor that it was really another woman, Chalimbwai, who had complained about Wangembor's pig.

In this case, protesting the injustice of Fuku'asa's gift in private had a quite different meaning than a similar, but public, complaint would have had. A public protest would have signaled to others that Kwahapa and Henry did not want to receive a gift from their umweminga, which could only mean that they were lazy and without the resources to return the gift. Kwahapa's private protest to her brother with whom she did not have to maintain "face," however, delivered a double message: that she was happy to receive Fuku'asa's pig and could easily make a similar return gift, and that she and Henry had not complained about Wangembor's pig.

YAM GROWING PRIVILEGES

The tambaran cult is associated with an elaborate set of markers of social status. For instance, there are many rules governing how initiates of various tambaran grades can organize their gardens.[21] Men also gain rights to grow different kinds of yams as they progress through the grades of the cult.[22] Initiates of the ambwa mwe grade, for example, can grow a particular kind of short yam called *apkwase*. This yam apparently produces no better yields and tastes no better than other varieties; the right to grow it is just a marker of cult status. Furthermore, my informants said that people who had not yet been initiated into ambwa mwe could grow apkwase yams as long as they were not planted in the section of the garden nearest the public path. They could even give these yams to their anumbo as long as they put them in a basket and covered them with something else. In short, people who had not been initiated into the ambwa mwe grade could do anything short of making a public display of growing apkwase yams, as this would constitute a claim to having the right to do so.

In fact, making a public display of growing forbidden yams was a conventional way of goading the other initiation class into performing a tambaran initiation. One class would start assuming the privileges of the next highest grade as a challenge to the other. The rules are a language of claims. By conforming to the rules in public, people signal that they respect the authority of the next highest grade; by breaking the rules publicly people signal that they no longer respect the position of the more advanced initiates. Private, or backstage, violations of the rules, however, have quite a different meaning since symbolic attempts to hide these violations signal respect for the other moiety.

TAMBARAN SECRETS AS A LANGUAGE OF CLAIMS

The tambaran cult is shrouded with secrecy; women and uninitiated men may not see or speak of various aspects of the cult on pain of death.[23] But much of this secrecy is primarily a marker of social status. Interviews with various people revealed that many women and uninitiated boys knew the secrets. Several boys said that their fathers (and in one case even a mother) had told them tambaran secrets but had warned them not to tell anyone else. One young uninitiated man even said that fathers and older brothers had to tell the uninitiated men about what went on in the tambaran so that boys would be prepared to face the ordeals with proper dignity. Several children said that their fathers had brought home pork from the cult house for their wives and children, warning them that they must consume the meat in the house and not speak of it to anyone since the fact that men consume pork in the cult house is supposedly a secret.

That this is quite a common practice is indicated by a case in which the death of a man, Kolai, was attributed to the fact that he brought some pork home from the tambaran house and several people saw his young daughter eating it in front of his house. Interestingly, informants stressed the fact that Kolai did not properly hide his deed as much as his violation of tambaran rules. For instance Henry described the incident in an interview:

Kolai carried some pork up and gave it to his wife and children and his children carried it out and ate it outside the house and a lot of people saw. Hapandi saw, Kwaru saw, and they said: "Oh this thing we hide, this man here has revealed it. Everyone knows about it now." . . . He brought a piece of pig to his wife and his children carried it outside. First Kwaru saw it, then Hapandi saw it. He [Hapandi] stood up in Haganatapa [hamlet near where Kolai lived] and said: "This place Haganatapa is in the dark and there are pig feces all over it." He said that and Kwaru knew that he had seen the children eating the meat. . . . The reason for the death was over this pig. His children came and ate it outside and all sorts of women and children saw it and said: "Where did they get this pig?" [Elderly men at the top of the tambaran system] like Hilanda and Numu, they can do this sort of thing. But us and all the younger men, this is forbidden; you must eat the meat in the bush; you can't bring it home.

Henry stresses the fact that Kwaru and Hapandi saw what Kolai had done. Both men are members of the ambwa initiation class and initiates of the ambwa mwe tambaran whereas the dead man, Kolai, was a member of the gwar class. Seeing Kolai's children eating meat in public did not reveal any secret information to Hapandi and Kwaru since the pig was part of a festival sponsored by the ambwa class. But Kolai's lax attitude toward the supposedly secret pig was a sign of disrespect for the ambwa people and Hapandi's comment that Haganatapa, a hamlet associated with the ambwa class, was "in the dark and [had] pig feces all over it," stressed this disrespect. It was as if Kolai was treating Haganatapa, the hamlet of the ambwa people, like a rubbish heap by throwing pig feces there.[24] He was treating the ambwa class like rubbish. (Henry did not explain this metaphor. I interpreted it in light of my general knowledge of standard rhetorical images in Kwanga speeches.)

Henry's concluding remark that men like him cannot bring tambaran meat home to their wives and children is also interesting since, on several other occasions, he and his children (separately) told me that Henry himself brought meat home from the tambaran. This indicates that it is not the deed that is important but the manner in which it is done. If a man brings meat home secretly and his children consume it in the house (backstage), it is not a sign of disrespect for the opposite moiety, not a "claim" that they are unimportant, and, therefore, is all right. Publicly flaunting the violation of cult rules, however, shows a profound disrespect for the other initiation class.

CLAIMS AND THE REVELATION OF TAMBARAN SECRETS IN THE REVIVAL

Tambaran secrets were revealed in Inakor in the summer of 1984 during the course of the revival. Kwahapa (and Henry on another occasion) told me that the pastors had just hinted at the secrets without "explaining" fully. They probably revealed much less than many of the women and uninitiated men present already knew. Henry, for instance, said that he had told Kwahapa everything that went on in the tambaran during an initiation in 1978 and even said that it was all right for the wives of the initiators to know cult secrets. The public revelation of secrets during the revival, however, created great controversy and received a great deal of attention because it constituted a claim that the women and uninitiated men had a right to know about these secrets. That undermined the authority of initiated men. It is not important if uninitiated men and women know the secrets, as long as they do not claim the right to know them by speaking of them in public. One informant insisted that, since the revival, all the women knew the cult secrets but would not speak of them in public for fear of sorcery. It is the claim to knowledge rather than the knowledge itself which is important. Secrecy is a language of claims by which the authority of the initiated men is either acknowledged (by not mentioning the secrets) or challenged (by mentioning the secrets).

The Role of Meetings

The Kwanga have a complex code of communication which allows people to signal their intentions. A public world of claims about the relative status of individuals and of categories of people is distinguished from an underlying reality that is universally recognized but only spoken of directly between close kin. By publicly conforming to rules associated with the tambaran and exchange relations in speech and action, individuals acknowledge the status quo; by breaking the rules publicly, people challenge the existing distribution of authority. As long as there is no claim to challenge the existing balance of authority and prestige, people can break the rules in everyday interactions with close kin. When people hint and gossip they can communicate information without making "claims" that they do not want to make and which may have serious consequences. Hint and gossip signal respect even when the message is a disparaging one.

But as the case of Kenamini's house indicates, these rules leave plenty of room for misinterpretation and doubt. In the many discussions of the affair of Kenamini's house, people tried not only to establish the facts—who said what, when, and to whom?—but also to interpret these facts. Were they serious challenges, or were they just idle boasts by irresponsible "pigs, dogs, coconut and betel palms"? As in funeral meetings, the discussion of the facts seems to be mostly a vehicle for finding out a more important truth, that is, people's intentions and attitudes. Thus, for instance, people discussed what Rambuli and Ainumu said to each other at great length but what they really wanted to know was if either moiety was claiming superiority or was prepared to escalate the scale of the exchange. The discussion allowed people to reveal their intentions by issuing challenges or retracting them.

This is important because what is often at stake is not merely relationships between individuals but also between groups. When people are in different moieties, initiation classes, or even lineages, an insult is more than personal; it can also involve a claim that one group is superior to the other. Such a claim could only be answered by a large prestation or by an initiation that would demonstrate the worth of the challenged group. Private and veiled insults avoid this danger; by preserving a public face of respect while attacking covertly, people signal that the challenge is purely personal.

The dense, complicated network of social relations in the Kwanga village creates a powder keg that can easily be set off by any minor remark or conflict. The result is an interpretation of what happened which is less concerned with the "facts" than with maintaining a balance between different groups in society and insuring that everyone's "honor" is intact, so they will not have to go to great (and potentially disruptive or expensive) lengths to prove themselves.

Institutionalized Duplicity in
Melanesian Cultures

The case in this chapter and those in previous chapters have shown that the Kwanga take a dark view of human nature. When anything happens that is in the least bit out of the ordinary people are sure that it is a sign of a hidden sorcery plot. Likewise, people look for veiled insults in every remark and are quick to believe that others are spreading slanderous rumors behind their backs.

In a society where everyone looks for the concealed meaning, rumors are quick to start and quick to distort the truth. Furthermore, because of an institutionalized distrust between members of different groups, people are predisposed to think that alarmist rumors of slander and attack might be true. Kin ties provide ready channels for the transmission of rumors that bring to life latent rivalrous sentiments between groups, and soon small matters become large fights involving the whole community. This can cause such serious problems that people believe that it is necessary to hold long meetings to check the rumors.

In this chapter I have addressed some of the reasons why the Kwanga look for hidden meanings. Public behavior often conceals a substantially different reality. People do spread slanderous rumors and cast insults in innuendo and metaphor; this is actually the most acceptable form of behavior between exchange partners, kandere, and distant kin. Likewise, the tambaran system requires that people play out a public drama that may bear little relation to their less visible behavior.

Furthermore, individuals know that anything they do could easily start a conflict involving a lot of people since if they insult a member of another moiety, lineage, or initiation class (or even seem to do so), that entire group will leap to the defense of their fellow. Consequently, everyone prefers to hint and to gossip so as to avoid starting a large conflict or exchange, or to avoid being held responsible if one does start.

But as we have seen, a preference for covert or ambiguous forms of attacks fosters distrust and suspicion, and so people are inclined to seek a hidden meaning even when statements should, in reality, be taken at face value. Sometimes a cigar is just a cigar and sometimes when young men complain that they are owed one chicken they are not conveying a veiled challenge from their initiated elders. When people look for veiled meanings, however, they can usually find them. And then large numbers of people are obliged to defend the honor of their lineage, moiety, or initiation class and so are drawn into conflicts or exchanges in which they have no wish to participate. When everyone is prepared to believe the worst, then irresponsible boasting on the part of "women, children, coconut and betel palms, pigs, and dogs" can create problems for the whole community.

Kwanga culture and social structure pattern rumors in particular ways. But there are also things in other areas which generate rumors and ensure that they have serious consequences. In most societies, certain categories of people are not supposed to fight or criticize each other. And, as among the Kwanga, fears of covert attack tend to be associated with such relationships. Marwick (1965), for instance, reports that among the Cewa, sorcery accusations are most frequent among fellow lineage members who are not supposed to fight with each other. People suspect covert aggression from those whom they know would not express anger openly. Hau'ofa (1981), similarly, says that Mekeo brothers do not fight openly but each fears the other may attack secretly. In fact, covert attacks on brothers are common in myths. In short, where people know that anger cannot be expressed directly, they fear that others are harboring hidden grievances and engaging in secret attack.

The distrustful ethos of many Melanesian cultures might also stem in part from the emphasis on secrecy associated with male cults. Again, people have good reason to suspect a hidden meaning because there often is one in matters associated with male cults. Men lie to the uniniti-ated about what goes on in cults and reveal to initiates that cult symbols have hidden meanings.

Similarly, people often cast insults, challenges, or reprimands in veiled language (e.g., McKellin 1984; A. Strathern 1975; Weiner 1984). And rivals in competitive exchange sometimes prefer to attack covertly by, for instance, secretly giving a particularly large yam to an enemy's exchange partner (Tuzin 1976).

In short, Melanesians know that many things cannot be taken at face value. This provides a fertile environment for rumors since people are prepared to believe that benign surfaces mask a quite different reality.

To make matters worse, conditions in many small communities guarantee that rumors will have serious consequences. Kwanga com-munities are divided into lineages, initiation classes and moieties that coalesce into fiercely loyal groups in the face of perceived insults from the outside. In other communities, kin groups can act in the same way (e.g., White 1990) and so can less formal factions such as "church" and "chapel" people in the small Welsh village described by Frankenberg (1957). When there are divisions within the community, whole groups of people will spring into action when they suspect that one of their number has been insulted or might be attacked by an outsider. Thus, few quarrels remain private matters for long.

In short, as chapter 5 indicated and as is commonly stressed in the literature on Pacific meetings, there are many things to "get out into the open" in meetings. When people do not want food exchanges and tambaran initiations, the conventional outlet for the tensions generated by rumors, they must hold many long meetings to stop the gossip.

CHAPTER SEVEN

The Power of Stories

In this chapter, I will further examine the ways in which unsubstantiated stories become "truth" in Kwanga villages. I will move beyond examining rumor to investigate ways in which stories about recent events influence people's interpretation of future events and their memories of the past, and can ultimately constitute much of their knowledge about their social world. Rumors are one such story; stories told in public meetings can have similar careers.

I will argue that sorcery talk among the Kwanga is an instance of a much more pervasive kind of behavior that occurs everywhere. When people are faced with an ambiguous and anxiety-provoking situation about which they have little good evidence, they try to interpret whatever facts are available to them in light of generally shared beliefs about that type of event, in order to convince themselves that they can understand and, perhaps, can even control the situation. Sorcery deaths in Kwanga villages represent situations that are both anxiety-provoking and ambiguous *par excellence*: deaths are anxiety-provoking because they usually indicate to people that a murderer is at large in the community, and they also have the potential to lead to violence as the aggrieved family searches for a culprit. Moreover, as was evident in chapter 3, people believe that there is never any good evidence in sorcery cases since sorcerers and their accomplices take great care to hide their identities. In this situation, villagers make up stories in which they attempt both to explain the death and to neutralize its disruptive potential.

But we have also seen that sorcery stories have political consequences in Kwanga villages. Pocock (1984: 28), among others, has noted that telling stories can be an act of power because stories redefine events and reputations and change people's ideas about their social world. Work on disputes in other small communities has also suggested that disputants and adjudicators try to influence others by carefully crafting stories about the events in question (Brenneis 1984; Just 1986; M. Strathern 1974). By defining situations in particular ways, stories can be very influential. As previous chapters have revealed, stories also deliver messages about the moral status of the events reported and also affect the reputations of both the speaker and those he or she comments on. Kwanga sorcery stories convince people that initiated men work hand in hand with sorcerers and turn death into a lesson about the consequences of challenging their authority. In these ways, stories strategically redefine events and, in doing so, they create and maintain the authority of initiated men.

But, as I suggested in chapter 1, in order to fully understand the ways in which telling stories defines social reality in Kwanga villages and elsewhere one must look beyond the meetings in which the stories are initially voiced. Looking at the fate of stories over time in Inakor and Asanakor showed that the process of defining a situation was a communal one (see also Brenneis 1986; Duranti 1986 on the importance of considering what the audience makes of an utterance). Speakers suggested many alternative interpretations of events in meetings but most of these had little influence on the audience. A few stories, though, seemed to capture people's imagination and were repeated many times over the months and were used to make sense of future crises. It was common, for instance, to consider broad patterns of dispute and sources of tension in the community when trying to figure out the cause of a death, and people often mentioned accounts of past deaths in the attempt to uncover such underlying sources of strain. Accounts that were repeated and reinvoked in this fashion influenced people's ideas about general patterns of tension and so had a much greater impact on the way people viewed the community than did the many other stories that were told once and never repeated. In some cases people even forgot their initial skepticism and came to view at least some stories as fairly well-established fact. Consequently, in order to understand how stories define situations and alter social relations one must examine the process whereby certain stories circulate through a community, are distorted as they are used to explain future incidents, and come to be regarded as truthful accounts over time. Taking such a view of Kwanga sorcery talk will show how stories are an even more powerful device for transforming social and political reality than has previously been appreciated. But we must look beyond the motives of, and rhetorical devices used by, individual speakers and examine the fate of stories over time.

Looking at the fate of stories after their initial telling also allows us to examine ways in which social relations and cultural beliefs are altered. Speakers in meetings often suggest novel ideas which challenge the distribution of authority, such as that God is more powerful than sorcerers, in this case by implying that good Christians need not fear big-men and their sorcerer henchmen. But audiences tend to be skeptical of such novel ideas and to repeat only the most stereotypical kinds of stories. I will argue in a concluding section that although novel ideas do have some impact on Kwanga society, change in relations of authority, and in the cultural beliefs that support these, is gradual. This process of change, therefore, can only be examined by following stories over months and even years as they circulate through the community.

Background

The Inakorians had been trying to control their sorcerer, Hapandi, for many years. Most people thought that he was malicious and often killed for petty, selfish reasons. Furthermore, several recent changes had led some people to question whether murder through sorcery should ever be considered legitimate. First, the villagers believed that the local government council and village court system should replace the old system of justice through sorcery. Instead of hiring sorcerers to punish wrongdoing and to redress grievances, people were supposed to take their problems to the magistrate or Councillor who would hold court hearings or mediation sessions. Second, when the villagers stopped performing tambaran initiations they also questioned the sorcery system that supported the cult. Third, Inakor and Asanakor Christians said that magical paraphernalia could make women and children ill, and, furthermore, that all magic was associated with the tambaran cult, which involved worshiping a "false idol" and was, therefore, sinful.

Villagers had tried various ways to stop Hapandi. They had taken him to court several times and had him jailed on charges of possessing sorcery paraphernalia. But this did not seem to work. Several people told me that sending Hapandi to jail just made him angry and that he would kill someone as soon as he returned home. More recently, the Christians had tried their hand at controlling Hapandi. They participated in an area-wide sorcery purge in the spring and summer of 1984 and Hapandi was sent to jail along with many of the other sorcerers in the region. A few months after Hapandi returned to the village, a group of committed Christians from a neighboring village visited Inakor to hold a revival meeting; they persuaded Hapandi to convert to Christianity and he renounced sorcery in front of a large crowd. No one died for several months after that but when a woman and a baby died in October 1985, and Hapandi's own stepson died in December of that year, people were sure that Hapandi had returned to his evil ways. In the inquests, the Inakorians tried to find out why Hapandi had taken up sorcery again and why neither the courts nor the Christians had been able to stop him.

The First Death

Kimbasumwa, a middle-aged woman, died in October 1985. Her husband Teimu and her seven children (the eldest was a young married woman with two children and the youngest was a three-week-old baby) survived her.

They buried Kimbasumwa the next day, and, on the day after that, most of the residents of Inakor and many people from Asanakor assembled for the first inquest. The discussion was of general issues since many of the community leaders and several of the people most closely related to Kimbasumwa, who would normally have led the search for her murderer, had been inadvertently delayed in a neighboring town and could not attend the meeting.

Several of the speakers tried to put the death in a long-term perspective by discussing past deaths. Four people had died in 1983 and 1984 in the course of a controversy over a tambaran festival. In 1983 Inakorians started a festival to complete the cult cycle that had begun with the 1978 initiation; when two people died, everyone thought that they had been ensorceled for violating cult rules. Many people thought that the cult was not worth the lives that it cost and wanted to abandon the festival, but others disagreed and the resultant conflict was believed to have led to two more sorcery murders. But the deaths had stopped after Hapandi converted to Christianity. People said that Kimbasumwa's death indicated that Hapandi had taken up sorcery again and that the Christians were losing their power over him.

People suggested various reasons why Hapandi might have taken up sorcery again. An old man suggested that a sorcerer could have legitimately punished the Christians for revealing male cult secrets, since traditionally sorcerers punished those who violated cult rules. But since Kimbasumwa was not a Christian, she could not be held responsible for the activities of the revivalists, and so her murderer must have had a different motive.

Some people blamed the village government officials, the Councillor and magistrate (who were not there to defend themselves). They said that the current community leaders were weak men and compared them unfavorably to the "hot" leaders of the past who had frightened sorcerers into good behavior.

The discussion continued in much the same vein for several hours, and people gradually dispersed and returned to their homes.

The next day, the village of Inakor gathered in Kimbasumwa's hamlet for a second discussion. Several of the men who had missed the first meeting gave their views. Henry, Kimbasumwa's brother's daughter's husband, opened the discussion by suggesting that the fight over pig hunting (described in chapter 5) had brought sorcery back to Inakor. Later that day he explained his theory about the death to me. Briefly, after a communal hunt failed, some young men had accused the initiated men of sabotaging the hunt with their magic. Henry felt that when the young men criticized their initiated seniors Hapandi had decided to kill someone to remind the community that sorcerers supported the authority of tambaran men. Henry thought that this was a legitimate reason for murder and that the principal fault lay with the young men who had been insubordinate. Henry's chief evidence for his theory was that birds, which were perhaps the familiars of sorcerers, had started to cry out at night on 26 September, the day of the opening of the aid post in Inakor.

Kimbasumwa, the victim, had not been involved in the fight over hunting magic, but Henry thought that this fight had reminded Hapandi of a longstanding fight he had with her husband Teimu over land and hunting magic. (The Kwanga believe that sorcerers often kill women and children to punish one of their male relatives.) Henry said

that Teimu and Hapandi had fought over some land several years before and after that Hapandi had had little success in pig hunting. He
thought that Teimu had secretly stolen some of Hapandi's hunting
magic and was using it to sabotage Hapandi's hunting. Teimu had always denied this, but Henry said that after Kimbasumwa died Teimu
had sent his son-in-law to retrieve the magic from its hiding place and
return it to Hapandi, thus proving that everyone's suspicions had been
correct. (I also heard this theory from several other people.) According
to Henry, when the young men criticized their hunting magicians,
Hapandi thought he could kill Kimbasumwa without being detected
since everyone would be thinking of the recent uproar and would forget
about the past quarrels. This would teach the whole community a lesson and would allow Hapandi to get back at Teimu at the same time.

The Councillor and Ronald both thought that Kimbasumwa might
have died over land disputes. The Councillor pointed out that Kimbasumwa and Teimu had fought with several people over land, and that
they had often been warned that their contentious behavior might result in sorcery. Ronald said that a few months before her death Kimbasumwa had told him that her neighbor Walafuku had been so furious
over a recent quarrel over land that he had threatened to "break all her
ribs with the blunt end of an axe." Ronald said that Kimbasumwa had
asked him to hold a court hearing to look into the matter, saying something to the effect of: "If I die or one of my children dies this is what
will have killed me," implying she thought Walafuku might hire a
sorcerer to kill her. But Ronald had not taken her seriously and so had
put off the hearing until it was too late.

They also discussed recent signs that sorcerers were active. An old
man said that when the magistrate of a village to the north had recently
visited Inakor, he had commented on bird cries that reminded him of
two sorcerers from his area, long dead, who had trained Hapandi. The
magistrate guessed that the pupil had taken on his masters' cries and
that he must now be active in Inakor. A young couple who had returned to the village from town the same evening claimed to have been
followed by a sorcerer, and a man who had been sitting on his veranda
when the couple arrived in the village said he also thought he had seen a
sorcerer lurking around an empty house. Later, a woman heard noises
in an empty room of her house and called to her husband who was
playing cards nearby. When her husband came he saw someone jump
out of the empty room and run away. The same night a young man

thought a sorcerer shot him when he returned home from the card game. The young man had fallen down on the road and had felt sick in the morning. But he eventually recovered and so he concluded that the sorcerer had realized that he had shot the wrong person and had reversed the spell. Kimbasumwa fell ill the next day, and so people speculated that she must have been attacked by the same sorcerer when she went to the toilet alone. A man said that his three children had been chased by a sorcerer when they went to the woods to pick greens. There were also many stories about disputes between Hapandi and Teimu.

Some of the suspects tried to defend themselves. Hapandi said that he was afraid to practice sorcery because the police had beaten him several times in the past when he was jailed on sorcery charges. Walafu-ku objected that his disputes with Kimbasumwa and Teimu had not been serious. As the sun set people gradually left and went home.

A Second Death

Less than two weeks after Kimbasumwa's death a four-month-old baby died. Ordinarily there are no inquests after infants' deaths, but since this baby had died so soon after Kimbasumwa people were worried that Hapandi was on a murderous rampage and might kill several more people unless they stopped him. A small group of Inakor men met in the hamlet of the baby's paternal grandfather to try to find out why Hapandi had abandoned the church and returned to sorcery after so many months of good behavior. They decided that some Christians were angry with the non-Christians in the community and so were no longer trying to stop Hapandi from practicing sorcery. Some men suggested that, in fact, the Christians would be pleased if Hapandi killed a non-Christian and taught the rest of them a lesson. In the meeting, they examined incidents that seemed to indicate that prominent Christians had encouraged Hapandi to ensorcel someone.

Henry[1] told several people that he believed the trouble had started with a fight between Wangembor, a young non-Christian man, and Bwalaka, a prominent Christian. Bwalaka's wife Mary had been "possessed by the Holy Spirit" during the same revival meeting in which Hapandi had converted to Christianity, and she led a campaign to rid the community of all magic. The non-Christians publicly supported her, but sometimes when she divined the presence of a magical item the alleged owner would say that she was lying. This annoyed the Christians. These tensions came to a head when a young married woman fell ill. Mary divined that Wangembor had some love magic that was making the woman ill. But he said he did not have any love magic. In a village meeting, Bwalaka called Wangembor a troublemaker, and he was furious and hit Bwalaka. Henry believed that Mary and/or Bwalaka had been bothered by the fight and had stopped trying to rid the community of sorcery and other harmful magic and may even have asked Hapandi to kill someone to teach the non-Christians a lesson, thus paving the way for Kimbasumwa's death.

At the meeting, Henry tried to put the recent deaths in a wider perspective, claiming that the fight over hunting magic, Wangembor's quarrel with Bwalaka, and Teimu's fights with Hapandi over land and hunting magic had all contributed to reviving sorcery in Inakor. He said that none of these things, in their own right, were sufficient to provoke Hapandi. But together they had amounted to "a big problem," and so Hapandi had murdered Kimbasumwa to satisfy his old grievance and to teach the whole community a lesson. Henry said:

All the little problems from before, all the little fights over land and sago and water, they kept adding these things up. . . . I told you guys: "The Christians are working [to rid the community of sorcery] but they are unhappy. They are bothered by the time Wangembor hit Bwalaka. Their work is slowing down now because they are [brooding about this incident]." After that, the Councillor started this project of opening the new aid post. We started hunting pigs. Then . . . all the young men got mad at the big-men [for allegedly sabotaging the hunt]. All right, this new trouble went now and they added it on to the problems from before. So now it was a big problem. So sorcery started. You can't just go and think: "I haven't done anything. Why do we have sorcery?" You must think of all the trouble you have made before. I tell you all the time . . . [at weekly community meetings] that you shouldn't fight over little things. But you fight and look, the village is in a mess now.

A few minutes later Abel, the village pastor, followed up on Henry's remarks about Wangembor and Bwalaka. Abel speculated that Bwalaka started sleeping with Mary after his fight with Wangembor, thus diminishing her prophetic powers. Just as men believed they had to avoid contact with women to use magic, now women possessed by the Holy Spirit tried to preserve their powers by avoiding contact with men. Abel criticized the non-Christians for provoking the Christians:

It all started when Wangembor hit Bwalaka. It's Wangembor's fault. Mary was bothered by this. It was her own husband they hit. And Bwalaka was bothered by it too, so he started sleeping with her, and this pushed down her power, and her power went away. Sometimes she saw things but Bwalaka told her not to reveal them. This is because you non-Christians threw stones at us Christians. It's because of that the village is in trouble now. This power comes from God. It's not something you can buy with money. The man slept with his wife now, and God wanted to take his power back again. You threw stones at us, and we were troubled, so we couldn't work well. The power of God slackened, and now we're in a mess. God makes this power. If we argue and fight, he will take his power back. This power doesn't belong to any man. It belongs to God. So the power stopped at this time, and now sorcery is shooting people all around.

Later, Abel's father Suroho provided further proof that Bwalaka was the kind of person who hired sorcerers, implying that he might have a reason to want to preserve sorcery. Several years before, Bwalaka had been the chairman of a village coffee buying group in which most of the community had shares. He was accused of stealing group money and was removed from the board of the group. In the course of the controversy, one of Suroho's sons had punched Bwalaka. Suroho said that Bwalaka was still angry and had given Hapandi two hundred kina to kill Suroho and all of his children. According to Suroho, Hapandi refused the money because Suroho was his classificatory brother and warned Suroho that Bwalaka was after him. Suroho was frightened and he invited the Christians from the other village to come and rid the community of sorcery. They succeeded in converting Hapandi but then the non-Christians of the community provoked him, and he resumed his evil ways.

As evening fell, people drifted off to their homes.

The next morning Henry got up early and went around the village to invite the senior men to reassemble and discuss the reemergence of sorcery in Inakor so that they could decide how to stop it before it got out of hand. Several people had already gone to their gardens, but a small group of men gathered in the hamlet of the dead baby's parents. Once again, they concentrated on the fight between the Christians and the non-Christians which had supposedly driven Hapandi from the church and weakened the revivalists' power. Several people also suggested that Hapandi had returned to sorcery after being warned of a plot on his life. Several older men chastised the younger men for bringing back sorcery by making trouble and insulting big-men.

The participants gradually dispersed after several hours of similar discussion and agreed to reassemble the following Sunday to decide how to stop sorcery once and for all.

On Sunday they discussed Bwalaka's role in aiding and abetting Hapandi. They talked about a time when Mary had "seen" that Hapandi had a sorcery spear hidden in a tree. They said that the pastor, Abel, had wanted to go get the spear immediately, but that Bwalaka had told him to wait until morning. But there was nothing there in the morning, and everyone was sure that Bwalaka had warned Hapandi who had secretly removed the spear and had hidden it somewhere else. They also discussed evidence that Hapandi had been angry at Kimbasumwa and Teimu. Several people reported that after a day of unsuccessful pig hunting before the aid post opening, Hapandi had threatened to break Teimu's neck as if he were "a wild fowl," indicating that he thought Teimu had sabotaged that hunt.

In the ensuing discussion they returned to many of the themes of the previous meetings. Finally a rain storm sent people scurrying for cover and broke up the meeting.

People spoke of having another meeting but this never happened, and no one seemed sure that the evidence was sufficient to convict Hapandi or Bwalaka in court. It was better just to let them know that everyone knew they were guilty and disapproved of their actions, and then the two men would be afraid to kill anyone in the future.

The Third Death

Hapandi's stepson Samwa died on 1 December 1985. He was a young married man (in his mid-thirties) who had suffered from a lingering illness (probably tuberculosis) for many years. He had been sick for some weeks before he died but no one had been very concerned about him because of his long history of ill health. In fact, Samwa's wife Kenuku was in a neighboring village attending a celebration for the opening of a new church when her husband died.

Within a few hours of the death, stories began to circulate about Samwa's final weeks of life. My neighbor (who was Samwa's half-sister) said that Samwa had told several people about the fatal attack. A few weeks before his death, Samwa had gone alone to his garden leaving Kenuku at home caring for a sick child. Hapandi and Samwa's mother had gone to a nearby garden on the same day. When returning home, Samwa felt a sharp pain in his side and, some people said, had turned and seen Hapandi standing close behind him.

They discussed Hapandi's alleged attack on Samwa at the first meeting. People thought that Hapandi had killed Samwa because he coveted Samwa's wife Kenuku. Some neighbors claimed that they had seen Hapandi leave his garden to return to the village while Samwa was still working. But Kenuku said that Samwa had arrived back in the village before Hapandi. People felt that this proved that Hapandi had hidden somewhere along the path in order to ambush and ensorcel Samwa. Several witnesses were called to state the order in which the two men had, first, left their gardens and, second, arrived in the village. There was also a great deal of discussion of various things Samwa had said which indicated that he was angry with his mother and Hapandi. They also discussed the more general conditions that had provoked Hapandi to take up sorcery again. They returned to many of the themes of Kimbasumwa's inquest, including the fight over hunting magic, the rift between the Christians and non-Christians, and Bwalaka's role in aiding and abetting Hapandi. Samwa's classificatory father pulled together all of these themes and suggested that Samwa's death was one of a series that had started with Kimbasumwa and had all been related to similar issues such as the fight over hunting magic:

We hunted pigs . . . and [one man] set up his net and a pig nearly went into it and then turned and ran away. They came up and talked about it. Hapandi said he'd like to kill Teimu, to hit him with an axe. Teimu heard this and was afraid and took [a young man] and went home. We went home and slept. The next morning we hunted again. We didn't get any pigs. . . . We fought and we fought and then we opened the aid post. Then after a little while Teimu escaped and the sorcerer killed Kimbasumwa. Bwalaka and Hapandi must have promised. . . . The talk came up and that very time they killed Kimbasumwa. The first death was [a baby], then Kimbasumwa, then [another baby], then [two women and an old man were ill for several weeks], now Samwa. All of them have the same sickness. It's exactly the same sickness.

People decided that, although it was obvious that Hapandi had killed Samwa, this was Hapandi's own concern since Samwa was a member of his family, and so the villagers should not do anything about it. Several people, however, warned Hapandi and Bwalaka that everyone knew that they were murderers now and that the two men would surely meet a violent end if they killed anyone else.

Telling Stories about Sorcery Deaths

The discussions of the three deaths followed a by now familiar pattern. Faced with ambiguous evidence, the participants in the inquests used their knowledge of unusual incidents, tensions in the community, and past disputes to construct elaborate theories about the conditions that might have led to the murders. They interpreted unusual events such as the fight over hunting magic and the bird cries at night after the opening of the aid post in light of such generally shared beliefs as that fights between young men and their initiated elders provoke sorcerers, sorcerers making their rounds emit bird cries, and sorcerers may choose victims almost at random to serve as an example to the whole community. In this way, speakers such as Henry produced accounts of what might have happened. But the participants in the inquests devoted little time to discovering whether their theories were true or false and did nothing to punish the alleged culprits, Hapandi and Bwalaka.

People were probably aware that their theories about the death would not hold up in court but they seemed to think that just voicing their suspicions in public would stop Hapandi and Bwalaka from killing again. Several people said, for instance, that once Hapandi and Bwalaka knew that the community suspected them they would be afraid to commit another murder, knowing that the family of their victim would be likely to take violent revenge (see chapter 5).

Speakers also wanted to remind everyone else in the community that they were not blameless. Indeed, several of the most vocal participants seemed more interested in lecturing the rest of the community than in chastising the murderers. Henry, for instance, had an additive theory of sorcery, and I heard this from many other people as well: Henry told me that the sorcerer watches over the community for fights or challenges to the authority of initiated men and to the tambaran cult. Individual offenses seldom prompt the sorcerer to action but eventually twenty or thirty instances of misbehavior will create a general impression that the community is in disorder, and then the sorcerer strikes. In the inquests, Henry showed how many fights might be related to the two deaths and then went on to forcefully state the moral of his story: "You can't just go and think: 'I haven't done anything. Why do we have sorcery?' You must think of all the trouble you have made before. I tell you all the time . . . that you shouldn't fight over little things. But you fight and look, the village is in a mess now." Abel similarly warned the community that their fighting caused trouble.

Just (1986) argues that the Dou Donggo of Indonesia are often less concerned with literal truth than in constructing accounts of disputes which will deliver moral messages to the community. A similar logic seemed to inform these inquests. People seemed less interested in discovering the truth about the deaths than in drawing certain messages from them. They did not try to prosecute anyone but, instead, told elaborate stories about how everyone in the community had contributed to the trends that had culminated in the deaths. Speakers prompted people to forget the murderer and to think of the ways they themselves had contributed to the problem. In this way, the participants in the inquest got a great deal of rhetorical mileage out of an emotionally charged event to try to "strike the fear of sorcery" into people's hearts and get them to behave better in the future. The by now familiar message was that fighting of any kind, whether the instigator was right or wrong, could lead to trouble for everyone.

Storytellers like Henry also assert that the leadership of initiated men and sorcerers is legitimate and beneficial for the community when they suggest that sorcerers only strike troublemakers. As Ronald and Gwarambu hastened to assure everyone, sorcerers did not kill for no reason, they visited only the "troublemakers and the sinners."

In short, as was evident in previous chapters, the Kwanga know that the evidence that they use in inquests would never be accepted in extra-local courts where magistrates insist on eyewitness accounts, confessions of murder, or "smoking guns." They also know that circumstantial evidence can be misleading (as is evident in the fact that they often will interpret the same piece of evidence in several ways at various points in the inquests) and that theories based on such evidence as bird cries at night must, therefore, be taken with a grain of salt. But people believe that publicly telling stories has benefits even if these stories cannot be conclusively proven.

Furthermore, as was also evident in previous chapters, people probably realize that it is better if no one can be sure about the facts of the murder. Identifying and prosecuting a murderer could start a fight since his kin would almost certainly come to his aid unless the case against him was conclusively proven. Telling cautionary tales, however, frightens everyone into good behavior and upholds the authority of village leaders. Thus, Kwanga accounts of death turned a potentially volatile situation that, in many areas where people believe in sorcery, would lead to violence and feuding, into "proof" of the destructive potential of everyone's own bad behavior.

Stories and the Construction of the Truth

Telling stories about sorcery is clearly a form of political action in Kwanga communities which "transforms" social reality by neutralizing the destructive potential of death and by reinforcing relations of authority. But to fully appreciate the way stories define social reality in Inakor and Asanakor one must look beyond their first telling. People take sorcery stories with a grain of salt on first hearing. The fact that people initially regard sorcery stories as fictional is important to the way they work. But I will argue that some stories come to have an insidious and pervasive impact on the audience's memory of past events and their interpretation of future incidents. Furthermore, because stories conceal their arguments, most often people do not realize the effect stories have on their perceptions of situations but, instead, think that they are simply remembering the unadulterated facts of the matter. Below I will examine several ways in which unsubstantiated stories come to be regarded as truth.

First, stories give people a framework for understanding ambiguous incidents, and so once someone suggests a plausible story about one situation people are inclined to use this framework to explain other related events. Bennett and Feldman (1981: 8) suggest that in American courts

stories solve the problems of information load in trials by making it possible for individuals continuously to organize and reorganize large amounts of constantly changing information. New pieces of evidence can be fit within the structural categories in an incident . . . Once the basic plot outline of a story begins to emerge it is possible to integrate information that is presented in the form of subplots, time disjunctures, or multiple perspectives on the same scene . . .

In other words, juries and other audiences interpret new information by extending the framework of the story.

This process was evident in Kwanga inquests. Henry's story of Kimbasumwa's death is a good example. Before Henry told his story people were at a loss about what sort of evidence was relevant to figuring out the cause of Kimbasumwa's death. But after Henry suggested that Hapandi had killed Kimbasumwa as a warning to insubordinate young men, people came up with all sorts of incidents that also showed that the young men in the community had gotten out of hand recently. Henry himself remembered that several months before Kimbasumwa's death a young man had publicly punched Bwalaka, a senior man, and called him a liar. Then someone suggested that Bwalaka might be secretly encouraging Hapandi to kill people in order to remind every-one that they should show more respect for senior men. And this led to a reconsideration of the Christian revival movement in which both Bwalaka and Hapandi were involved. People came up with various incidents that seemed to indicate that Bwalaka was the kind of person who had hired sorcerers in the past and so might conceivably want to preserve sorcery now, and they also discussed incidents (like the failed divination of Hapandi's spear) which possibly showed that Bwalaka was trying to protect sorcery.

In short, Henry's story influenced what sort of evidence people con-sidered and what meaning they attached to the various incidents they discussed. People started with the "story" that Kimbasumwa's death had been related to a dispute between young men and their initiated elders and added in various "subplots" as they considered other things. Were it not for Henry's story, incidents like the time when a young man had punished Bwalaka and called him a liar would have had no apparent relationship to Kimbasumwa's death, since she was not closely related to either man.

Stories also influenced the way people interpreted future events. For instance, when Samwa died a couple of months after Kimbasumwa, people suspected that Hapandi and Bwalaka were conspiring to punish the young men, and so people looked for evidence of this. There was a great deal of discussion of incidents that could have indicated that Hapandi and Bwalaka were in cahoots and that both of them were angry at the young men. In this way, the story of the conspiracy be-tween Hapandi and Bwalaka shaped the evidence that people con-sidered in the next inquest and what they made of it.

Furthermore, when people interpreted incidents in light of the theory, it began to look like there was a great deal of evidence to sup-port it. None of the incidents that seemed to fit into the pattern were very conclusive. But when people interpreted a number of incidents in the same way, it seemed pretty clear that Bwalaka and Hapandi were angry with the young men and that they got along very well with each other. When they found many incidents that appeared to show similar patterns the explanation seemed plausible, even if it was not conclusively proven. Thus, by providing a meaningful framework to interpret confusing and ambiguous events, stories draw people's attention to certain aspects of situations and prompt them to ignore other things. When people interpret many incidents in the same way, it begins to seem like there is a lot of evidence to support a theory.

In a recent book on modern witches in England, Tanya Luhrmann (1989) argues that once people begin to use a particular theory to interpret their experience, events seem to confirm these theories. This also seems to be the case in Kwanga inquests: as people used a story to interpret other events it began to look as if events were confirming the story.

A second way in which stories systematically distort people's perception and memories is also related to speakers' tendency to interpret particular events in light of general beliefs. I noted in chapter 1 that verbal accounts often refer to underlying propositions or knowledge structures. Storytellers generally leave a great deal unsaid and rely on their audience to "hear" all sorts of related information and to infer causal connections between the lines (Hutchins 1980; Leitch 1986: 34; White 1990) by using their background knowledge. Listeners "instantiate" specific information in stories into "schemas" that suggest the typical features of that sort of situation. When speakers relate particular events to more general schemas, the audience can infer all sorts of related information and can reach conclusions about matters that are not explicitly addressed by the narrative.

The process of referring to underlying knowledge structures influences people's ideas in several ways. First, the stories people remember are the ones that accord best with such general beliefs. For instance, no one was very interested in Ronald's story of Walafuku's alleged threat to "break all of [Kimbasumwa's] ribs with the blunt end of an axe," even though this appeared (in the local view) to be a death threat followed by a death. I suggest that people had little interest in this story—even though it was much more straightforward than the more popular alternatives and there seemed to be more direct evidence that it was true—because it violated one of their most basic beliefs about sorcerers and their accomplices—that is, that sorcerers are most likely to act at the bidding of prominent village leaders. Walafuku was a relatively young man and so people had more trouble believing that he would have hired a sorcerer than they did believing the same thing of

Bwalaka, a much more prominent man. Thus, people are more likely to find plausible, and more likely to be influenced by, stories that accord well with their general beliefs.

This may be particularly true in the case of sorcery because people have little or no direct evidence in such cases. Consequently, they try to get at the truth by interpreting signs that might indicate a motive or opportunity for murder.[2] But these signs could mean many things, and so speakers have to explain how they think each was related to the murder. Since there is so little (if any) conclusive evidence, however, people have to make judgments based on the characteristics of the story itself: does it accord well with their general knowledge of individuals, and of sorcerers? does it seem to explain many recent events?[3] This means that people have a tendency to "like" stories that accord with their general beliefs about sorcery. Thus, although people often discussed quite a number of novel theories in the course of inquests, when I asked them about deaths from past years they most often ascribed these deaths to very stereotypical causes such as fights over "land, pigs, and women," as one man put it.

Second, people tend to forget elements of situations which do not accord well with, or are irrelevant to, their sorcery death schema. For example, Henry linked the fight between Bwalaka and Wangembor to a general category of events, that is, fights between young men and older men. This type of event is believed often to lead to sorcery. Henry claimed that Bwalaka had continued to brood over his fight with Wangembor because the two men had never settled their differences. But I (with the aid of field notes) pointed out to him that the two men had, in fact, exchanged pigs and yams to settle their quarrel. Henry then remembered this incident, but he said that although the two men had exchanged pigs Bwalaka must still have been angry. Henry had remembered aspects of the earlier incident which were consistent with the general scenario—that is, fights between young and old men lead to sorcery deaths—and had forgotten things, such as the reconciliatory feast, which did not fit this more general scenario. Moreover, when the incident was discussed in the inquest no one questioned Henry's assertion that Bwalaka was still angry at the young man, even though the feast seemed at least to create the possibility that the two men had made peace. Perhaps this was because once Henry suggested that this particular incident was an instance of a more general scenario with which everyone was familiar, people remembered the aspects of the events which were consistent with the scenario (that the two men fought and then someone died) and forgot the rest. In this way, stories altered people's memory of past events.

Furthermore, people seem to have gone to some effort to make the death fit into the general schema to begin with: the victim, Kimbasumwa, was not directly involved in any fight between young and old men and so it required a certain amount of oral gymnastics to conclude that her death was the anticipated (and if informants were telling the truth, predicted) outcome of the fight over hunting magic. Thus, people not only remember stories that accord with general ideas but they make some effort to show how reality fits into these general patterns. They probably do this for the reasons outlined above: they are making use of the only models available to them to make sense of a mysterious and potentially dangerous reality; they want to assure themselves and others that death does not strike randomly but occurs in certain regular and, therefore, predictable patterns; and they want to pull the moral out of disturbing events in order to prompt people to behave better in the future. But speakers' words have the (perhaps) unintended consequence of also proving to people over and over again that events confirm general beliefs.

Third, sometimes people actually "remember" things that did not happen, but which could well have happened if reality conformed better to their general beliefs. The rumors that Samwa had told his wife Kenuku that he had seen Hapandi make the fatal attack are a good example of this process. When I later asked Kenuku about this incident she claimed that Samwa had felt a pain in his side but had not seen Hapandi on this occasion. She thought it was probably true that Hapandi had attacked Samwa but said that Hapandi must have put a spell over the victim to prevent him from seeing or remembering his attacker. Furthermore, the fact that Kenuku went to a church opening in another village and left Samwa in Hapandi's care a few days after the alleged attack makes it seem unlikely that Samwa had really told her that he had seen Hapandi ensorcel him. I suspect that when people heard that Samwa had felt a sharp pain in his side a few days before he died, they filled in what, in the local view, was the obvious inference (and was probably the conclusion that whoever told the story intended them to reach), that Hapandi must have ensorceled him at this time. As the rumor spread around the community, people did not distinguish fact from inference. They "remembered" that someone had actually seen Hapandi ensorcel Samwa when, in fact, people had only guessed that he might have done this after hearing that Samwa had felt a sharp pain in his side a few days before he died. In short, just as storytellers prompt their audience to relate particular events to more general scenarios and, thus, to "hear" much more than was actually said, so, through a similar process, after many months people "remember" much more than they actually heard; they remember the story—which comprises both what they saw and heard and the information they inferred "between the lines"—and do not distinguish fact from interpretation.

There is also a general tendency to remember stories and to forget the evidence altogether. This may be because the evidence is almost always so ambiguous as to be meaningless in its own right. People are more likely to remember good "stories" that make sense of mysterious events or words than they are to remember the evidence that inspired these theories, since the evidence is at best suggestive and could mean any number of things. For example, in speaking of deaths from the distant past, people could often remember several stories that had been told in inquests but could seldom tell me very much about the evidence for each of these stories. They would only say that certain of the stories had been true and others false but usually could not say how people had decided which was which. Thus, stories form people's principle knowledge of many past situations.

These tendencies were exacerbated when people gossiped about things. As Andrew (the Asanakor court clerk) and others were fond of saying, if many people are saying the same thing, it will seem to be true although, in fact, everyone may be repeating a groundless rumor they have all heard from the same source. People have the impression that there is much independent evidence pointing to the same conclusion but, in reality, all anyone has seen in most cases is suggestive incidents that everyone has interpreted the same way because everyone has heard the same rumor. In this way, what starts as a theory can eventually take on the appearance of a well-established fact. Stories, once established, seem to take on a life of their own.

Beliefs about the way speakers hide evidence also encourage people to focus on stories and ignore the evidence. We saw earlier that speakers often purposely leave their remarks ambiguous: they mention a few suggestive facts but do not tell people what they should make of these facts. This sort of behavior is part of an elaborate complex of beliefs about sorcery talk. People believe that no one ever tells the truth, particularly in sorcery cases.[4] Those who have what is considered to be definitive information about the death, such as a confession from a sorcerer, just hint at what they know, fearing that if they tell all the

sorcerer will kill them. Instead they may discuss suggestive but ambiguous types of evidence in public. So theories, which may be based on
good but concealed evidence, are believed to be of greater relevance
than the less definitive evidence that is discussed in inquests, and, as a
result, people tend to remember the stories that were told in previous
inquests and forget the nature of the evidence which supported the
stories.

In short, for many reasons, even if a story is not conclusively proven,
it can have a far-reaching impact on what people will believe and what
they will do in the future.

This process not only makes stories look much better grounded in
evidence than they really are, it also, over the long run, tends to create
the illusion that many instances of the same general class of events, like
sorcery death, follow a similar pattern. Sorcery is a somewhat special
case because people see few sorcerers killing people but hear many
stories about sorcerers. As a result, a great deal of people's past experience of sorcery comes from stories. If the most plausible story is one
that accords with previous experience that, in turn, consists of other
stories we would expect sorcery stories to follow stereotypical patterns.
Indeed, this seems to be the case. People often favored novel explanations during the first discussions of a death but then gradually dropped
them in favor of more stereotypical explanations. For instance, when
the two brothers died in Asanakor people initially thought that Jeremiah had poisoned them because he thought they were interfering in
his marriage. This was quite a novel explanation. But as the months
passed, people decided that someone else had killed the two men because of a fight over land, perhaps the most standard of explanations,
even though there was much stronger evidence that Jeremiah was angry
at the victims than there was evidence that those who had been involved in the land dispute harbored a grudge. Similarly, when I interviewed Henry about all the deaths he could remember, he attributed
most of them to fights over land, pigs, or women (or in the case of
women, to the fact that men had been fighting over them).

These processes are particularly important to understanding the
political impact of sorcery stories. I argued in chapter 1 that the primary
impact of individual sorcery stories is in reproducing the general belief
about the relationship between initiated men and sorcerers. Even if no
one is sure who killed someone on a particular occasion, the fact that
they hear many stories implicating initiated men, reinforces their general belief that sorcerers are the henchmen of big-men and that, therefore,
people should not challenge their authority. The fact that people are

more inclined to believe stereotypical stories makes it difficult to challenge the authority of initiated men. People can and do tell novel stories that suggest, for instance, that God is more powerful than sorcerers so that good Christians need not fear initiated men and their sorcerer henchmen. But such stories have minimal consequences because people do not believe and repeat them. In short, when investigating the political impact of stories it is important to realize that "all stories are not created equal." Hearing any account of events shapes people's views and behavior but following stories over time suggests that some stories influence individuals much more than others do and that it is highly stereotypical stories that are most likely to have such a lasting influence.

I do not suggest, however, that there is no possibility of change. Pocock (1984) and Bruner (1984, 1986) both argue that "meaning" emerges from discussion and performance. Each time a symbol or story is evoked in a particular context it takes on new meaning. It was evident that the cultural principles or scenarios that stories invoked to explain death underwent subtle alterations. For instance, when people invoked the idea that insubordination to initiated men led to sorcery to explain Kimbasumwa's death they changed general ideas about what sort of behavior counted as such insubordination. The fight between Wangembor and Bwalaka over Christianity, for instance, was very different from the fights over secret knowledge and hunting rights which had been believed to activate sorcerers in the past. Initiated men now became the defenders of Christianity whereas insubordinate young men were "heathen" troublemakers. Thus, although people have trouble swallowing the suggestion that God could protect Christians from sorcerers, they accept without question the proposition that sorcerers might collude with Christian big-men. In this way, ideas about the close association between sorcerers, initiated men, and the men's cult were subtly altered.

Similarly, Henry had to go to elaborate lengths to show how Kimbasumwa's death was another instance of sorcery striking to maintain the authority of initiated men—since Kimbasumwa had done nothing to challenge this authority. In trying to fit the particular into the general scheme, Henry stressed that a victim need not be the obvious instigator since sorcerers struck randomly in a community to warn troublemakers and preserve order. The fact that Henry restated this idea several times in public meetings indicates that this might be a revision to the general scenario—since if it were part of people's taken-for-granted knowledge of the behavior of sorcerers it could have gone unstated like so many of the other ideas that underpin sorcery stories.

Narrative and Society

Sorcery talk is an instance of a more general category of behavior that is found in many situations: people tell stories about socially and psychologically troubling events, or things that are just plain confusing, in order to transform them into "more ideal constructions" (White and Watson-Gegeo 1990: 5) and to convince themselves that they understand and, therefore, can control an ambiguous and potentially dangerous reality. The Kwanga tell stories about sorcery deaths simply to try to figure out what happened and to assure themselves that, as they tell each other over and over again, people do not die for no reason. They resist the idea of arbitrary death that could strike at any time and assure themselves that each instance of death is understandable and could have been avoided if people had only behaved themselves. Furthermore, their stories turn an event like death, which leads to feuding and violence in many societies, into "proof" of the potential consequences of everyone's bad behavior.

Although scholars have noted the ways in which people give events new meaning when they talk about them (see chapter 1), few have analyzed the implications of this, particularly in small communities where communication networks are very dense and gossip spreads readily. Stories that give events meaning not only allow speakers to convey certain messages about themselves, about others, and about the consequences of certain kinds of behavior, they also make ambiguous and confusing events intelligible. By doing this, stories make events memorable and, over time, people often remember stories and forget the more confusing evidence on which they are based. Furthermore, people often "swallow" fact and theory as one in stories and so do not think to question the speaker's interpretation of events. Consequently, much of the information people have about individuals and events comes in the form of stories. People do not "see" events; instead, they hear stories in which these events have already been interpreted in terms of general beliefs about how the world works and what people are like. Moreover, individuals build on stories they have heard before to explain new things and also find plausible accounts that are similar to familiar ones since such stories form their principle experience of things like sorcery and adultery that are largely hidden from view. Thus, experience seems over and over again to confirm people's culturally derived suspicions about reality. These processes have political im-

plications since typical sorcery stories reinforce the authority of initiated men.

But examining Kwanga sorcery stories has also shed light on the role
of individual creativity in altering views of particular situations and
changing more general cultural ideas. Speakers in inquests fashion impressive accounts of events which link together many apparently unrelated events and point to the broader implications of these events. In
this way, speakers bring a great deal of individual creativity to their
interpretation of social relations. Individuals also often attempt to
introduce new ideas about the behavior of sorcerers and to change
political relations by doing so. But following stories over time shows
that many of these novel and creative ideas do not, in fact, seem to
have much impact on the audience, who remembers only the most
general and stereotypical aspects of explanations. It is precisely because
people regard stories told in inquests as "just so stories"—or fictional
accounts—that speakers can take such creative license in producing
them. Such fictional accounts do influence people—by, for instance,
striking the fear of sorcery into them—but they may be quickly forgotten and are less influential than the few stories that are remembered and
repeated. The process of changing "social and cultural worlds" is a slow
and communal one. Ideas about different categories of people change
only when alterations are subtle enough to pass unobserved by a group
of people who are inclined to be skeptical of ideas that are different
from ones they have heard before. Thus, individuals may "shape" and
"reshape" social reality when they talk about it but they do not do so
just as they choose.

To the outside observer the Kwanga seem to be obsessed with talk.
They spend many hours in meetings and think rumors are so serious
they have long public discussions to look into them. As shown in this
chapter, and in previous ones, it was evident that the Kwanga have
reason to be concerned about what people say. Once people start to
look for confirmation of a particular theory, they forget things that are
inconsistent with it and so the theory begins to seem well proven when,
in fact, it is just based on many ambiguous signs that have been interpreted the same way. When theories circulate in gossip, it is even more
difficult to know the evidence on which they are based, and a story will
come to seem true just because many people are saying the same thing.
Rumors can make trivial events seem much more ominous and can
escalate conflict rapidly. Beliefs about duplicitous behavior in meetings
make matters worse since everyone suspects that speakers hide their

best evidence, and so people pay attention to accounts of disputes or deaths even if there is little obvious evidence to support them. In short, once someone implants a suspicion in others' minds there are many ways that it can come to look like a proven fact.

The Kwanga are not unique. In many societies in Papua New Guinea and elsewhere, people spend a great deal of time talking about disputes, deaths, natural disasters, and social scandals. They hold meetings just to look into rumors. Perhaps this is because in small communities where politics is a matter of reputation management, and where rumors spread rapidly and take on a life of their own, what people say, and what they convince others of, has serious consequences.

In the last three chapters, I have explored the Kwanga preoccupation with various forms of talk and the social conditions that foster this pervasive concern in Inakor and Asanakor and in other similar environments in Melanesia and elsewhere. Because of various pressures associated with life in small isolated communities, people spread rumors and voice strong injunctions in public speeches which they later disclaim in order to influence events without facing reprisals. They create the impression of a complex reality that only initiated men can understand and control, and by doing so, bolster the authority of community leaders. But initiated men can also be "trapped" by their own talk. Their duplicitous behavior fosters distrust and suspicion: everyone looks for the hidden meaning behind every word or action. This starts rumors that can damage reputations and escalate conflicts and competitions. Initiated men believe themselves to be the victims of sorcery attacks because of false rumors; more concretely, they can be caught up into large communal exchanges they say they want no part of when rumors convince them that their honor has been impugned.

In the next three chapters I will move to a broader examination of leadership in small Melanesian communities. In chapters 8 and 9 I will look at the conditions that subvert hierarchy in Kwanga villages. This will add to the profile of the sociological conditions that create the preoccupation with talk in Melanesian villages and which lead to long, apparently inconclusive meetings to discuss rumors. Then I will move on to an analysis, in chapter 10, of the ways in which leaders are constrained by gossip and rumors.

CHAPTER EIGHT

Two Models of Government

In Inakor and Asanakor, initiated men and their uninitiated followers alike frequently complain about the absence of strong
leaders in their villages. People bemoan the inability of New Guineans
to follow the directives of leaders, claiming that it is their nature to
suspect the motives of their appointed leaders and to disregard their
words (Brison 1991).

The Kwanga are not alone. Other Papua New Guineans also complain about the same characteristics of their own societies, particularly
when they compare themselves to "white men." For instance, in Manus
Province, the leader of a movement for wide-ranging social and economic change, Paliau, complained that his followers were not like white
men who "could make a group decision and carry it out" (Schwartz
1962: 263). Paliau scolded his followers for being unlike the people of
other countries where "if [leaders] were men with good ideas who gave
their ideas to the rest, [they] are obeyed by their followers. Whatever
they say is listened to and carried out" (Schwartz 1962: 352). Paliau
also urged his followers to try to maintain unity and harmony within
the group (Schwartz 1962: 264) in order to become more like white
men.

This chapter explores Inakor and Asanakor people's ideas about how
their "government" differs from that of white men and also investigates
the villagers' frustration at their apparent inability to emulate Europeans. The next two chapters will explore in greater detail the factors
that produce and maintain an egalitarian ethos and make it difficult for
anyone to lead the community effectively for very long.

Two Models

Kwanga meetings often contain a great deal of talk about the correct way to conduct a discussion. An examination of this "meta-commentary" reveals an ongoing debate about the merits of two models of social control and political power, one associated with tradition and the other with the Australian colonial administration and the new national government. Interestingly, local speakers seem to think that what distinguishes the new and old ways of doing things the most is the kind of talk associated with each. The old ways are associated with gossip and innuendo (see also Goldman 1980, 1983), whereas under the new law one should speak straightforwardly and reveal everything that one knows. This is not uncommon: Marilyn Strathern (1972: 102–103) says that people of the Hagen area of the New Guinea Highlands similarly contrast the veiled speech of the past with the "straight talk" required in modern courts (see also Rosaldo 1973, 1984). Two speeches from inquests illustrate the Kwanga commentary. George, the Asanakor pastor, said in a meeting:

Are you listening? This meeting we are hearing now, we are not following the customs of before. No don't do this. I make some point and immediately you guys break it down again. Now I don't want us to talk and talk and follow this way of first making the water dirty and then waiting for it to clear so we can see. For myself, I am telling you now. What I want is for right now the truth to come up. And I will put it in Ronald's [that is, the village court's] hands, and Ronald must throw out this thing; throw it out. I don't want to stay here and question another suspect. I don't want you guys to say: "Wait for the water to clear first and then we will see." If you talk about the water clearing then another person will die. No, right away. This is the time of the Bible here. Everything is out in the open now. So now you must talk straight. You mark some man and then we will say: "All right, just you will go. Ronald will show you now and it will finish." You want to follow the law of before and say: "Hide it first, then later we will retaliate." This no, no.

Ronald expressed similar ideas in another meeting. He said:

Whoever of you knows something about Inakor and Asanakor . . . call their names so we can look into it. This is the true way to find out about sorcerers. . . . From one thousand years ago to now, we have not seen even one sorcerer come out into the open so we could take him to court. No, not at all. Someone dies. Talk comes up, but we don't jail a man. Never. You want to change and live under the law. All right then, when the law talks you must reveal the sorcerer. I want this kind of custom to take over. But no one does it.

We always hide sorcerers. . . . There are hundreds of sorcerers. All these sorcerers are around, but you and me come here and just tell stories and fight among
ourselves without accomplishing anything. I don't like this way of just talking
without evidence and accusing people. If you do it this way I will take you to
court. You must get the story. . . first before you talk. You can't just guess with
no good proof about all these men. You can't just sit there and talk without
evidence. This is all just rumor. I won't listen to this kind of story. I want you to
get up and show me the men. Asanakor, too, you must say who you think it is
and we can talk about it and find out about it.

Both speakers complain about the local way of talking. George ac-
cuses people of making misleading points to conceal the truth. Every
time he tries to discuss the truth, people "break down" his point by
introducing new topics. He tells people not to "dirty the water," that is,
obscure the truth with lies, because the resultant confusion allows
counter-sorcery. He says that, instead, people should put what they
know "out into the open" where the village court can evaluate it.

Ronald criticizes the practice of hiding knowledge about sorcerers
and of telling lies based on little evidence, something people do either
to conceal the truth or to frighten a reaction from the suspect. These
behaviors prevent prosecution of sorcerers.

In Kwanga rhetoric, sorcery and the intentional creation of ambiguity and confusion through gossip, hints, and lies are seen as part and
parcel of a traditional system whereas straightforward public revelation
of information symbolizes the "new law" of courts and centralized government. What are the characteristics of these two systems?

Gossip, Innuendo, and Sorcery: Power without Responsibility

The traditional system is decentralized and indirect. People look after themselves instead of appealing to a central authority.
They can almost always rely on the support of kin and fellow lineage,
initiation class, and moiety members. Epstein (1974a: 26) notes that
this kind of automatic support by kinsmen is common in Melanesian
societies (see also Young 1974: 65), and Lawrence (1971) terms this
group the "security circle." But individuals, and their support groups,
are checked by the knowledge that an attack on or an invasion of the
rights of others will bring retaliation from their security circles.

This is not an amoral contest of strength. There are principles of justice.[1] Instead of being tried before an impartial jury, as in Western law, the suspect is, in effect, tried before a jury divided into two camps: those biased in his favor (inside his security circle) and those biased against (outside his security circle). Thus, on the rare occasions where there is an airtight case against someone (such as when adulterers are caught in the act), the security circle will sometimes fail to come to his or her aid. But airtight cases are rare where everybody takes care to hide their actions. Alternatively, if the suspect has such a bad reputation because of past misbehavior that even his own kin will not find it difficult to believe that the current charges are true, they may fail to support him. For example, Hapandi's relatives often said in meetings that they would turn a blind eye if he was attacked.

The traditional order is predicated on protecting individuals from reprisals. To escape the consequences of their actions, people pursue their goals in ways for which they cannot be held accountable. They take hidden measures such as hiring sorcerers, or probably more commonly, attacking the reputation of their victim by implying that he is involved in sorcery or other bad deeds. In public they bluff. They tell long "stories" about recent events with clear implications for what people should do. But then if anyone challenges them, speakers say that they were "just guessing" and have no evidence to support their theories. For the most part, this kind of "talk" is the primary political tool. They avoid more direct measures like taking people to court since this is dangerous, and, instead, try to incite others to action as when Deborah was told to make the final determination in the Naifuku and Ambusuroho case.[2]

Out of the apparent anarchy created by these strategies, a semblance of order emerges. Interpretations of events in meetings warn people that antisocial behavior can lead to sorcery or accusations of sorcery, and, less dramatically, to malicious rumors, shame, and attacks on one's reputation. The ambiguity and confusion surrounding the "truth" create the impression that only big-men are knowledgeable and control sorcerers, and so the only way to be safe is for other people to behave themselves.

This is a rather indirect method of social control. Wrongdoing seldom leads to conviction and punishment because everyone fears the culprit's kin. Instead, suspected culprits, guilty or innocent, are greeted with a buzz of gossip and speculation and this may or may not stop them. In each instance there is always an element of doubt about what actually happened. But over the long run there is a cumulative impact. Repeat offenders may never be convicted on any particular offense, but after many accusations people come to believe they are troublemakers. Similarly, no one can ever be sure in each instance that people died because they revealed cult secrets, but if they hear such theories many times they will fear that violating cult rules invites sorcery.

The system has drawbacks. Because people are reluctant to act without consensus and this is difficult to achieve, many disputes drag on for years and seem almost impossible to resolve, such as the cases of Tewamwa (chapter 5) and of Haumele (chapter 4). Decisions on matters of communal concern, such as the affairs of the coffee buying cooperative, are both hard to reach and hard to enforce and, perhaps as a result, such communal ventures often fail. It is also difficult to coordinate communal action since people are reluctant to take the lead in making decisions, and when someone does step forward to do this, his assertive leadership is likely to arouse resentment and resistance.

But, conversely, if disputes are not resolved and decisions are not made, potentially divisive situations seldom lead to violence. Thus, for instance, Jeremiah came to no harm after being accused of murdering Naifuku and Ambusuroho. Similarly, Hapandi, the Inakor sorcerer was frequently accused of murder and threatened with violent death but was protected by kin. But as recent comments by kinsmen like Hilanda indicate, Hapandi may not be able to count on their support much longer. This is important because violence could easily lead to retaliation, feuding, and village fission. The raison d'être of the traditional system seems to be keeping the village together, and the local people still think a large village is desirable for defense in an area where warfare was traditionally endemic.[3]

Problems with the New Law

If traditional order is associated with ambiguity, indirection, and decentralization, the local people associate the "new law" with straightforward public revelation of knowledge and obedience to a central authority.

But many speakers complained that their fellow villagers did not follow the new ways very well (a suspicion that seemed to be confirmed by the examination of the village court in chapter 4). In an inquest,

Henry revealed that he thought his fellow villagers were not entirely clear about the "new way" of doing things. He said:

You guys don't discuss things properly. You talk and talk and tell plenty of lies. You should make the discussion short, say Hapandi did it, and tell him to throw out his sorcery spears. A lot of us here aren't clear on the laws of meetings. We are breaking a new trail through unfamiliar territory [Neo-Melanesian: *brukim bus*]. So we are still dying.

In another inquest, Ronald also indicated that his fellow villagers had not completely grasped the ways of the new law. He tried to explain it to them:

You made me your leader so now you must obey me. You made me your leader so when you wrong another man and I charge you compensation then you must pay it. . . . This is the way of leaders: you elect me, then when I prosecute you in court, you must follow my orders. If you follow my orders then this trouble will finish. If you don't then this trouble will come back and get you. You have to pay your compensation quickly. If you don't then he will have this pain in his stomach. You didn't satisfy him. So when you do it again. . . . It doesn't matter if the law is here, you will die. Obedience is the way to close the road of dying [through sorcery]. . . . There is just one road, following orders. That's the only thing that will save your life. . . . If you don't obey you will continue to have trouble. When you don't obey and you have trouble you can't blame us leaders. You must evaluate yourself first: are you a bloody bigheaded man or are you a good man?

The two men comment on the new way of doing things. Henry contrasts the traditional way of hinting at knowledge with the new way of revealing evidence in clear and unambiguous ways. The new way of speaking clearly will shame the sorcerers into stopping.

Ronald says that following the new law involves relinquishing the principle of self-help and referring disputes to a centralized authority. If people's grievances are satisfied in court, they will have no need to hire sorcerers. People are told to reveal what they know and want straightforwardly and to let the leaders decide. Giving up the power of self-determination also means ridding oneself of the dangers of others' self-determination, that is, of covert attack through sorcery and other means. Secrecy is not necessary if everyone is following the orders of leaders. Ironically, Ronald also points to a key problem with this system; that is, the magistrates have no power to enforce their decisions and must rely on the cooperation of convicted culprits. There is no centralized power to punish those who ignore magistrates' decisions. People continue to disobey leaders, and leaders continue to fear reprisals. Covert maneuvering, and the fear of hidden agencies that it engenders, still prevails. People bemoan the apparent inability of New Guineans to follow their leaders. A new system of social order predicated on centralized authority seems impossible. What prevents it?

Conditions Underlying the Gossip, Innuendo, and Sorcery Model

Many ethnographers have described a complex of behavior, in Melanesia and elsewhere, in which individuals try to influence others by casting particular interpretations on recent events. Brenneis (1984) and White and Watson-Gegeo (1990) describe meetings to address conflict which often avoid punitive action or even definitive conclusions. Instead, an "official public version" of problematic events is the aim, and this may do more to stop conflict from spreading and escalating than to resolve the initial dispute (White 1990). Similarly, Keenan (1974, 1975) and Arno (1980, 1990) comment on the use of gossip networks. People avoid responsibility by making charges in safe contexts such as conversations with kinsmen and accuse people publicly only when everyone agrees on the person's guilt (Keenan 1974). Hinting and the use of figurative language in public meetings (see Atkinson 1984; Knauft 1985; A. Strathern 1975; Weiner 1984) have a similar effect. Individuals cannot be held responsible for their words since no one can really be sure of their intentions. "Just talking" is evidently part of a complex of behaviors predicated on avoidance of responsibility which is found in a number of societies. What creates this complex?

First, people try to influence others by manipulating their impressions of events because there are high costs to more direct strategies. Previous chapters have revealed the inhibiting effect of kin networks and other social divisions. The community is divided into lineages, moieties, and initiation classes, each jealously guarding its autonomy and resenting outside interference. Any action creates an automatic opposition. In fact, Epstein (1974a: 33) argues that effective centralized leadership is impossible in "multicarpellary parishes"[4] in Melanesia since leaders will have difficulty winning recognition from the whole group.

A dense web of kin ties in a village with a high level of endogamy has a similar effect since people loyally defend their kinsmen unless there is conclusive proof of guilt, which is almost never the case. As well, people must be careful that their actions do not violate kin obligations, and this often makes it difficult for leaders to be impartial.

A preference for indirect and invisible strategies could also result from a lack of centralized power and authority (Rosaldo 1973). But is this characteristic of Kwanga villages? In the modern system the magistrate and Councillor have authority but little power to enforce their decisions. Traditional leaders such as initiated men have authority and also the power to reinforce it in the forms of hunting and gardening magic, and sorcery. But their power is still apparently ineffective. Indeed, previous chapters have revealed that at least in Hapandi's case, the person who has coercive powers is very vulnerable. Hapandi had been chased out of the village several times, was often accused of murder, was the focus of malicious gossip, and his life had been threatened at least once.

Young (1971, 1983) argues that contradictory principles of hierarchy and egalitarianism exist in a Goodenough Island society, and perhaps this is true of the Kwanga as well. Read (1959) and White (1978) also argue that an "ambivalence" about power exists in many Melanesian societies. Chapters 9 and 10 will examine principles of hierarchy and more egalitarian mechanisms in Kwanga villages.

CHAPTER NINE

Leadership, Authority, and "Egalitarianism"

Kwanga leaders seem to have legitimate authority and even are believed to have magical powers to control life, death, and communal prosperity which they can use to punish violations of their authority. Yet when leaders try to take forceful action on a problem they lose their support and may even face reprisals. In this chapter I will examine principles of hierarchy and mechanisms of equality in Kwanga society.

In the process, I will reexamine some of the literature on Melanesian leadership. The relative "egalitarianism" of Melanesian societies is often noted but the concept is ambiguous and takes on different meaning in different contexts. Sahlins (1963) argued that hereditary ascription was relatively rare in Melanesian societies where big-men achieved prominence through clever manipulation of social relations and display of prowess in competitive exchanges. Leadership achieved through demonstration of superiority had intrinsic constraints and was unlikely to last even for an individual's lifetime. Expanding his dominance involved the big-man in increasingly large prestations and it was likely to alienate his supporters, whose harvests he tapped; this also became increasingly difficult as his physical strength waned with age. It was only where an ambitious individual "came to power" by attaining an "office" of legitimate leadership (as in Polynesia) with associated sanctions, that power could be consolidated over time and space (Sahlins 1963: 295). Displays of superiority might be necessary to win the office but the leader then "came to power" and no longer had to demonstrate that he was worthy to lead.

Ethnographers have questioned the extent to which this portrait can be generalized to all of Melanesia. There are hereditary leaders in many societies particularly in coastal and insular areas (Douglas 1979; Hau'ofa 1971). Others have argued that even where there are no hereditary offices of leadership, there may be other legitimate bases for leadership. Michael Allen (1981: 108), for instance, says that graded male cults, such as those found in the Sepik and Vanuatu, may provide a basis for legitimation and consolidation of power. These cults

may . . . be said to provide leaders with a somewhat more viable and enduring basis for legitimation of their authority than is common elsewhere in western Melanesia. The high level of specification of rules, procedures and stages has important implications for the degree of control it gives those at the top of the hierarchy. The pervasive importance of the institution in virtually all aspects of social, political, and economic life indicates that status defined in its terms has an exceptionally high level of legitimacy. [M. Allen 1981: 108]

Nevertheless, in many areas of Melanesia, far from commanding respect and obedience, leaders tend to become scapegoats who are blamed for any communal misfortune. To avoid this fate, prominent men are careful to solicit and respect everyone's opinion and so decisions about matters of communal concern are usually made through consensus. Below I will take a close look both at principles of hierarchy and the leveling mechanisms that subvert them in Kwanga villages.

The Bases of Hierarchy

Tuzin (1976) has shown a close connection between political power and the male cult among the Kwanga's eastern neighbors, the Ilahita Arapesh. Initiated men claim the power to punish violations of cult rules by calling on sorcerers and cult spirits. Initiates control hunting, gardening, and war magic necessary to communal survival and prosperity, and the most prominent men in society are the "divine artists" of the cult. In short, ambitious men in Ilahita may have to prove themselves through displays of prowess. But once they have shown their worth, they can "come to power," that is, achieve a social position of authority which does not require them to continually demonstrate their worthiness to lead.

Among the Kwanga, initiated men also claim to control the policing powers of sorcerers. Ritual power and knowledge, important for the well-being of the community, is in the hands of tambaran initiates.

As in Ilahita, Kwanga men are given hunting magic and gain the ritual "heat" to empower it in tambaran initiations. Hunting magic is distributed among several men, but each moiety selects one man as the group magician. Traditionally this man had a great deal of prestige since he had to observe stringent taboos on food (he could only eat food cooked over a fire and could not drink cold water) and on contact with women (he could not eat food cooked by women and could not sleep with them) for several months before the hunt. People recognized that this was difficult and that not every man had the necessary self-discipline.

There are many hunting methods that are not dependent on magic, and young uninitiated men often particularly excel at these. But they can run into trouble if they are too successful. When a young woman died, for instance, people said that this was because her husband was conspicuously more successful than his cult seniors in hunting. Only initiated men can safely "win" in competitions for prestige.

Initiates of the gwar grade of the tambaran cult are given yam magic, used for the benefit of their group, and acquire the ritual heat necessary to empower it. Prowess in yam growing is important to winning prestige and, again, young uninitiated men invite sorcery attacks if they produce more impressive harvests than their cult seniors. The death of a baby, for instance, was attributed to the fact that his father, an uninitiated man, had displayed a larger yam harvest than many initiated men at a recent competitive exchange.

In short, this is not an unrestricted free-for-all competition for prestige and power, as Sahlins's model suggests. Only certain people have the right to win.

Oratorical skills were also taught during seclusion in the ambwa mwe initiation (Tuzin 1980: 104). Although traditional style has been replaced by plainer "modern" ways of speaking, meetings are still dominated by initiated men. Uninitiated men make unimpressive contributions, probably because they have less practice than their cult seniors. I counted the speeches made by Inakor people in a sample of seven Monday meetings and eleven funeral meetings (seven in Inakor and four in Asanakor). This gives only a rough estimate of the variation in participation among individuals and categories of people because speeches vary greatly in length. But those who speak more frequently also generally make longer speeches, so in most cases, taking into account the length of contributions would increase differences.

Women do not often speak in meetings. They contributed only 42 of 910 speeches. Initiated men are much more vocal (792 speeches) than uninitiated men (76 speeches). Men who had been initiated into the gwar grade of the tambaran cult (that is, fifth or second highest grade) gave many more speeches (615) than men who had only been initiated into the ambwa mwe (that is, the fourth) grade (177 speeches), even though there are six more men in this ambwa mwe class. Patterns of participation were similar in each of the three types of meetings observed.

In Inakor, as in Ilahita, many of the most influential and outspoken men were cult house artists. Artists made a total of 334 speeches in meetings as compared to 281 contributions by other gwar initiates, even though there are only 8 artists and 12 other gwar initiates. Artists include the current Councillor; Henry, one of the community's most successful "businessmen";[1] Suroho, a leader in the Christian church; and Hilanda, an outspoken elderly man. Most men over sixty are relatively quiet in meetings and uninvolved in community decisions but Hilanda was an active contributor. He was also a former Councillor, leading businessman, and father of the current village magistrate. Almost all of the artists are in the "top ten" of Inakor speakers (determined by participation), and all are initiates of the gwar grade of the tambaran. Interestingly, the most vocal speakers and many of the divine artists were also named by Henry (chapter 3) as most commonly suspected of hiring sorcerers. The "top ten" speakers in Inakor meetings were Gwarambu, a gwar initiate, sacred artist, and the current village Councillor (he made 118 speeches in the 11 sample meetings); Ronald, a gwar initiate and the current village magistrate (he made 93 speeches); Hilanda, a gwar initiate and sacred artist (he made 89 speeches); Walafuku, a gwar initiate (he made 74 speeches); Henry, a gwar initiate and sacred artist (60 speeches); Hapandi, an ambwa initiate and the village sorcerer (43 speeches); Bwalaka, a gwar initiate (38 speeches); Abel, an uninitiated man and the village pastor, Mwanchambor, an ambwa initiate (23 speeches); and Suroho, a gwar initiate and sacred artist (22 speeches).

In short, there is a strong relationship between tambaran position and participation in meetings. The authority of initiated men reaches beyond the realms of magic and the tambaran and into the secular world of everyday politics, even though there is serious doubt about whether initiations will be performed in the future. The political authority associated with the tambaran seems to have outlived the cult itself.

LINEAGE HEADMEN

Kwanga villages comprise a number of totemic patrilineages and the genealogically senior male of the group is (at least in theory) the headman. There are 19 lineages in Inakor (population 390) each with between 1 and 12 adult male members (with an average of 3).[2] Lineages own an estate consisting of residential, gardening, and hunting land, a set of names given to babies, sometimes a myth (usually the origin myth of the group), and hunting magic. The headman allocates resources and decides on when and how group exchange obligations should be met.

The genealogically senior men of lineages also gain access to secret group myths and magical items when they are initiated into the ambwa mwe grade.[3] Mythical ancestors of each group were believed to have carried certain things "out of the ground" with them when they first appeared on earth, and these items, which are believed to have particularly potent magical powers, are also controlled by the headman.[4] One group had a particularly powerful form of love magic, another possessed the power to cause famine, and a third group had powerful war magic and also magic to control the rain.

Egalitarian Mechanisms

Initiated men and lineage headmen have authority over others and their fellow villagers speak of how they preserve order within the village and protect it from enemy attack. Moreover, the tambaran system establishes a hierarchy of power and authority within the community of initiated men (see Tuzin 1976: 287–291; 1980: chap. 6, chap. 8). But coexisting with this hierarchical organization are more egalitarian principles.

Many leadership roles, like lineage headman and magician, are

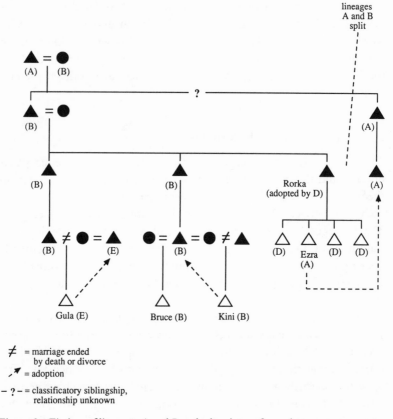

Figure 2: Fission of lineages A and B and adoptions of members

ascribed. Younger brothers are subordinate to their elders. But, in practice, there are many ways to circumvent genealogical ascription. Liberal
adoption practices and the tendency of lineages to fission mean that
many men end up as headmen of their own small groups and few remain subordinate. Lineages tend to be small. Genealogical links between members can most often be traced and seldom extend back more
than two or three generations beyond the present living members. At
the point at which genealogical links are forgotten, groups tend to
fission. For example, A, an Asanakor lineage, originally comprised two
classificatory brothers (whose genealogical relationship has been forgotten), and their offspring (see fig. 2). The elder brother married a
woman from another village, whose lineage totem was B. Totemic
emblems are used to identify food in exchanges, and my informant

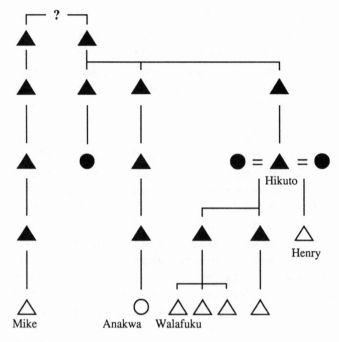

Figure 3: Lineage C

explained: "*A* was too big; it was confusing for our exchange partners to sort out which food belonged to whom." Consequently, the elder brother and his descendents decided to take on the totem *B*. They did not join the lineage of their wife and mother but formed a new group taking her totem as a marker. Groups *A* and *B* now have separate exchange obligations, have separate gardening and residential land, and share a common hunting bush. Residents of Inakor, including *B* and *A* kin, seemed to be unaware of the historical relationship between the two groups.[5] When lineages fission, people often remember that there is a genealogical relationship between the groups, but the apical ancestor is not a prominent figure (and, indeed, is seldom even remembered) and the relationship is not used to rank the two groups.

   In other cases, groups retain a common totem while taking on a degree of structural independence in exchange obligations and ownership of resources. In the case of the Inakor group *C*, for instance (see fig. 3), the genealogical relationship between Mike and the rest of the group has been forgotten. He and Anakwa, whose genealogical connection with the rest of the group is remembered but distant, retain *C* as their totem but have separate resources and exchange obligations from the rest of the group.[6] Henry, the genealogically senior male, has the group's myth. He told me that he will not pass on his knowledge to Mike, the senior member of the next generation, but instead will give it to his brother's son Walafuku, the senior man of the next generation in Henry's own line, thus furthering the structural separation of the branches of C.

Why do lineages fission? My informant stated that A and B divided because the original group was "too big." But this explanation seems a little mysterious in light of the fact that in many areas there are corporate groups with similar functions that are much larger than even the original A, which had, at the most, six or seven adult male members when it divided. Among the neighboring Ilahita Arapesh, each clan has about thirty-eight people (Tuzin 1976: 162). Lineages seem to divide when ambitious younger brothers want to become headmen. In the C case, for instance (see fig. 3), Hikuto, the most junior of the three "grandfathers," was clearly an ambitious and successful man. He had three wives, which is almost always a sign of success, and numerous offspring. The fission of C put his descendents in a prominent position as evidenced by the fact that his son Henry was a ritual artist, is in the "top ten" of Inakor speakers, and intends to pass on the group magic within his own, junior line.[7]

Tuzin (1980: 201–202) describes similar processes within the Ilahita subclan where junior branches attempt to assert their autonomy by introducing a new spirit statue into the tambaran house. Scaglion (1976), working among the Western Abelam, also notes that the basic corporate unit of Abelam society, the lineage (1976: 65), is prone to fission: "After a time, the eldest brother's authority is challenged by a younger brother as the lineage becomes too large and unwieldy to administer" (1976: 66). Kaberry, too, mentions the tendency of Abelam corporate groups to fission when they "become too large" (1940/41: 254).

ADOPTION

Lineage fission is one way of circumventing genealogical ascription. Ambitious younger brothers become the headmen of new groups. But a more common way for younger brothers to become the equals of their elders is to be adopted into another lineage. Theoretically men become members of the group of their fathers. A census of

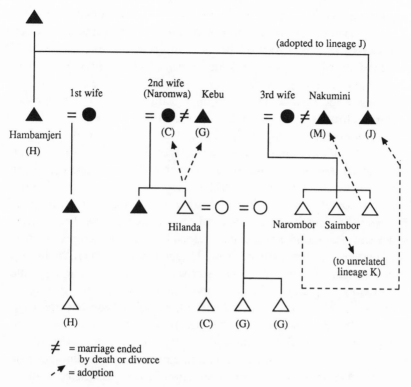

≠ = marriage ended
     by death or divorce
⟋⟍ = adoption

Figure 4: Adoptions of Hambamjeri's sons

Inakor, however, revealed that only 67 percent of adult married men are, in fact, in their father's lineage. Ten percent were in the group of their father's brother (because of frequent adoption, in many cases, the father's brother will have been adopted into a different lineage and so will not be in the same lineage as ego's father); 7 percent were in their mother's brother's or father's mother's brother's group; 3 percent were in the group of their mother's second husband (i.e., stepfather), and 11 percent were in an unrelated lineage. Many men have "taken places" or, as the Kwanga say, are "filling holes" in other groups.[8]

The case of A and B illustrates this process (see fig. 2). Rorka, the youngest son of the B line, was given by his father to group D, which was short of men. Rorka, in turn, had four sons, three of who remained in D. But since B was now without heirs, they took back the second son, Ezra. He was also given a position in A, the brother lineage of B, which had no male heirs, and he said that his son will inherit both positions. Rorka's two brothers remained in their father's group, B. One of their grandsons, Bruce, is now in B. The other grandson, Gula, however, has left B to take the place of his stepfather (his mother's second husband) in group E. When a man dies leaving young children it is quite common for these children to become affiliated with the lineage of their stepfather. Accordingly, Kini, whose widowed mother married Bruce's father, a B man, is now a member of B.

Adoption has varying implications. The move is arranged by the parents. Though the agreement is often made when a boy is still is child, the actual transfer does not occur until he marries and takes an active role in the exchange system. When asked for their lineage affiliation, men almost always give their natal rather than adopted group, and they often use the resources of both natal and adopted groups. They usually live with the adopted group and their children often become members of that group. But if a man's natal lineage is short of men the lineage may reclaim his sons. Men almost always take on the exchange and initiation obligations of their adopted group. Most often they relinquish the obligations associated with their natal lineages but ambitious and promising individuals may hold exchange and initiation obligations associated with both the natal and adopted groups simultaneously.

There are several reasons for adopting members. Since lineages tend to be quite small there are many structural "slots" (associated with resources). The fewer the members of any group, the greater will be the probability (particularly in the traditional situation where many infants died) that some groups will lack sons and will need to fill "holes" by recruiting from other groups. The alternative, allowing the group to disappear with its population, could easily lead to conflict over resources.

Adoption also satisfies the demands of the exchange and initiation system. Since exchange relations are inherited, if one partner has three sons and the other has only one, the imbalance will have to be corrected by adoption.[9]

In the past, endemic warfare brought many refugees to the village and the adoption system also facilitated the integration of immigrants into the village. The system of "hole filling" also provides another way for ambitious and promising younger brothers to become the equals of their elder siblings. For instance, Hambamjeri was by birth a member of H, a group that had recently migrated to the village and had a relatively small amount of land (see fig. 4). Hambamjeri married and had a son who took a place in H. Later, Kebu, a man of a native Inakor lineage G, died leaving a widow, Naromwa. Since G was short of men, they invited Hambamjeri to marry Naromwa and take Kebu's place in G. Naromwa and Hambamjeri had two sons. Her father asked that one be given to his lineage C, which was short of men. So the elder son took his father's place in G, and the younger son took a place in C. When the older son died, the younger son, Hilanda, took both his own place in C and his older brother's place in G. Hilanda himself had several wives and passed on his C place to the son of his first wife and the G place to his second wife's sons. Hambamjeri acquired a third wife by stealing a young woman who had come to marry another man, Nakumini of G (this was another branch of the G lineage). In compensation for the loss of the girl, Nakumini asked for one of her sons to become his heir in G. So Hambamjeri gave him his youngest son by this woman. Hambamjeri's older two sons by his third wife were also given to other groups. The eldest, Narombor, was given to Hambamjeri's brother who was himself filling a place in the J totem, which had no heirs. The second son, Saimbor, was given a place in K totem, which was also without heirs. Thus, the five sons of Hambamjeri all became senior men of different lineages. Two of them were ritual artists; two had hunting magic. This case is extreme but not unique in kind. The four surviving sons of Hupakumba, who was another prominent big-man of Hambamjeri's time, also are each senior men of different lineages.

Ambitious men do not themselves arrange to be adopted into another group. The senior generation identifies promising individuals and puts them in advantageous positions. Both Ezra, from the A and B example, and Hilanda from the H case, for instance, were given places in two groups, which almost certainly indicates that they were thought to be particularly promising. Both Hilanda and Ezra were active participants in community meetings during the period of my fieldwork although they were both elderly men and members of this age group were seldom very vocal. Both were also ritual artists and had held positions as village leaders under the Australian colonial system. Neither was the eldest of his sibling set.[10]

Although ambitious men cannot on their own initiative claim membership in another group, they can choose whether or not to remain active members of more than one group. Hilanda, for instance, retained memberships in both G and C even though C had too many men. It seems likely that a "lesser man" would have relinquished his membership in C long ago since extra exchange partnerships involve more work in gardening and pig husbandry.

The Equality of Big-Men

Scaglion (1976: 66) suggests that Western Abelam big-men may rise above others through recruiting followers from outside their lineage (see also Kaberry 1971: 60). Among the Kwanga the adoption system is designed to ensure that groups are of roughly the same size and so it is difficult for one man to become "bigger" than the rest through building a faction.[11] Group fissioning and adoption provide ways for many people to become lineage headmen but at the same time it prevents anyone from becoming "too big" since few remain subordinate. A man becomes one of a number of relatively equal big-men.

Furthermore, tambaran initiates may have authority over others but none can interfere in the internal affairs of other lineages (or of the other moiety). Each headman reigns supreme in his own small group, and his followers resent outside interference. Initiated men and group headmen lead the uninitiated and genealogical subordinates, but they must cooperate with each other.

The success of communal pig hunting, for instance, is governed by the magic of a number of lineage headmen,[12] each of whom has a bundle of magical items which is believed to enable him to control the spirits of the pigs in that area. A communal hunt will only succeed if everyone opens and ritually treats his magical items. Anyone can sabotage the whole hunt by secretly retaining a leaving such as hair or bone from a pig caught on someone else's bush land and failing to perform the appropriate ritual over it.

This is part of a more general emphasis on consensus among initiated men. Each invites sorcery attacks if he disregards the others' opinions. A case will illustrate these themes.

THE DEATH OF TANA

An Inakor man, Tana, died soon after a village-wide food exchange that had been the subject of much community debate. It was part of a tambaran-associated festival that had been interrupted when Kongiya died. Many people felt that the festival should be abandoned after Kongiya's death, and there was a village meeting to decide what to do. They discussed whether to hold the competitive yam display normally associated with the festival or to replace it with a simpler noncompetitive food exchange. Those in favor of the noncompetitive exchange, a group that included Tana and his younger brother Gara, won out. Shortly after the exchange, Tana died. An informant, Henry, explained the reason for this death to me in an interview. He spoke of "a stick" that symbolized the competitive yam display since such sticks are used to construct the bins in which short yams are displayed. Henry said:

After Kongiya died, his brother Techambu said: "I'll turn my back on this [death]. Let's go ahead and display our yams." We had a big meeting. Gara got up with a stick and said: "I'm throwing away this stick. We won't do it." [Later when Tana died] we said: "He threw away the stick and threw away Tana at the same time." Lots of people were bothered by [Gara's talk of throwing away the yam display]. Hapandi was bothered too. . . . We [some of us] wanted to do the yam display. So when Tana died we put the blame on Gara.

Gara tried to place himself above the others by autocratically deciding to abandon the yam display. Later, Tana's death was attributed to this imprudent action. Henry said that both moieties must agree on matters relating to the tambaran since they both owned it. He said of Gara:

It's your fault. You took the stick and threw it away and threw Tana away at the same time. This is a big thing, a big thing belonging to all of us. . . . When we want to do a tambaran we will make an agreement with [the other moiety] first. If they do it without asking us first we might talk and kill them. . . . We found out that it was Gara's fault and scolded him: "It's your fault. This isn't a little thing. This is a big thing belonging to the whole village. You should ask around and see what everybody thinks before you do this. You just acted on your own wishes and you will die." [Here "you" refers to Gara or someone in his group, in this case Tana.]

Sorcery struck when Gara disregarded others' wishes. The correct and safe way to proceed, as Henry suggested, was to "ask around and see what everybody thinks" first. A decision on a community enterprise should be made through consensus. Big-men are equal and none should claim superiority over the others.

Jealousy

Lack of equivalence is generally thought to be dangerous. People, for instance, fear that superior achievement can lead to covert attack. A group of ten informants (five male, five female) were asked to respond to questions on a number of hypothetical scenarios (devised by Theodore Schwartz, personal communication). In one, a village man ran a conspicuously successful trade store and people began to talk about him. Informants were asked what the people said and what the store owner would do. Almost unanimously, they replied that people complained that the owner had more money than everyone else: "Why only him and not us?" They were likely to hire a sorcerer to kill him. In response, the store owner would either die (in the view of fatalistic informants!) or close down the store. Similarly, when Yuanis, a big-man from a village to the south, was severely crippled by disease, some-one told me that his fellow villagers had hired sorcerers because they were jealous of Yuanis's success in commercial enterprise.

The exchange system also emphasizes equivalence. Ideally, both sides should give and receive the same things; lack of equivalence can lead to sorcery attacks. The more competitive the context of the ex-change, the more exact will be the demand for equivalence. Those who return less than they receive run the risk of angering the recipient by implying disrespect. Conversely, those who give more than they receive may make the other side jealous.

Lack of equivalence can also be dangerous for the whole community. When there was a great deal of rain in the normally dry planting season after one initiation, people said that Narombor, a rain magician, was angry because the initiates from his moiety had been judged less im-pressive than those from the other moiety.[13] The Councillor, who told me this story, said that in subsequent tambaran festivals the decorations of the initiates from both sides had always been pronounced equally beautiful in order to avoid similar disasters.

In short, there are principles of hierarchy in Kwanga society associ-ated with genealogical position and also with the tambaran cult. But these hierarchical principles are subverted by the division of the com-munity into lineages, moieties, and initiation classes. A headman may have authority over his own lineage but most matters concern people from many lineages and so involve negotiation of consensus between relatively equal headmen. Similarly, initiates of high tambaran grades still risk arousing resentment and covert attacks if they interfere with the concerns of the other moiety or initiation class, or with other lineages. Thus authority is tightly circumscribed and in most situations the only safe course is cooperation and consensus.

Patrilineal Principles, Hierarchy, and Change

The egalitarian ethos of political relations in Kwanga villages is at least in part due to flexible principles of recruitment to lineages which allow men to circumvent the authority of their older brothers. This flexibility, in turn, seems to have been related to particular social and demographic conditions, namely, frequent warfare and a low population to land ratio.

In Kwanga villages, flexibility and order are simultaneously achieved by manipulating descent group membership. Patrilineal principles create a "structure" but more flexible principles provide the rules for recruiting people to fill structural slots. The case of L lineage (see fig. 5) will illustrate this process. Relationships within the original L patrilineage are used to structure relationships between the current members of L, several of whom were recruited from outside the patrilineage. Originally L comprised two classificatory brothers. When the elder brother had no sons, a man was recruited from lineage M to take his place. The M man had two sons, creating two new structural slots. The

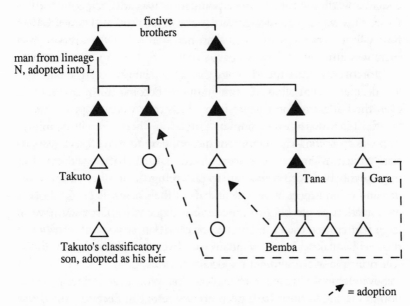

Figure 5: Adoptions of lineage L

elder son has been succeeded by his son Takuto who, having no sons, has recruited his mother's brother's son's son to take his place. Takuto's father's brother had no heirs and so Gara, a member of the junior branch of L, has taken this place. The junior L grandfather also had two sons. The eldest son's son had no male descendents so Bemba, a descendent of the younger grandfather, has taken his place. The younger son had two sons, Tana and Gara, and so the extra son, Gara, was given to the senior line of L. In short, each father must be replaced with a son so those without male children must recruit heirs from other sources and those with more than one son often allow the younger sons to be adopted into other groups. Patrilineal descent provides the structure; the structural "slots," however, can be filled by anyone, regardless of whether he was born into the patrilinage or not.

This system was advantageous in a world where intervillage mobility was common. In a situation of endemic warfare there were inevitably refugees.[14] When these immigrants were assigned to slots in a preexisting structure they took on a whole series of kin and exchange obligations and were given access to resources. They became an integral part of the community with ties to other village members. This bound the village together, something that was clearly desirable in a situation of endemic warfare where a larger population was advantageous for defense. This was advantageous for the immigrant and also benefited the host village. Traditionally, there was no shortage of resources and so there was little cost to this system.

Moreover, despite the ideology that gave primacy to "true natives," the flexible system allowed immigrants to become full members and even the leaders of the villages into which they were adopted. Again, this flexibility was advantageous in a situation where intervillage migration was common. The immigrant did not have to face life as a second-class citizen. Members of a host village realized that they themselves might easily be forced by warfare to take refuge in another village some day and could expect to be full citizens of their new village. In short, a combination of plentiful resources and frequent warfare may have in large part created the egalitarian ethos of Melanesian social relations in the past by making it advantageous to subvert patrilineal descent as the sole principle of recruitment to social positions.

Several things have led to changes in this system. First, since pacification in the 1920s there have been no war refugees. Second, coffee was introduced in the area in the 1960s, and most villagers now have coffee gardens. Coffee gardens are most often planted on prime land close to the village. There is no absolute shortage of land in Inakor and Asanakor but most villagers prefer to plant gardens on land that has been used within the last generation (as small bush is easier to clear than larger bush) and which is close to the village. Coffee gardening has created a shortage of this most desirable type of land and has led to land disputes. Third, improvement in medical facilities has lowered the infant mortality rate. More children survive and, consequently, there are fewer empty "slots" to be filled by recruitment outside the patrilineage. Finally, the land policies of the national government have been a source of concern to villagers. The Kwanga say that the new land courts recognize only patrilineal rights to land and believe that the national government is in the process of returning all land to its rightful owners—that is, to the descendents of those who emerged from that ground. Thus they worry that land their group captured in warfare that they have used for generations will be taken away from them and they must then find their own "true" land to return to at this time.

All these changes increase the costs of flexible principles and decrease the benefits and, thus, have led to a shift toward a more rigid model of social organization. The increased pressure on resources created by cash cropping and the decreased infant mortality rate means that there are greater costs to adopting new members to groups. Perhaps for the first time there are shortages in valued resources. At the same time, pacification has decreased the benefits of a flexible system. People no longer fear that they will be forced to seek refuge in other villages and so no longer value the principles that facilitated this. Furthermore, a large village is no longer necessary for defense and so additional population is not beneficial. In short, changes in migration patterns have led to new emphases in ideas about social organization.

There are indications that patrilineality as a principle of recruitment and as a criterion determining access to resources is becoming stronger. People are more reluctant to give their sons to other groups saying that these sons will have inferior rights as adopted members. There are also cases now of "true" (that is, patrilineal) members of groups attempting to evict adopted members. Tomba, for instance, the "true" member of lineage N (see fig. 6) had lived and worked for years in Maprik, a local town, where he had three wives and numerous children. In 1986 he returned briefly to Inakor bringing with him one of his sons, Al, whom he left in the village. Before returning to Maprik, Tomba went to the village Councillor asking that the widow Tembwai and her two adult sons be ejected from N. He said that they had no right to use N's re-

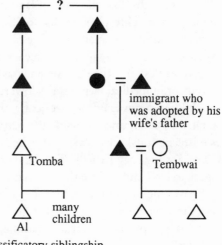

— ? – = classificatory siblingship,
         relationship unknown

Figure 6: Lineage N

sources because they were not "true" members of the group and, in fact, Tembwai's husband's father had been adopted into N, when he came as an immigrant to the village and married the daughter of a man who had no sons. Tomba's attempt to evict Tembwai and her offspring had met with little success when I left the village.

The system of transferring people among lineages creates a community of many, relatively equal, big-men. Now people are more reluctant to adopt group members from outside the patrilineage. As this generation matures, and others succeed it, these changes could lead to a more stratified society in which younger brothers remain subordinate to older brothers.

CHAPTER TEN

Leaders as Bad Men and Victims

I have shown that flexible principles of recruitment and frequent division of lineages subvert ascribed hierarchy in Kwanga villages. Examining the careers of leaders will reveal other leveling forces.

Many ethnographers have noted that Melanesians seem to be ambivalent about power (Hau'ofa 1981; Read 1959; Young 1983: 166, 201; White 1978). Everyone admires strong leaders, takes vicarious pleasure in their achievements, and sees them as necessary for protecting the community against enemies and for keeping order within the village. But at the same time people resent those who take autocratic attitudes (Read 1959; Watson 1971) or are visibly more successful than everyone else (Burridge 1975; Young 1971). People also suspect leaders are abusing their power to pursue selfish goals at the expense of their fellows. Hau'ofa (1981), for instance, says that even though the concepts of rightful hierarchy and strong leadership seem to be stronger among the Mekeo than in many Melanesian societies, Mekeo sorcerers, valued for their ability to preserve law and order and defend the village against enemies, are also suspected of killing fellow villagers for malicious reasons or for money. In fact, the Mekeo seem to be preoccupied with this hidden "dark side" of power (see also Young 1971: 182 on Goodenough Islanders).

Such contradictory principles of egalitarianism and hierarchy put Melanesian leaders in a "double bind" (e.g., Young 1983: 166, 201 on Goodenough Island leaders). They can do nothing right: they are expected to lead but their attempts to do so inevitably meet opposition and criticism.

Read (1959) suggests that participating in meetings is one way in which Melanesian leaders can satisfy the conflicting demands on them. The Gahuku-Gama of the Eastern Highlands of Papua New Guinea admire strong and forceful men, of whom warriors are the prototype, but they also resent those who disregard the opinions and desires of their fellow community members. In meetings, Gahuku-Gama orators can display "strength" by haranguing the audience and by making forceful speeches. But they can also gauge public opinion and, in the end, will suggest courses of action that they think everyone will support. In this way, leaders can demonstrate strength but also show a "nice appreciation of the opinions of others and of their right to express them" (Read 1959: 433) and, thus, avoid offending people.

Read's remarks also seem to apply to Kwanga leaders who make forceful speeches in meetings but then later say that they were "just talking." In this chapter, I will explore the conditions that create an ambivalent attitude toward leaders and cause them to do things like haranguing the audience in meetings but then mysteriously "forgetting" their own injunctions afterwards or spreading rumors that they publicly deny. I will then look at cases from other areas and will suggest that the social conditions in small isolated communities make it difficult for anyone to be a strong leader.

I will also argue that gossip, rumor, and innuendo constrain Melanesian leaders in many ways. First, the atmosphere of suspicion that goes along with rumor and innuendo helps foster the much noted "ambivalence about power" of Melanesian communities. Suspicions about leaders are part of a pervasive distrust of everyone that, in turn, stems from a real preference for devious and hidden strategies. Second, distrust of leaders leads to backbiting and slander. Almost anything a leader does creates resentment and slanderous rumors that frighten many prominent men into trying to get rid of their powers. Furthermore, those who hold firm and ignore the backbiting become the victims of increasingly negative rumors that erode reputations, make the victim a social outcast, and can even leave him vulnerable to attack. Third, individual initiated men, just like women and children, can be duped into believing that suspicious events and statements conceal dark plots against them. They, like everyone else, have been taught to look for a more ominous hidden world behind innocent surfaces, and so they also can be frightened into altering their behavior to avoid sorcery attacks. In short, initiated men use gossip, innuendo, and other sorts of talk to influence others without being held responsible. But individual initiated men are just as much controlled by this "talk" as are women and children.

The Contradictions of Leadership

Young (1983) argues that Goodenough Island myths and legends contain a standard script for the career of leaders which seems to be reenacted in actual events. These stories portray leaders as victims of their own societies. People are never satisfied and often suspect leaders of abusing their powers. Almost anything leaders do provokes malicious gossip and possibly secret attack through sorcery. Finally, in a fit of towering rage, the much maligned men use their magical powers to destroy both themselves and everybody else by creating drought, famine, or some other natural disaster.

Kwanga stories about powerful men reveal similar themes. Henry, for instance, told me about his stepfather, Suroho, who had died several years before I came to Inakor. Suroho defended his village by ensorceling enemies who tried to encroach on village land. Henry described these events in an interview: "He chased them all out. He was a really rough man. When he brought sorcery to some village he really finished them all off. He was a strong man. He had a big name and was known everywhere. He did it in his own village too. All the other families were under him."

But Henry also said that Suroho was accused of ensorceling fellow villagers, and this made him so unpopular that his sons had to find wives in other villages.

Henry said that Suroho's downfall came after he had hired a sorcerer to kill a man whose wife he coveted. Suroho married the widow but, according to Henry, when some men told her of Suroho's role in her husband's death, she joined with them in a plot to kill him. Before he died, Suroho had a dream in which this plot was revealed to him and in the morning he told his wives: "The hawk that before made its home in the bamboo [his lineage's totem], now they have taken a net and caught it." Henry interpreted these words:

He meant that he was sick; he was going to die. They had injured him. The hawk is a symbol of himself: he was a rough man before. Hawks are no good. Men don't touch them. He could fight with a whole family or another village. Before [the other big-men] weren't fit to oppose him. They didn't come and talk with him. He would have shot them if they did that.

Henry's story should not be taken as literal truth but it does reveal several pervasive ideas about leaders. First, as in many areas of Melanesia, there is a fundamental ambivalence built into the image of

the leader. Suroho's "roughness" benefits the village by driving away
outside enemies, but he is also "no good" and acts selfishly in ways that
harm others, as when Suroho killed a man to marry the widow. In other
words, people admire forceful leaders but believe that the very strength
that enables these men to keep order in the village and to defend it from
its enemies can also be used to ride roughshod over fellow community
members. In fact, it seems to be virtually inevitable that anyone
"strong" will also be seen as a "bad man" who pursues selfish goals at
the expense of others. Second, leaders come in for a great deal of criticism and, in many cases, this backbiting and resentment destroys them in
the end. Their actions will inevitably provoke malicious gossip, resentment, sorcery accusations, and hints of sorcery attack. Suroho was
relatively thick-skinned and ignored the backbiting but he also faced
other difficulties: he became a virtual social outcast and his sons were
unable to find wives in the village. Third, even the most powerful are
vulnerable to covert retaliation. In this case, Henry thought retaliation
came through supernatural means, but in two other cases I heard about
sorcerers were secretly ambushed and killed.

I saw the themes of the Suroho story reenacted many times. Leaders
always seemed to provoke an ambivalent reaction. For instance, people
frequently complained that when Bwalaka had been village Councillor
he had bullied people and had not hesitated to send them to jail for even
the smallest offense. He was not reelected. But, ironically, complaints
about the present Councillor, Gwarambu, who was viewed as overly
mild-mannered and reasonable, were almost as virulent. People said
that sorcery and other kinds of mischief were rampant in the village
because no one was afraid of Gwarambu.

Leaders, particularly those believed to have supernatural powers,
also often complained about malicious gossip and said that they feared
sorcery or outright attack. They seemed to be scapegoats who were
suspected of abusing their powers and were blamed for any communal
misfortune. Fembor, one of the two most powerful hunting magicians
in the village claimed to have thrown away his hunting magic and converted to Christianity. He explained his reasons in a meeting that followed the death of his infant granddaughter (this meeting was also
described in chap. 5):

They talked about me and talked about me whenever we hunted pigs. I got sick
of this and went to the church. I confessed my sins and threw [my hunting
magic] away in my garden house and then I was baptized. I did this because of
this talk. They were always talking about me and I was sick of it, so I converted.

Because I was tired of this talk. Whenever they went hunting and didn't get anything they would say: "It's Fembor. It's Fembor." I threw all these things away because of this. I threw them away in my [garden] house. I think they must have rotted by now. The house too must have rotted and covered them up. I did it because of this talk.

By his own account, whenever a communal hunt failed, Fembor was accused of sabotage. Finally, irritated by all these complaints, he threw away his magic. Two lineage headmen who had possessed particularly potent magic (one, magic to create famine, the other, particularly strong love magic) also said that they had thrown away these powers because of malicious gossip (that they had created natural disaster in one case, and unfairly monopolized the women of the community, in the other), and because members of their group were dying from sorcery commissioned by jealous villagers.

Leaders are not only gossipped about, they also face real dangers. The vulnerability of those with power is perhaps most dramatically evident in the case of sorcerers. Some sorcerers, particularly when there is only one in a village, gain the reputation of killing fellow villagers without good cause. They are the object of continual backbiting, are excluded from social circles, are often accused in public gatherings of killing people, are jailed, have been known to flee the village fearing for their lives, and in a couple of cases from long ago which people told me about, were ambushed and murdered. In short, leaders feel vulnerable to backbiting and sorcery, and there is some evidence that they are, indeed, resented and this can be dangerous.

In summary, like many of their counterparts in other areas of Melanesia, Kwanga leaders seem to be in a double bind. People expect leaders to be strong in order to protect the community against enemies and to frighten their fellow villagers into good behavior. Those, like Gwarambu, who do not exhibit the expected forcefulness of character are severely criticized. But strong men are also resented and suspected of misusing their power to pursue personal goals to the detriment of others in the community. It seems that leaders can do nothing right: people expect them to lead and criticize those who are not forceful; but when anyone does take strong action, people say that they are abusing their powers, and they also may be blamed for the failure of communal ventures.

Furthermore, leaders can be frightened into compliance by talk. To escape the backbiting and the rumored sorcery attacks that their actions seem inevitably to engender, many people, like Fembor and the two magicians, try to rid themselves of their powers. There are a few who ignore the complaints and the dangers (like Suroho), who can "rise above" the intrinsic constraints of the social structure, and are strong leaders (Young 1971: 113; see also Douglas 1979: 7). But they become social outcasts and sometimes are even attacked.

A Comparative View: Ambivalence about Power and Small Communities

Similar patterns are found in other areas particularly among people who, like the Kwanga, live in small isolated villages. I will examine leadership among two other groups, the Goodenough Islanders studied by Young (1971, 1983), and the Melpa of Mount Hagen (Highlands, Papua New Guinea), in order to suggest that there is a relationship between social structure and leadership styles. The Goodenough Islanders are in many ways similar to the Inakor and Asanakor people: Kalauna, like the two Kwanga villages, is a relatively large (by Papua New Guinea standards) and compact village that comprises several clans each with its own headman. Lineage headmen have magical powers and, as among the Kwanga, they are often blamed for deaths and other natural disasters. I will argue that Kalauna leaders, like their Inakor counterparts, are caught in an environment that engenders ambivalence about power and malicious gossip.

Melpa leaders, however, seem less constrained by the societies they lead. They seem to be more assertive and powerful than their counterparts in Inakor and Kalauna. I will argue that the greater power of Melpa leaders stems from a social environment that presents fewer constraints: the Melpa tend to live in small scattered family clusters instead of in large, compact villages comprising several lineages or clans. This social structure does not create either the same degree of ambivalence about power or as dense a gossip network, as do Inakor and Kalauna.

Although evidence from only two groups cannot, of course, prove that social structure creates certain leadership styles, examining two such well-documented and well-known cases as the Melpa and the Goodenough Islanders will perhaps suggest possible avenues for further analysis of how leadership patterns vary across societies in Papua New Guinea. A more comprehensive survey is beyond the scope of this analysis and, in any case, would be difficult to carry out since it is not easy—and perhaps is impossible—to assess such variables as how powerful leaders are, how much gossip there is, how ambivalent about power the local people are, and so on. These things call for subjective assessments and, thus, vary somewhat with the personality and background of the ethnographer. Furthermore, such things as gossip have not been the focus of many studies of Melanesian leadership and so many ethnographers do not supply information on this topic.

The village of Kalauna is in many ways similar to Inakor and Asanakor. The village comprises several clans, one of which is believed to control most of the magical powers governing harvests, weather, and life and death. Headmen of this group are prominent community leaders but also come in for a great deal of criticism when they are blamed for deaths and natural disasters (see, for instance, the case in Young 1971: 108).

The powerful also seem to be vulnerable in Kalauna. Young (1971) says that during the period of his fieldwork magicians were sometimes blamed for droughts and deaths and were forced to seek refuge in other areas. Indeed, the most powerful clan originally held all of the food magic for the community but gave some of it away after they were warned that they would die from sorcery if they continued their monopoly (1971: 30).

Like their Kwanga counterparts, Goodenough Island leaders complained bitterly about malicious gossip. For instance, when one leader, Didiala, was suspected of destroying a harvest, he defended himself in a village meeting (Young 1983: 163–166):

[My] wife told me what people were saying. So I grew ashamed of your talking. . . I was not angry. But you stopped me and I bowed my head. I expected my group to support me but they turned away . . . I did nothing . . . You blame me for nothing and I am ashamed. Yes, your gossip made me ashamed . . . All you whom I have helped in the past, have you forgotten? Why do you urge me to die? You make me cry. You wrong me. Afterward you will see the other side of the matter and you will say, "Oh, thank you, Didiala!" But when my sons grow up you will make them cry too.

Didiala, like his Kwanga counterparts, complains that others resent him and malign him behind his back.

Magicians and sorcerers almost always denied responsibility for particular deaths or disasters (1971: 84, 89). But one leader, Kimaola, whom Young deemed "most likely to succeed" after his first period of fieldwork, did blatantly take credit for such disasters (1971: 98), probably hoping to enhance his influence by demonstrating his coercive powers. When Young returned to the field some years later he found Kimaola a virtual outcast. He had been attacked and almost killed by angry villagers who thought he had ensorceled someone (Young 1983).

In Kalauna and Inakor, as in many Melanesian societies, the very exercise of power seems to invite suspicion that it is being misused. This leads to malicious gossip and backbiting and perhaps to more serious things. Leaders fear this suspicion and its consequences and so attempt to divest themselves of power, or to deny responsibility for specific natural disasters. But those, like Suroho and Kimaola, who ignore it, face more dire threats like jail, sorcery attack, exile, or outright attack and murder. Strong leaders seem almost inevitably to be perceived as "bad men" and to become victims. What creates this pattern?

A certain amount of ambivalence about power is probably found everywhere. But particular conditions in some Melanesian villages seem to intensify suspicions about leaders. I have already noted the ways in which the division of the community into lineages, moieties, and initiation classes inhibits leadership. Epstein (1974a: 26, 33) argues that such social structures make it difficult to lead effectively since almost any action strikes someone as unwarranted interference and meets virtually automatic resistance. People may desire a strong village leader but, at the same time, they resent it when someone outside their own lineage tries to order them around. Leaders are frequently in the position of having to comment on issues that concern members of other groups. Consequently, almost anything they do will provoke an ambivalent reaction unless they are very careful to show respect for the opinions of each lineage headman. But then they risk appearing to be weak and ineffectual.

The multistranded nature of social ties in small inbred villages also creates an environment in which almost any action is bound to offend someone. Everyone interacts with the same small group of people in a variety of contexts and this means that they are bound to be faced with conflicting demands. In Inakor, for instance, everyone is simultaneously part of a kin network, a lineage, a moiety, and an initiation class. It is, therefore, difficult to do anything that will please everyone since, for instance, an action that is appropriate to a moiety member may violate kin obligations. To take another example, although it is appropriate for a village magistrate to be impartial, such an attitude is never acceptable in a kinsman. As a result, any visible action is likely to offend someone. This is a particular problem for leaders because they are often in the public eye and therefore people are aware of their transgressions. Consequently, it is difficult for leaders to avoid criticism and they are often seen as "bad men" (see J. Hutson 1971 for a description of a very similar situation in a European village).

To make matters worse, since almost any action seems to provoke a negative reaction, people avoid doing things they can be held accountable for. Sometimes they do nothing, but often they work covertly. But, of course, everyone knows that everyone else is involved in covert schemes and, as was apparent in previous chapters, this creates a situation in which people are predisposed to distrust others and to believe that benign faces hide much more dangerous thoughts. As a result, they are inclined to entertain suspicions about leaders' characters.

Leaders are suspected of corruption and are the object of much backbiting in many societies. Why are such suspicions so particularly effective in curbing Melanesian leaders? Merry (1984) argues that small close-knit villages (like Inakor, and Kalauna) generate an unusual amount of gossip and that people are unusually sensitive to backbiting in small villages, particularly if they do not have ties outside the community. In Inakor and Kalauna where most marriages are made within the village (78.9 percent village endogamy in Inakor and 86 percent in Kalauna) people do not have many kinsfolk and affines in other villages. Moreover, village lineages are not part of an overarching, extra-local lineage system so that, again, people have relatively few ties outside the village. Both of these things mean that fellow villagers are dependent on each other for companionship and aid and so they try to avoid doing things that might offend each other. So when leaders hear complaints and nasty rumors about themselves, they are quick to change their behavior.

But what of the violent ends that befall those who are immune to the effects of gossip? Merry (1984: 285–286) says that in small communities a consensus eventually forms against those who ignore gossip and persist in offensive behavior, and they may be accused of witchcraft and perhaps expelled from the community or even murdered. Kimaola and Suroho both fit this pattern: they initially "rose above," that is, were uninhibited by, gossip and eventually were threatened with violent death.

Merry does not explain how this consensus forms and leads to violence. Perhaps it is because where there is no strong central power, people are often dependent on support groups to protect them from attack and to prevent others from infringing on their rights. Among the

Kwanga, for instance, kin and fellow lineage and moiety members usually rally to protect one of their own, and people, such as women who were born in distant villages and married into Inakor, who have no local kin, are at a noticeable disadvantage. But even if people have local kin, rumors of persistent misbehavior over many years can create a considerable consensus against them, and their kin hint willingness to turn a blind eye towards an attack. Hapandi's kin often hinted that if he were killed in a secret ambush, they would not avenge his death. In two similar cases, sorcerers who had the reputation of killing within the village were ambushed and murdered (long before I arrived in the field). Thus, people are sensitive to slurs on their reputations, and for good reason since unheeded gossip can eventually have serious consequences.

Anything leaders do provokes malicious backbiting, which can result in social exclusion, inability to make good marriages, and withdrawal of aid; it can also create more serious dangers in the form of sorcery accusations and even outright attack. Perhaps this is why the Kalauna villagers view *veyaina*, or malicious gossip, as almost as damaging as sorcery (Young 1971: 135). The power of sorcery fears in checking autocratic leaders in Melanesia has often been noted (see, e.g., Burridge 1975). But the power of malicious gossip, and fear of being accused of sorcery, are perhaps even more powerful constraints.[1]

THE MELPA

I have argued that small, isolated villages tend to foster an ambivalence about power and a great deal of malicious gossip, both of which inhibit strong leadership. Evidence from the Melpa of the Mount Hagen area of the Western Highlands of Papua New Guinea supports this analysis. They have a different pattern of local organization which seems to place fewer constraints on leaders.

Local organization among the Melpa differs from the conditions described above on almost all counts. First, the Melpa do not live in concentrated villages. Instead, small groups (usually of close kin) live in scattered family clusters (A. Strathern 1972: 55). Second, the local group among the Melpa comprises only one clan (A. Strathern 1972). Third, these local groups are exogamous (A. Strathern 1984: 15). Marriages become the vehicle for alliances with other groups, and this is part of a general pattern of cultivation of extra-local ties by big-men. Such extra-local ties are crucial for success in *moka*, the ceremonial exchange system in which big-men compete for prestige, and Strathern (1972) notes that big-men invest a great deal of effort in cultivating them. They travel a great deal and this is thought to be proper behavior for leaders (A. Strathern 1972: 84–87, 116). They may even maintain households in more than one local group and "commute" between the two (A. Strathern 1972: 115). Furthermore, the mutual dependence of local group members among the Melpa is not great. It is relatively easy to change local group affiliation (and many people do this to escape quarrels at home). In fact, if a man joins the group of his mother, he has status equal to agnatic members of the group (A. Strathern 1972: 128).

Correspondingly, Melpa leaders seem to be less vulnerable than in other areas. Big-men act assertively and forcefully. Strathern (1972: 150), for example, describes instances of big-men driving people from their local group. Strathern himself (A. Strathern 1984) contrasts the leadership patterns of the Melpa and the Wiru. Wiru live in villages that comprise a number of descent groups (A. Strathern 1984: 10) and at least some marriages are made within the local community (A. Strathern 1984: 15). It is more difficult for people to move away from their agnatic group among the Wiru since they have inferior status in other groups (1984: 15). Andrew Strathern (1984: 16) states: "There are Wiru big-men . . . but their power and influence seems in no way to have reached that of big-men in the central Hagen [i.e., Melpa] area."

Perhaps big-men among the Melpa are more powerful because they face fewer obstacles than their Inakor-, Kalauna-, or Wiru-speaking counterparts. Local groups comprise only one clan, so the segmental divisions that make village leadership difficult in Kalauna and among the Kwanga do not exist in Melpa local groups. Furthermore, local group exogamy among the Melpa means that the web of kin ties within the local group, which are another basis for factions in Kalauna and Inakor, is not as dense as in Kalauna or among the Kwanga. The fact that exchange partnerships are made between members of different communities instead of within one community also means that rivals are not (or at least not to such a great extent as among the Kwanga) party to the same gossip and so there is less of a tendency for gossip to be distorted and to escalate conflict than in Inakor and Asanakor. Strathern (personal communication) also suggests that relationships between men and women are different among the Melpa than among the Kwanga and that these differences also lessen (though they do not eliminate) the tendency for rumors to spread and be distorted. Melpa men and women are not likely to participate in the same gossip circles;

instead, women and men talk about different things. In addition, the big-man's extra-local ties mean that he can withstand temporary local opposition by moving away. Because of their extra-local support, Melpa big-men presumably have less to lose from alienating members of their local group than do their counterparts in Kalauna and Inakor. Finally, the dispersed residence pattern of the Melpa means that they do not have the frequent interaction and the ability to observe others which generate so much malicious gossip in Kalauna and Inakor. Strathern (personal communication), however, notes that, in fact, gossip and rumor may play a similar role in Kwanga and Melpa communities but that the effects of this "talk" may be somewhat more attenuated among the Melpa because of the social differences discussed above.

Melpa big-men also rely less on claims to supernatural powers than do their counterparts among the Kwanga and in Kalauna (Epstein 1974a: 30–31 says that this is a general difference between highland and lowland people in Papua New Guinea). This raises an interesting possibility. Covert action and secret attack are the rule in Inakor and Kalauna because people fear reprisals from the family of the victim and fear offending and alienating fellow community members on whom they depend. Chapter 3 demonstrated how hinting at control of sorcerers allowed people to influence events in ways for which they could not be held accountable. Perhaps it is in situations where power must be exercised in ambiguous ways that leaders will claim control of supernatural powers. Among the Melpa, where local organization does not present the same constraints, leaders act in more straightforward, secular ways.

Melpa leaders may avoid claims to magical powers because they are dangerous weapons. As previous chapters have shown, the veiled strategies of Kwanga leaders come back to haunt them in the long run. Claiming to have used supernatural powers for legitimate reasons on one occasion invites suspicion that these powers have been used less legitimately on others. Young (1971: 185), for instance, describes the dilemma of Kalauna leaders: "[Natural] misfortunes, or the threat of them, can be put to political advantage by leaders who lack other than ritual bases for their authority. Conversely, leaders can be embarrassed by natural misfortunes with which they do not wish to be associated but which others attribute to them—a fact which political opponents may capitalize upon."

Furthermore, being blamed for a number of deaths, instead of only

one, may alienate potential supporters and create the consensus necessary for violent action against the culprit. There are many cases of
sorcerers being jailed, expelled from their villages, or even killed after a
series of deaths due to an epidemic that was attributed to their actions
(see Hau'ofa 1981). Likewise, among the Kwanga, once a person was
implicated in one death, he was likely to be accused again (see also
Knauft 1985). The only cases I collected of sorcerers being murdered
involved individuals who were thought to have killed a sufficient number of people to arouse the hostilities of a large proportion of the community. Denying responsibility for particular events, as in most of the
cases above, is one way of minimizing this effect. In other areas leaders
do not themselves claim sorcery powers but instead say that they control the actions of sorcerer henchmen (Malinowski 1926; Hau'ofa
1981).

In contrast, among the Melpa, big-men do not emphasize their supernatural powers so they are not held responsible for natural disasters
as Kwanga and Kalauna leaders are. Indeed although it is community
leaders who are most often suspected of sorcery in Inakor and Kalauna,
among the Melpa deaths are often blamed on relatively powerless
people like women and "small men" who kill big-men out of envy
(A. Strathern 1972: 148).

Strong Men, Autonomous Men, Big-Men: Stereotypes of Melanesian Leaders

There has been some debate about how best to character-
ize the "typical" Melanesian leader, or even if such a thing exists since
variations within the region seem to be as great as commonalities
(Chowning 1979; Godelier 1986). Some scholars argue that, at least in
pre-contact times, the typical Melanesian leader was an autocratic
despot who ruled through violence (Salisbury 1964; Standish 1980;
Watson 1971). Others say that the influence of such despots was short-
lived (Read 1959); the more accurate stereotype of the Melanesian
leader was one who respected the opinions of others, treated them as
equals, and carefully negotiated consensus (see also Brown 1963).

Perhaps both portraits are to a certain extent accurate. Individuals
may adopt different strategies to gain power and influence events in the

same social environment (Kracke 1978). Similar communities may accommodate different "styles" of leadership. The "strong man" (Read 1959) or despot, and the "autonomous man" (Read 1959), or individual who carefully negotiates consensus, may be two styles of leadership adopted by different individuals in similar conditions.

Read (1959: 433) describes the "strong man" as

preeminently a warrior, a man who is quick to take offence, to suspect a slight or injury and likely to resort to force. He is a "hard" man, a proud man, an individual who is not likely to defer to others, a person who tends to act precipitately. He expects obedience, is motivated by a desire to dominate and cannot abide opposition. He is an individual who easily feels threatened by the quality of "strength" in others.

Suroho, in front of whom other Inakor big-men were afraid to speak, clearly represents this type and so does Kimaola. Whereas others hint at knowledge of, but publicly deny responsibility for, deaths and other natural disasters (through use of magical powers), Kimaola boldly and openly took credit for them and attempted to rule through fear. Perhaps the prototypic "strong man" is Matoto of the Tairora (Eastern Highlands of Papua New Guinea) (Watson 1971). This mythic leader (he had been dead twenty years by the time Watson conducted his research) ruled through violence; he was reputed to enjoy killing people, and people obeyed him without question. Like Suroho, he was renowned for his ability to protect his village from enemy attack, but was feared for his relentless indulgence of personal desires at the expense of others.

Conversely, according to Read (1959), the autonomous man demonstrates strength through forceful public oratory and sometimes through prowess in warfare, but also shows respect for others, carefully soliciting their opinions and acting only when backed by consensus. Similar strategies are described by Young (1971, 1983). For instance, Didiala hints that he may have created natural disasters with his powerful weather magic, but never openly acknowledges complicity.

Read (1959: 433) predicts that the strong man is unlikely to achieve "generalized authority or lasting influence," and the evidence tends to confirm his suspicions (see also Keesing 1985; Poole 1986: 304–305). Despots may have considerable power but their leadership is usually short-lived. Thus, Suroho was feared by all but eventually was (in the local view) killed by sorcery. Similarly, Matoto, after many years of despotic rule, was ambushed and murdered (Watson 1971). And Kimaola, whom Young (1983) predicted in his first period of fieldwork would be the strongest leader of Kalauna, was almost killed by his fellow villagers some years later.

These two styles of leadership are shaped by the constraints presented by small communities. (In other areas of Melanesia, such as among the Melpa, perhaps neither of these characterizations is very appropriate. In these areas the entrepreneurial big-man made famous by Sahlins (1963) may be a closer approximation to the truth.) Most people will fear malicious gossip and will try to avoid it. They will not try to coerce others but will influence events in more subtle ways. These are the "autonomous men." A few people, however, are impervious to gossip and slander. Thus, Suroho apparently ignored accusations of sorcery, and so did Kimaola. These are the "strong men" who manage to "rise above" the constraints of their societies (Young 1971 and Watson 1971 both argue that this is necessary for strong leadership in Melanesia) and gain power by disregarding the things that discourage most people: gossip, accusations of sorcery, fear of attack by sorcery, and withdrawal of aid and companionship. In the short run, there is little people can do to stop those who are proof against these normal sanctions. People fear reprisals from the kin and fellow lineage members of the culprit and so avoid violence. But, over the long run, the bad reputation of the strong man will erode his support and eventually someone will feel that it is safe to attack him.

Strong leadership over a long period of time seems to be difficult if not impossible to achieve in many Melanesian communities. Neither the strong man nor "autonomous man" is able to exercise much power or to consolidate it over the long run. Bold direct strategies not only create resentment but are also unlikely to work: people suspect that the leader is abusing his power and sometimes withdraw their support. As a result, strong men eventually lose their support.

Autonomous men, however, try to avoid the constraints imposed by their own societies by influencing others in veiled and ambiguous ways. But these strategies defeat them in the end because they are suspected of nefarious covert maneuvers. Then they try to rid themselves of their status and magical powers to avoid outright attack. Power without responsibility is probably universally desired but, at least in the Kwanga case, it has its costs since the very ambiguity that protects people from reprisals prevents them from ever conclusively proving their innocence.

The Death of George's Daughter:
Leaders as Martyrs

Papua New Guinean leaders have other problems as well. They are expected to show the community the way to an era of social harmony and material prosperity by introducing economic development projects and also programs for social reform that will bring the New Guinean way of life closer to that of the white man. Village leaders are criticized if they fail to suggest ways to attain these goals: people blame "weak" leaders like Gwarambu for the perceived lack of development in Inakor and Asanakor and also for the persistence of sorcery and various sorts of misbehavior in the village. They say that the Kwanga will never prosper without strong leaders to take the initiative in organizing communal development schemes and to get people to obey orders so that these ventures can succeed. But in practice, those who did take charge of such projects as the coffee cooperative were seen to be autocratic bullies and were suspected of stealing group money. Furthermore, people who took the lead in organizing a communal venture or suggesting a particular course of action were often blamed if these projects failed.

These patterns were particularly apparent in a case that occurred shortly before I left Inakor in 1986 and which I have referred to several times in earlier chapters, the death of Kichambwai, the ten-year-old daughter of George, the Asanakor pastor. George was one of the strongest supporters of the Christian revival. He led a campaign to undermine not only sorcery but also the system of gossip, innuendo, and inquests associated with it. George believed that a Christian lifestyle would stop fighting and death in the village and would also usher in a new era of material prosperity. (The link between Christianity and material prosperity was somewhat unclear: some people thought Jesus would be resurrected and would bring material wealth with him when he returned to earth after everyone converted to Christianity; others claimed that if people followed Christian practices they would not fight and that this would enable them to carry out communal business projects successfully.)

George's program for social reform was far reaching. He and the other Christian revivalists revealed tambaran secrets to women and children not only in Inakor and Asanakor but also in nearby Kwanga villages, including Apangai. The Christians tried to force people to throw away all of their magical paraphernalia, saying that all magic was associated with the tambaran and was, therefore, sinful.

George said that people should ignore the tambaran men and sorcerers and should look to God for justice and guidance. The Christians should concentrate on living a good life according to the laws of the Bible and then God would protect them from sorcerers. Furthermore, George argued that it was sinful for Christians to take action against those, like sorcerers, who wronged them. Justice should be left to God who would punish wrongdoing. An Asanakor Christian later explained this concept to me, using the hypothetical example of someone killing a dog. The owner should not retaliate but instead should pray to God and then later if the culprit's dog died then the owner would know that God had punished the original crime. George was, in short, trying to replace the decentralized system of self-help with one ruled by a central authority, God. People could do what they thought was right (in this case, revealing tambaran secrets) without fear of offending others, because the ultimate central authority, God, had the power to protect people from illegitimate attack.

George also urged Christians to avoid inquests, saying that in them people told lies about sorcery which scared the audience and, thus, perpetuated the dominance of tambaran men and their sorcerer henchmen. When a teenage boy died, for instance, many people said that he had been killed by people from another village who were angry because the Asanakor revival team had revealed tambaran secrets in that village. But George accused the proponents of this theory of making it up to frighten the Christians into abandoning the revival. This implicitly recognized the power of public discussion to "strike the fear of sorcery" into the audience. After all, at least to the outside observer, sorcery largely is the attributions and interpretations advanced after deaths. Even to the local people, who believe there are sorcerers, if this reality is unknowable, it has little power to influence behavior.

Furthermore, George tried to cut away the protective layers of ambiguity that surrounded sorcery and the system of diffuse, decentralized social control. Stripping away the ambiguity would leave people who hinted at control over sorcerers open to retaliation and, thus, would considerably diminish their power. George and the other Christians said that "prophet women," who had been possessed by the Holy Spirit, had the power to see hidden things such as sorcery implements. When several "visions" proved to be false, however, many people, including Christians, began to doubt that the prophets could really see hidden truths. People I talked to said that some of the things that the prophets "saw" did, indeed, come from the Holy Spirit; other visions were the work of Satan and bush spirits and were false. Since no one could definitively know a true from a false vision, ambiguity was restored.

Finally, George argued that some deaths were not caused by sorcery. Hunting magic, and yam magic, and tambaran paraphernalia could cause sickness and death and so could God, as a punishment to sinners. Thus people could not be certain that every death was an instance of sorcery punishing misbehavior.[2]

But even though George had acted with considerable support in both Asanakor and Inakor, when his daughter died everyone said that a sorcerer had struck her down to punish George for pushing through Christian reforms against everyone's will. They said he had been arrogant and foolish and deserved his severe punishment.

Furthermore, in the end George supported the system that he wished to abolish. He not only embraced the conclusion that a sorcerer had struck down Kichambwai to punish George's revival activities, but George also participated in the inquests to look into her death, thus reinforcing everyone else's belief in the sorcery system. This occurred despite the fact that George clearly had considerable insight into the system of gossip, innuendo, and inquests which made everyone afraid of sorcerers and prevented people from doing things that might offend others.

George's case shows Kwanga leaders as victims of their own society. They act forcefully because this is what everyone seems to want; but then their followers turn on them and blame them for all of the village's problems. Furthermore, leaders themselves cannot break out of the system of gossip and innuendo which makes strong initiatives impossible. They, too, are frightened into giving up their programs by gossip, innuendo, and inquests which make sorcerers seem both real and completely uncontrollable. The following account of the events after Kichambwai's death shows a slow change in George's position beginning first with his insistence that God, not sorcerers, had killed his daughter and that no inquests would be held. He later came to concede that a sorcerer must be involved—although he remained opposed to measures like a compensation payment which would encourage sorcerers. George also ended up holding and participating in inquests.

THE DEATH AND BURIAL

Kichambwai fell out of a tree while picking fruit and died within a few hours. She had been a healthy child, well past the dangerous infancy years when children often die, and, furthermore, there had been no period of illness to prepare her family and friends for the possibility of her death, so her parents and other relatives were devastated.

Within an hour of the event, a crowd had gathered in the central hamlet of Asanakor, where the body lay, and people began to speculate that the fall had not been the true cause of death. She had been ensorceled the night before and, in order to escape detection, the murderer had instructed her to fall from the tree. Moreover, many people said that if sorcery had struck it was because George had revealed tambaran secrets in other villages where people had been offended by outside interference.

George initially had a different view. His wife Naihuwa often criticized him for devoting too much time to church activities at the expense of his own gardens. In fact, the couple had quarrelled so bitterly about this issue on the night before Kichambwai's death that they had slept in separate houses. Holding his child's body on his lap the evening of the day she had died and crying, George claimed, in an impassioned speech, that God had killed Kichambwai as a punishment to Naihuwa for trying to hinder His work.

I want to give a short speech here. Are you listening? Listen good. If God had wanted this child to live she would be alive. Lots of things could happen but she wouldn't die. But God said that she should leave the earth, and she left the earth. . . . I have only one thought about this matter. This problem with my wife I have had for a long time. You all know about this cross which I carry. I cry. I cry. I cry. I cry in the church. I cry everywhere because of this problem with my wife. . . . This is all I can think of, that's all. . . . I didn't make any trouble. It's her trouble. It's this burden of hers that we feel all the time, me and my children. It covers us up altogether. . . . If you have any ideas you want to discuss [about the cause of Kichambwai's death] you must think of them yourselves. As for me, I have told you. I think it's because of her mother. So tomorrow we will just bury her and go home to our individual houses. We won't meet and talk about this [in an inquest]. If I have a problem, if I have a problem, whatever kind of cane God wants to give me, he can give it to me. . . . It's all right, let my child go. She will go first and I will follow her. Here on the earth, I am only working on contract [that is, he is only staying on the earth for a short time just as men who leave the village to work on plantations on two-year contracts only stay there for a few years and then return to their homes]. I will leave this earth and go to my home. Let my child go first. . . . I will follow my child. My true home is up in Heaven. . . . If I believe and follow the word of God right, sorcery can't kill me. Sorcerers are no match for the power of God.

Sorcerers cannot kill someone if God wishes them to live; therefore, God must have killed Kichambwai to punish her mother for her sins. Consistent with his position before Kichambwai's death, George claims that there is no reason to brood over or discuss the death. He will leave everything to God and will wait happily to be reunited with Kichambwai in Heaven.

George's faith in the paramount power of God was quickly eroded, however, and the next day as the body was buried, he lay on the ground crying and keening:

It was because I cried for Inakor and Apangai [villages where he revealed cult secrets] that my child has died. . . . Oh Mary, oh Abel [other Christian leaders], we went together and brought the revival team to them so they could live well without fights and arguments. So that they could be free. We thought of them, and we did this, and now my child has died, and my thoughts have gone crazy. So Mary and Abel, you can't leave me. You must pray over me all the time to stop my anger. You must pray over me so I won't brood too much over this child. She can die. God hasn't prohibited death. He says the road to death is open. It's not just her. Plenty of men die. God made two roads: to come and to go. The three of us made an agreement, and we brought the revival team everywhere. We didn't do this. It was the work of the Spirit. The Spirit moved and revealed all these things. You look: before Jesus carried this wooden cross. Now me, the father, I escaped it and now my child is carrying this wooden cross. Now you can't leave me. You must pray over me all the time and help me overcome this pain and anger. I am not going to leave the work of the Lord over this. If you don't pray over me, I will leave the work of the Lord and my old ways of thinking from before [when he was not Christian] will come back. Oh sorry, my child did not just die [a natural death]. They [i.e., sorcerers and initiates] must have conspired and killed her. If some other village had come to kill, they would have killed me, not my child. Someone from here must have conspired with them and killed her.

George had embraced the view that sorcery had killed Kichambwai because of his revival activities when he said that it was because he took pity on other villages (that is, tried to improve their lives by revealing tambaran secrets there) that his daughter died (implying that these villages killed her) and when he said he was now "carrying a wooden cross" like Jesus because of the revival. Just as Jesus tried to help people and was crucified by them now George had been punished by "heathen" villagers to whom he was trying to show the way to a better life. He asked his fellow Christians to pray to strengthen his faith in this time of crisis. He also expressed the common view that a local accomplice, who would have known that Kichambwai was George's daughter and could have pointed her out to a sorcerer from elsewhere, must be involved, since people do not know children from other villages, which again suggested that he suspected sorcery.

THE INQUESTS

George still insisted, however, that he did not want an inquest. Though he attended the first meeting of the inquest, he opened the meeting by declaring that he had not wanted to discuss the death because, since humans could never know for sure how a person had died, it was not worth discussing. But the people of Asanakor wanted to identify Kichambwai's killer before he struck again because they had heard rumors that three sorcerers had been seen lurking around the area and so he had agreed to hold this inquest. In the course of discussion, an Inakor man, Hilanda, said that he had heard Apangai people say several things that might indicate anger over George's revival activities, and the group disbanded after agreeing that Apangai should be asked to come and discuss the matter. At the meeting with Apangai a few days later, George's attitude had changed. He seemed convinced that someone from Inakor was responsible for Kichambwai's death as was shown when he interrogated Inakor men about statements they made indicating they might be angry about the revival (chap. 5).

George had heard that a group of Inakor men had demanded that the Christians pay compensation for exposing secrets. But Inakor people said that they had only suggested that the passing of such an important custom should be honored with a feast.

There was also concern over a rumor that an Inakor man, on hearing the Asanakor slit gong signal indicating a death, had said: "Oh a child must have fallen from a tree in Asanakor," indicating foreknowledge of the death. The man answered that since he had known that no one in Asanakor was seriously ill, when he heard the slit gong he had guessed that there must have been an accident.

Several other people spoke of complaints about George that they claimed to have heard in Apangai. They said that the Apangai people had threatened that if the revival did not "bear fruit," that is if Jesus did not return to earth soon with the cargo of the white men, they would take action against the Inakor and Asanakor Christians. Apangai people were alleged to have said:

If you want to reveal [tambaran secrets], you should do it in your own village. You can't come into my village and do it. You've done it so now this [revival] must come true and bear fruit. You can't bugger up my things and then let this work [come to nothing]. If you do that I will see you [that is, deal with you] some time in the future.

This comment pointed to the arrogance displayed by the Inakor and Asanakor Christians when they revealed tambaran paraphernalia to women and children in Apangai without the permission of the village leaders. The members of the Inakor-Asanakor team had acted as if they were so much more powerful and knowledgeable than the Apangai people that they need not bother to respect local wishes, so now they had better produce "fruit" to justify their behavior.

People also expressed reservations about the wisdom of the Christian campaign to rid the region of sorcery and magic. An Inakor Christian described a conversation he had had with non-Christians in his village after George suggested that they publicly reveal tambaran secrets and throw away the related magic:

When this talk of the Bible came up I went and talked to all [the people in Inakor]. I asked them about throwing away the [magicial and tambaran para-phernalia]. I went and asked them and [one man] said: "You can't just hear this new talk and get all excited about it and tell me to throw these things out. You didn't get to be a big-man on all these things of the white men. No, you got to be a big-man from [the ways of the ancestors and the male cult]. You bring a pig and [honor] these [traditional items] and then I'll throw these things out. . . . This is something of mine. My ancestors created these things. I am not a white man yet.

An informant later expressed similar sentiments in a conversation with me. He said that it was all right for the revivalists to try to get rid of sorcery but they should let people keep their traditional medicines and their hunting and gardening magic because the local people did not have "enough medicine or knowledge to live like white men yet," and so needed to keep the traditional magic to survive.

George said again that he was happy to have a member of his family die for a good cause and would not grieve too much over the death since he and his daughter would, in any case, be reunited in Heaven before long. He said that he had only been trying to help his people live a good life free of fights and arguments when he revealed secrets and had done nothing wrong. If people were offended and had ensorceled his daughter for that reason, George said he was willing to imitate Jesus and bear the "wooden cross" so that they could lead a better life. He again asked his fellow Christians to pray over him or else his grief and anger at his daughter's death would lead him back to the "old [pre-Christian] ways of thinking":

Before they killed Jesus and nailed him to a wooden cross and it's the same with me now. . . . My child died and I feel really bad. Oh my brothers if you have any good thoughts say something to me to cool me off a little.

After several hours, the Apangai men took their leave, saying that it was clear that Inakor had killed the child. But after their departure, Ronald, a classificatory brother of George's from Inakor, revealed that someone in Yubanakor had told him that Apangai sorcerers had killed Kichambwai. The Inakor men left soon after. George invited the Inakor men to come and discuss the evidence against Apangai, but they were angry because they had come under suspicion in the last discussion and refused to come. After Asanakor made a public apology and prepared a small feast, the Inakor and Asanakor men reassembled. Despite persistent questioning, the Inakor men refused to reveal what they had heard saying that if they exposed their sources the murderer might kill them. They said that George and his kin should just accept that someone from Apangai was responsible and give a prestation to Apangai to prevent them from returning and killing more people, without attempting to identify the sorcerer who had killed Kichambwai.

George rejected this solution probably realizing that such payments reinforced sorcery. He spoke, instead, of trying to find and jail the sorcerer since this would discourage sorcery. The Asanakor people invited Inakor to a second meeting to look for a local accomplice. They suspected that a local man must have been involved since no one from another village would have known that Kichambwai was George's child. Five non-Christian men who were rumored to be angry because their wives neglected their work and devoted themselves to church activities were questioned. Each denied that he was angry with the Christians, and the meeting gradually disbanded.

Soon afterwards, I left the field. There was talk of a second meeting with Apangai but this had not yet happened.

The Dilemma of Leaders

George who, in the height of the revival had had a great deal of power and renown, was quickly brought low after his daughter died and the Christian revival failed to "bear fruit"—that is, usher in a

new era of prosperity. People claimed that they had privately disapproved of George's actions all along, said that his ideas were foolish,
and that he deserved his punishment. Moreover, when George tried
to find and prosecute a murderer, people hinted that they felt that
the sorcerer had acted for legitimate reasons; they would not reveal
what they claimed to know about the sorcerer, but instead insisted that
George should pay off all the sorcerers in the area to prevent further
deaths. Not only would this have perpetuated the sorcery system but it
might have seemed to many people to be an implicit admission by
George that his revival activities were wrong and that sorcerers had
been justified in killing Kichambwai. In his own view, George became a
martyr for the community: he, like Jesus before him, had tried to lead
them to a better, Christian way of life, but they could not see the light,
and so his daughter died as a sacrifice to the old ways of paganism and
sorcery. From an outsider's view, George also seemed like a victim:
many people had wanted the revival but when it seemed to fail, they
blamed him. Even though George had acted with considerable support,
when his daughter died people said that it was his fault because he had
wrongly exposed tambaran secrets.

Furthermore, George, himself, ended up believing that the sorcerer
had killed Kichambwai because of the revival, and that this proved that
God did not have the power to protect people from sorcerers. He
ended up participating in inquests even though he realized that
inquests reinforced sorcery beliefs. Even though he had considerable
insight into the way gossip and innuendo supported initiated men,
George ended up reinforcing the system himself.

The Attack on Sorcery

George's statements about his daughter's death repre-
sented a broad attack on sorcery along with the whole system of decentralized and indirect power which was consistent with his ideas before
Kichambwai died. He argued first that sorcery was no match for the
power of God. This interpretation, however, received no support and
by the next day George himself had dropped it. Next, he said that
people should not fear death and the punitive power of sorcerers
since human time on earth was short in any case. Heaven was mankind's
true home.

George then argued that Kichambwai might have died because of his revival activities but there was no point in discussing it since mere mortals could never really know about such things, and inquests just made people fear sorcery without doing anything to control it. After Kichambwai's death, though, the rest of the community wanted to identify the sorcerer, and soon George was actively participating in the discussion.

By the second meeting, George seemed fully committed to finding the murderer and took the lead in questioning Inakor, maintaining that killing Kichambwai was not legitimate because revealing tambaran secrets was a good thing. He was still trying to do away with sorcery since, if sorcerers can be identified and punished, then sorcery may disappear. His attempts to identify and punish the culprit were, however, frustrated by the fact that most of the evidence came from rumor and reports of suspicious actions and statements. As each new theory was investigated it dissolved into a confusing morass of suspicion and rumor. In part, George failed to undermine the traditional system because no one believed his explanations. But in many of his speeches it was evident that George himself had doubts. This was apparent in the shift in George's keening from the first day to the second. The death of his daughter was a great blow to George's faith because he believed that God would protect him from sorcery. So, first, he tried to persuade himself that it was God who killed Kichambwai. When this failed, he was reduced to pleading with his fellow Christians to pray for him to prevent his faith in God from faltering in his anger and grief over his child's death. Similarly, he was progressively pulled into the public discussions that he had originally opposed. The position of sorcery, and the decentralized system it represents, remain intact partially because everyone, including George, believes that people use sorcery to punish those who offend them and that deaths should be discussed. Why did George abandon his own programs?

EVIDENCE

Most obviously, George, like everyone else, believed that all deaths were due to sorcery because his experience had proved this to be true. It is in the interests of initiated men to say that sorcery strikes to sanction tambaran violations and misbehavior; when someone dies, people make such interpretations; those who watch (and those who participate) see it proved again and again that sorcery causes death and it is unwise to do things that might offend others.

Moreover, the process of interpretation protects this belief from empirical disconfirmation. Direct evidence is not available, and so everyone relies on gossip and hint which could be interpreted in numerous ways. Just as the ambiguous and secretive nature of sorcery makes it difficult to take action so it also makes it impossible to prove conclusively whether or not it was at work.

Nor are initiated men entirely cynical in their explanations. They too must deal with a lifetime of experience which seems to confirm the power of sorcery; they too must deal with the gossip, innuendo, and beliefs about the way people conceal evidence, which all exaggerate the importance of tenuous and circumstantial evidence and make it seem that more definitive information is being concealed. George, for instance, claimed that he had not believed that Kichambwai had been ensorceled until he had remembered several signs that indicated unnatural intervention. Among these had been a report that Kichambwai had told her cousin that she had been bitten by three insects "of the ground" who had called out her father's name and the "suspicious" statements of the Inakor men that might have indicated concealed anger at George and the other revivalists. George, like everyone else, had grown up in a society where people constantly suspected others of concealing their intentions and knowledge. Like everyone else, he had learned to find the hidden meaning behind veiled statements. Moreover, he himself had probably made veiled threats, and insults, and had hinted at evidence he did not want to reveal publicly, since these are preferred forms of behavior in many situations. In short, for various reasons, it was difficult for George to resist the notion that strange events like the insect bites and ambiguous remarks indicated a secret plot to kill his daughter. Big-men, like everyone else, know that benign surfaces often conceal more menacing interiors.

Perhaps sorcery is believable to people because it is an element in a more pervasive complex of beliefs about covert aggression which, at least in part, reflect real behavior patterns. In an environment that encourages covert attack it is not difficult to believe in sorcery, the ultimate act of covert aggression, and, indeed, given a belief that it is present it would be difficult not to suspect others of using it. That sorcery beliefs reflect such tensions in Kwanga villages is demonstrated by the fact that almost all attributions of sorcery are made within the village. In the case of Kichambwai, people maintained that there must have been a local conspirator and this is not unusual. Extra-local suspects are often accused in early funeral discussions but final consensus almost always labels a fellow villager. It is because fellow villagers often attack each other in covert ways that they believe each other capable of attack through sorcery.

The Bittersweet Life of Intense Sociality and the Problem of Anger

George not only came to believe that God was no match for sorcerers but he also acted in such a way as to reinforce everyone else's belief in the power of sorcerers and tambaran men. Why did he do this despite his own insights into the way inquests reinforced the fear of sorcery?

George himself attributed the "old ways" to the problem of anger: he asked his fellow Christians to pray for him so that his intense anger over the death of his child would not cause him to abandon Christianity and go back to the "old way of thinking." Why are anger and the "old ways" so closely linked in his mind?

Local beliefs emphasize the rage felt by the bereaved after a death. For instance, funerary customs include an attack on the dead person's possessions by his cross-nepotic relatives. The public reaction to death probably intensifies this anger. When George, with considerable support from local Christians, publicly revealed tambaran secrets, people said that this caused his child's death. In fact, even those like his brother Mando who had supported George's revival activities blamed him for Kichambwai's death. Moreover, when George tried to prosecute the murderer, people refused to reveal what they knew about the murderer and told him just to make a payment to the Apangai sorcerers to stop them from killing another Asanakor person.

George's experience also suggests another source of anger. Life in a small close-knit village can be intensely frustrating since anything anybody does meets resistance or has repercussions. Cases in previous chapters have shown these patterns. When Ronald tried to prosecute Jeremiah for murdering Naifuku and Ambusuroho, many of those who had initially encouraged him later accused him of conspiring to kill the brothers himself. Probably everybody in the community had many similar experiences but leaders, since they were more visible, suffered most. These conditions make anger particularly problematic since expressing it often leads to severe reprisals, particularly when victims have large networks of local kin to support them (see for instance White

1985: 365; 1990). Furthermore, when bad feelings arise between kinsmen, which is common since they often live together and share resources, normative prescription of amicable relations may prevent direct expressions of anger. Hau'ofa (1981: 82) notes that this is a problem among the Mekeo. White (1990: 84), White and Watson-Gegeo (1990: 14), and Young (1971: 34, 43–44) make similar comments about other Melanesian villages.

Mansbridge (1980) describes a case that is an interesting variation on the theme of small communities. "Helpline" (a fictional name) is a community service organization in a large American city. The organization was set up with the explicit goal of breaking down hierarchical, bureaucratic structure. All workers were paid equal salaries and all decisions were to be made by consensus. Both dislike of bureaucratic roles and the egalitarian procedures for making decisions increased the resemblance of the organization to small communities where people deal with each other as "whole persons" rather than in terms of specific roles, and where decisions are often made by consensus. This resemblance, however, is only approximate because no organization, whose members leave work every day and where people can quite easily withdraw from the group altogether, can completely mirror conditions in a village where people must continue to deal with each other in a wide range of contexts.

There was evidence that Helpline meetings were plagued by some of the same pressures toward public concealment of attitudes and information that characterized those in the villages. Mansbridge estimated that Helpline workers devoted at least seven hours a week to meetings. Many people found meetings stressful and worried about others' reactions. One very active participant, for instance, reported that she frequently suffered from violent headaches after meetings and was very upset after taking strong stands, feeling that others would resent her assertiveness. Others expressed a dislike of criticizing people in public. Mansbridge attributes the reactions of her informants to the desire to maintain harmony and good feelings within the organization, the pressures of face-to-face interaction, lack of powerful roles for women (in the case of female informants), and to the egalitarian ideals of the group. These emotions are undoubtedly important in shaping public behavior in all of the cases described and probably in all small communities where people deal with each other in a wide range of contexts as "persons in the round" rather than in terms of specific roles. Indeed, when Mansbridge interviewed people after meetings they stressed the difficulty in criticizing someone they knew "as people"; that is, they felt that since they dealt with people in a number of different contexts and because they explicitly avoided bureaucratic roles, that any criticism was likely to be perceived as an attack on the whole person.

Not surprisingly, given the constraints on expressing it, the experience of anger is described as like being "knotted up" or "like a turtle caught in a net" (White 1990: 69) in some Pacific communities. The Kalauna villagers of Goodenough Island similarly describe the emotion, *unuwewe*, as being like a pig caught in vines. These metaphors evoke the image of an animal tangled in ropes that will only harm itself by struggling. This nicely captures the dilemma of people who will only harm themselves by expressing anger. In fact, one very common way of communicating anger in Melanesian societies is through self-directed aggression. Jeremiah, for instance (chapter 3), destroyed his own house and coconut trees when he was angry at his brothers-in-law. Tuzin (1976) and Young (1983) describe similar incidents. Where direct expressions of anger are dangerous, people get at others indirectly by hurting themselves. This shames the culprit by displaying the effects of his actions. The sarcasm characteristic of so many of the speeches quoted in previous chapters perhaps operates on a similar logic. In sarcastic speeches, people criticize others indirectly by criticizing themselves. In this way, they display to others the effects of their own behavior or attitudes. Hapandi, for instance (chapter 1), yelled at his audience: "I am not a Christian! I am not a Christian!" when he really meant that they were abusing him by treating him as if he were not a Christian. In this way, he criticized them in a backhanded way by seeming to criticize himself.

White and Watson-Gegeo (1990: 13) have argued that concepts of "anger" and "shame" recur in meetings to address conflict in small Pacific communities. Perhaps it is in the very nature of "the bittersweet life of intense sociality" (Young 1971: ix) to engender these emotions. The conflicting expectations involved in multistranded social relations make it inevitable that anything anybody does is bound to offend someone. At the same time people are reluctant to antagonize their fellow community members because they are dependent on them. This combined fear of repercussions and desire to have others think well of you is "shame." Anger, the inevitable product of such constant interaction becomes problematic whether expressed directly, indirectly, or not at all. So it is the focus of elaborate cultural beliefs.

One of the few safe ways to express anger is by making impassioned

speeches in meetings. Afterwards people can always disclaim responsibility for their words by saying they were "just talking," and the elaborate beliefs about how people bluff in funeral discussions to cover up the
truth or to test the reactions of the suspects also protect people from the
implications of what they say. So the very system that prevents people
from expressing the intense rage aroused by death and other experi-
ences in violence or by prosecuting a suspect makes it very easy for them
to make empty threats and accusations in inquests. As the Kwanga say,
the intense rage felt by the family just after the death will eventually
come to nothing. George, for instance, could accuse people and make
impassioned speeches in public meetings but could never be sure
enough of the identity of the murderer to prosecute him. People participate in funeral discussions because it allows them to vent their anger,
but in doing so they perpetuate the system by reinforcing the impression that all deaths are due to sorcery and that sorcerers are safe from
reprisals. The rage that makes the family want to attack and destroy the
system is neutralized and subverted since their impassioned speeches
reinforce the power of sorcery fears over the rest of the community.

Pressures of community life give rise to a complex of ideas about
hidden aggression which make sorcery believable. At the same time,
funeral discussions and other sorts of meetings allow for nondestructive
venting of emotions since beliefs about the deceptive nature of public
speech mean that people never know whether to take speakers at their
word or not. People can express unacceptable emotions without being
held accountable for them. Meetings, bluffing, and malicious gossip are
not only good strategy in small communities, they are also emotionally
satisfying. But by participating in inquests and gossiping about sorcery,
people preserve the system that they may, like George, wish to undermine. Big-men, just like everybody else, are trapped by a system of
gossip and innuendo which convinces them that sorcerers have acted
for particular reasons, but prevents the family of the victim from
retaliating.

Conclusion

In this chapter, and in the last two, I have moved beyond
behavior in meetings to a broader examination of leadership in small,
relatively egalitarian communities, particularly in Melanesia. Kwanga

big-men and other Melanesian leaders seem to be in a double bind. They are expected to lead the community and are criticized if they fail to do so. But, at the same time, almost anything they do creates resentment, opposition, and suspicions that they are abusing their powers.

The solution to this double bind for many is to hint that they are powerful and demonstrate their guardianship of society by bluffing in meetings and by spreading rumors—but to avoid doing anything for which they could be held accountable. They seem to be forceful leaders and "strong men" when they accuse people of sorcery and threaten to prosecute them. But when they do not follow through, they avoid offending people. Even this, however, is an imperfect solution since it leads people to distrust leaders.

Furthermore, big-men themselves are often fooled by the system of gossip, innuendo, and forceful speeches. They also believe that hinting and bluffing often conceals deeper knowledge and dark plots. Gossip, innuendo, and the specter of sorcery may allow initiated men power without responsibility. But this sort of influence has its costs and, in the end, big-men, perhaps even more than the others, are the victims of the system.

Sahlins (1963) directed a whole generation of studies of Melanesian politics when he suggested that the big-man system was a dead end in the grand scheme of political evolution. He suggested that intrinsic constraints in a system where there are no "offices" of leadership prevented leaders from consolidating their power over time and space. Melanesian polities would always remain small, fragmented, and acephalous.

Sahlins argument has been attacked on a number of counts. Andrew Strathern (1971), for instance, persuasively argues that big-men, at least among the Melpa of the Central Highlands of Papua New Guinea, are not dependent on the production of their local support group. Thus, Sahlins's evolutionary check does not seem to apply. But still it is evident that leaders in many areas of Melanesia lead through persuasion rather than coercion and that they are often unable to extend their power much beyond their local group for extended periods of time.

My analysis of the Kwanga and other groups suggests that "offices" of leadership are not the crucial variable. Indeed, leaders in societies that do seem to have some sort of notion of a legitimate office of leadership seem, if anything, to be less powerful than their counterparts in areas, like the Highlands, where there are no chiefs, divine artists, or village sorcerer-policemen. Instead, what inhibits Melanesian leaders is a particular form of local organization, that is, small isolated villages, comprised of many lineages, with a high rate of in-marriage. In such societies, leaders are always evaluated as "persons in the round"—a role that they can never play to everyone's satisfaction since people have conflicting desires and expectations. Perhaps only a strong office of leadership and ties with outside groups would allow the leaders to resist the social pressures of small communities.

CHAPTER ELEVEN

Conclusions

People in small communities in Melanesia and elsewhere evidently take gossip and rumor seriously: they hold long meetings just to look into slanderous rumors and make sure to deny publicly allegations of sorcery, adultery, or other sorts of misbehavior. In some places, people are so afraid of malicious gossip that they try to keep out of the public eye altogether, will not speak in public meetings, and may even avoid them (Bailey 1971; Frankenberg 1957; Mansbridge 1980; Young 1983).

I have argued that these beliefs arise from a social environment in which rumors have unusual power. In small communities without strong leaders the same small group of people interact with each other in a variety of contexts and will continue to do so over many years. Consequently, individuals are reluctant to offend their fellow community members, and so they avoid strong measures, preferring to drop hints, spread rumors, and develop elaborate theories in public meetings but then say they have no evidence to support their charges. In this way they can sway others without committing themselves to a potentially controversial position.

Furthermore, conditions in small communities ensure that "talk" can easily have consequences no one intended. First, everyone realizes that people often hide their true feelings in public. Indeed, this is the way people are supposed to act in certain situations. Consequently, people suspect hidden meaning behind every remark and they are prepared to believe that innocent surfaces conceal much more dangerous reality. This pervasive spirit of distrust creates a fertile environment for rumors.

Second, it is perhaps intrinsic to the nature of gossip and rumor that they distort the truth. Scholars have recognized the political importance of gossip as a mechanism of social control in small communities (Bailey 1971; Gluckman 1963; Merry 1984), as a means of defining an in-group who are allowed to gossip about each other (Gluckman 1963), and as a tool for attaining individual goals by strategically spreading information about oneself and one's opponents (Bailey 1977; Paine 1967, 1970). But these studies tend to overlook the ways in which gossip, as a means of communication *par excellence* through which people can avoid responsibility for their words, has an intrinsic tendency to distort the truth, cause alarm, and escalate conflict. When people gossip, they speculate irresponsibly because they know they will not be held accountable for words that no one can be sure were even said. Those who hear the rumor can never be sure they have the full story, and so they often suspect that the rumor is based on much better evidence than is immediately apparent. This is especially true where people believe that others hide their best evidence when they speak of things like sorcery and adultery. If many people repeat the rumor, it will look as though there are several independent sources confirming it even if, in fact, everyone is just repeating the same unfounded rumor. Gossip may be a political and social tool but, because it is largely hidden from the public eye, it has unique properties that distinguish it from kinds of political talk.

These processes occur everywhere. But they are of particular concern in small communities that foster gossip because everybody shares a common set of acquaintances who can be talked about.

Examining Kwanga politics has revealed something else about the political implications of gossip. Scott (1985), Spacks (1985), and Harding (1975) have suggested that gossip tends to be a "weapon of the weak," but examining the Kwanga has indicated that this is not always so. In Inakor and Asanakor, initiated men bolster their position in society by spreading rumors of sorcery. But gossip can also defeat leaders. Perhaps gossip, instead of being associated with any particular group in society, is primarily a leveling force: in small communities, where gossip matters, backbiting and rumor prevent anyone from consolidating power and foster a consensual system where it is difficult for any individual to lead effectively. Gossip, then, is a weapon used by all, which has the effect of distributing power throughout the community.

Powerful Words in Pacific Societies

In Inakor and Asanakor, the concern with gossip and rumor is part of a more pervasive fear of the power of words and there are indications that this is true in many Pacific Islands societies. Trobriand Islanders, for instance, speak of "dangerous words" (Weiner 1984), that is, forceful direct expressions of anger, or public statements of embarrassing truths, which can destroy social relations and start wars between villages. The fact that Brenneis and Myers (1984) adopted this phrase as a title for a volume on political language in the Pacific suggests that Trobrianders are not alone in their assessment of the power of words.

The local belief in the power of words is manifested in various sorts of behavior. In many Melanesian communities, people select "men of talk" as their leaders and think that the ability to "talk hard" is essential to preserving order in the community and protecting it from enemy attack. They also make the right to speak a key marker of social hierarchy that places men above women and children (Lederman 1984). Indeed, perhaps one of the most telling indicators of the almost mystical power that Melanesians attribute to public speaking is its close association with male cults in many societies. At the same time as men gain the ritual "heat" to empower the hunting, gardening, and war magic that brings them prestige and allows the community to survive and prosper, they learn how to speak effectively in public. Words and power are closely linked.[1]

Scholars who have addressed such material have spoken of the power of public speeches and other sorts of talk in defining a polity, relations of dominance, and the meaning of particular situations (Brenneis 1984, 1988; Gewertz 1977; Just 1986; Lederman 1984; Myers 1986; Myers and Brenneis 1984; White 1990; White and Watson-Gegeo 1990). But these studies often fail to locate speech events sufficiently within a broader context of social action and, therefore, have given an incomplete picture of the politics of meetings and gossip in small communities.

I have tried to move beyond local statements about gossip, meetings, and other kinds of talk to examine the social context that fosters these beliefs. Examining the social context has revealed many things. First, I have attempted to show that the power of rumors and other sorts of stories to change people's impressions and thus alter their behavior is even more powerful than is usually suggested. To fully understand the ways in which people alter reality when they talk about it, one must follow stories as they move away from their source and spread around the community. Examining this process has shown that at least some stories have a powerful impact on people's memories of the past and interpretation of the future and that people receive much of their information about the community in the form of stories, instead of through direct experience. In this way, stories largely constitute people's maps of their social world and have a strong impact on their behavior.

Second, I have tried to show that examining the broader social context reveals that many analyses of the "power of words" are incomplete. Focusing on rhetorical strategies is not enough; one must also look at how the audience reacts to speeches and what the long-term impact of stories is, as they circulate through a community. Scholars have suggested, for instance, that talk helps to create and to reinforce relations of dominance. But in Inakor and Asanakor the very words that initially suggest that big-men are powerful and worthy of respect can eventually backfire and lead to their downfall. Indeed, I have suggested that gossip and innuendo can be used by groups and individuals to build positions of dominance but that differences in power created this way were not likely to be either extreme or long-lasting. Following "official versions" outside the meetings in which they are voiced shows that they are but one moment in a continual struggle to understand and strategically define events. People tell stories about recent events in meetings to enhance their own power and comfort and these stories do have implications for social relations and particularly for relations of authority. But the audience does not swallow such stories whole. Stories are incorporated into people's oral history of their community only after they have been retold and have been systematically and inevitably distorted in the process. Thus, to understand how words come to constitute "worlds" it is necessary to follow stories over time. Speakers may maneuver to define situations strategically but they often have less control over their words than they anticipate.

Furthermore, I have tried to suggest previous studies on local beliefs about words have been incomplete because they do not fully take into account the extent to which many of these beliefs reflect reality. For instance, scholars have suggested that participants in meetings are primarily concerned with building their own reputations, and there is indeed a great deal of apparently petty bickering and "scoring points off one another" in Kwanga meetings. But analyses that focus on meetings as an opportunity to build reputations often do not explore the many good reasons people have to be concerned about their reputations. A reputation for hiring sorcerers for instance, could, in the local view, leave one vulnerable to sorcery attacks, and eventually, even to murder. Less dramatically, anyone who gained the reputation of being a trouble-maker might lose the support of kin and fellow moiety or initiation class members. Analyses have tended to focus on the positive benefits of appearing knowledgeable or "wise," but the equal or perhaps greater concern with avoiding a bad reputation and disproving negative allega-tions should not be overlooked. The Kwanga seemed to be concerned with their safety as much as with prestige.

Similarly, others have suggested that meetings address hidden ten-sions and construct an official public interpretation of problematic events. Again, these explanations are, for the Kwanga, not so much inaccurate as incomplete. An official public interpretation implicitly is contrasted with a presumably more dangerous unofficial private one. But why are private interpretations thought to be dangerous? Examina-tion of Kwanga villages has shown how gossip and rumor can be dangerous.

I have argued throughout that in many cases, local ideas about the power of words reflect reality. I have located meetings and gossip squarely in their social context and have tried to show the social experi-ences that shape the cultural beliefs about meetings and gossip, and have suggested that broadly similar notions about meetings, rumors, and "dangerous words" are found in many places where similar social conditions lead people to act and to experience social conditions in similar ways. Perhaps, for instance, the Kwanga, along with so many people in Melanesia and other areas of the world, admire and value elaborate veiled speech because they live in an environment that causes everyone to appreciate the art of being able to hint at things without being held responsible. They experience similar social pressures, act in similar ways, and their beliefs about talk at least in part reflect a com-mon reality that people have experienced.

The Conversational Marketplace[2] and Melanesian Politics

Debates about Melanesian politics tend to focus on the institutional bases of leadership and on grand events such as initiations, exchanges, and war.[3] In Kwanga society, and apparently in other areas is well, initiation, exchange, and secret knowledge are all important elements of leadership but one of the main ways in which Kwanga leaders influence others is through making speeches and spreading rumors. They manipulate people's impressions of events in order to prompt them to act in certain ways. Control over the interpretation of events perhaps explains the value of prestige gained in exchange, secret knowledge learned through such things as initiation, and the reputation for wisdom associated with "offices of leadership." Prestige, knowledge, and wisdom may increase credibility and thus the ability of some people (and categories of people) to make their views prevail. It is in these ways that prestige and institutionalized advantages are translated into power.

This process is particularly important in so-called "great men" societies (Godelier 1982). Recently scholars have stressed the importance of claims to specialized secular and ritual knowledge in many Melanesian societies and have argued that these things are often more important to a man's influence and prestige than are things like success in exchange. I have tried to show that specialized knowledge is, in its own right, of little consequence, unless people hint that it has been used in certain ways on certain occasions and, by implication, could be used again. Thus the study of "knowledge based societies" (Modjeska 1982) should lead to an examination both of public meetings (see Lindstrom 1988), long recognized to be an important arena in which Melanesian big-men built reputations (Read 1959; Sahlins 1963; A. Strathern 1975; Lederman 1984), and of gossip and rumor—which scholars often note in passing but seldom see as central to the operation of the political system. Gossip and innuendo are crucial both to creating and, ultimately undermining, the position of many Melanesian leaders.

Leaders in small, relatively egalitarian Melanesian communities have been variously characterized as "big-men," "strong men" (Read 1959), "great men" (Godelier 1982), "managers" (Burridge 1975), "chiefs," "despots" (Salisbury 1964), and "directors" (Salisbury 1964). Scholars stress the ways in which talented and ambitious individuals can earn prominence in societies where all men are basically equal by displaying their productive powers and by presenting themselves as forceful characters who are worthy of respect. But this array of images excludes one that Melanesian leaders themselves commonly evoke in their public speeches, that is, the leader as martyr, or as victim of his own society. This tragic figure who manages to temporarily "rise above" the constraints posed by his own society and culture, only to be blamed for deaths, droughts, or any other disruption to the orderly flow of social life, is a very common one in Melanesia. Leaders speak forcefully and take the lead in organizing public ventures, because this is what everyone seems to want. But then they are blamed when their projects fail; if they persist, despite the backbiting, they face social ostracism, or even outright violence, and they also fear sorcery attacks.

In many small Melanesian villages, then, it is "talk" that ultimately "wins." Ways of speaking are shaped by the pressures of a particular social environment, the small isolated community. But these ways of speaking also constitute the environment: as any Kwanga big-man could tell you, it is "just talk" that they have most to fear. Gossip and rumor are the most powerful forces in creating and preserving the egalitarian ethos of social relations. Talk, then, does more than reflect the nature of social relations, it plays a large role in creating them.

Notes

Chapter One: Gossip and Politics

1. Chowning (1974: 161; 1987: 187–188), Counts and Counts (1974: 121, 130, 137), and Young (1974: 60) all describe meetings held to address slanderous rumors.

2. There has been some debate on this question in Melanesia. See, for instance, Stephen (1987) and Chowning (1987).

3. The Papua New Guinea kina was worth about 1.10 American dollars in 1984.

4. See the preface for an explanation of the transcription method.

5. "Sin" is associated with traditional ways and particularly sorcery, and many people think that in a Godfearing, Christian village there would be no sorcery and, therefore, no untimely death.

6. Here I use the word "heathen" as a literal translation of the Neo-Melanesian term "haiten" which Inakor and Asanakor residents use to refer to non-Christians. I have avoided this literal translation in most cases because the English word "heathen" has many connotations that are not associated with the Neo-Melanesian term. But I have used "heathen" in translating Hapandi's speech because it captures well the derogatory way in which he is using the term "haiten."

7. Irvine (1979: 782), for instance, outlines various ways in which speech is structured to mark out certain contexts such as meetings as being "onstage" and others as "offstage."

8. Myers and Brenneis (1984: 19), for instance, state: "In the process of resolving a difficulty, actors reproduce the categories and resources through using them. . . . They are reproduced as the axioms of the moral and social universe of the actors, everything that 'goes without saying' or is 'taken for

granted,' the transcontextual basis of the polity. Thus, the public identities taken up by parties in resolving a dispute are reproduced in the process of resolving the dispute as real, natural, and in some sense what the world is really made of."

Richards makes a similar point. She suggests that meetings, like religious rituals, serve an important function in "reinforc[ing] social obligations by constant repetition, teach[ing] the young, inspir[ing]to action" (1971: 5) and making "men conscious of the power of the society to which they belong" (1971: 9).

9. White (1990: 74, 75) makes a similar argument. He suggests that among the A'ara of the Solomon Islands disputants try to relate their behavior to more general shared ideas about human behavior.

10. He speaks here specifically of general beliefs about emotions. But other sorts of general understandings or "schemas" probably also contain implicit moral evaluations.

11. Other things are also accomplished when people comment on experience by telling stories: Schwartzman (1987, 1989), for example, argues that stories told by workers in an American community service organization create a sense of communal tradition and identity.

12. Inakor and the other seven villages of the same language group hold such meetings (Brison 1989), and Schindlbeck (1984) mentions weekly council meetings in the western Kwanga village, Bongos. As well, many of the Abelam speakers to the east have weekly meetings (Noel McGwigen, personal communication). But many other groups in the area, including the Bumbita Arapesh (Stephen Leavitt, personal communication), Ilahita Arapesh (Donald Tuzin, personal communication), and the Urat (Stephen Eyre, personal communication) did not find such meetings necessary. Brenneis (1984), Chowning (1974), Counts and Counts (1974: 12), Epstein (1974a: 36 on Melanesia in general; 1974b: 101 on Matupit), Gewertz (1977), Kahn (1986: 30–32), Lederman (1984), Lindstrom (1990a), Myers (1986), Myers and Brenneis (1984), Read (1959), Watson-Gegeo (1986), White and Watson-Gegeo (1990), Young (1971: 145; 1974: 43–44) all comment on apparently inconclusive meetings in other areas of Melanesia. Statements by Richards (1971) and Kuper (1971) about Council meetings in Africa, as well as Turton (1975) on the Mursi, and Keenan (1974, 1975) and Bloch (1971) on the Merina of Madagascar indicate that this pattern is not confined to the South Pacific.

13. Thus, Myers and Brenneis (1984: 11) argue that "speech events in situations where egalitarian relations prevail seem strikingly concerned with the construction and maintenance of a polity, with the constitution of a *context* [italics in original] within which interaction can occur." In "egalitarian communities," individuals are relatively autonomous and there are "no defined relations of subordination or superordination" (Myers and Brenneis 1984: 11). In such situations, the political arena is an "achievement" (1984: 11) and the "actors' linguistic work" must create and maintain the "political arenas in which they contend" (Myers and Brenneis 1984: 11). Myers and Brenneis (1984: 14) state that "while demonstrating that the collective arena does not simply exist but must be achieved and sustained by actors' work, these accounts also show

that the goal of political discourse may be neither a decision nor coercion but rather the sustaining of an appearance of autonomy while at the same time constituting or reconstituting a polity." Brenneis (1988: 229) again refers to the constitutive function of speech events in "relatively egalitarian Pacific communities" claiming that "society above the level of the coresident family is instantiated only through shared participation in various speech events." In this contexts: "Creating contexts for such activity is a critical social accomplishment."

14. Many scholars have commented on the use of "veiled" speech styles in relatively egalitarian environments to avoid provoking fights and to demonstrate respect for others' autonomy, including: Atkinson 1984; Bowen 1989; Goldman 1983; Keenan 1974; Kulick and Stroud 1990; McKellin 1984, 1990; Rosaldo 1973, 1984; A. Strathern 1975; M. Strathern 1972; Weiner 1984.

15. See note 12 for mention of long unproductive meetings in Melanesia. In many societies there are also inquests in which various theories about the cause of death are discussed, and participants may be unable to reach a consensus. See, for instance, Brison 1988, 1989; Counts and Counts 1974; Darrouzet 1985; Knauft 1985; Riebe 1987; Rodman and Rodman 1983–1984; Tuzin 1974. In other areas people speculate about the cause of illness and death in gossip but seldom make public accusations (Bowden 1987; Forge 1970b; Hau'ofa 1981: 276; Stephen 1987). Young (1971, 1983) also mentions meetings on Goodenough Island to discuss the cause of drought and poor harvests, and such discussion apparently also occurs in the Trobriand Islands (Leach 1982).

16. A close association between politics and the interpretation of misfortune is also evident in societies in other areas of the world. See Bleek (1976), Harwood (1970), Goody (1970), Middleton (1960), Turner (1957), and Van Velsen (1964) for descriptions of moots and gossip concerning the causes of illness and death.

17. Favret-Saada (1980) also notes that witchcraft and sorcery are constituted through verbal behavior and that when we study such supernatural aggression we are largely studying talk. In a recent article Favret-Saada (1989) examines the social impact of stories about sorcery. "Unbewitchers" tell people who believe that they have been attacked by witches to do certain things (such as not exchanging greetings with the suspected witch) to guard against further attack and, in this way, turn helpless victims into active aggressors. Favret-Saada argues that this behavior also draws the family together and helps to balance power relations within families in various ways and, consequently, can help improve family relationships.

18. Allport and Postman (1947) argue that people are most likely to gossip when they are trying to make sense of events that are of some importance to them and about which there is no good information.

19. All of the Inakor and Asanakor people mentioned in the main body of the text have been given pseudonyms. I have given some people Christian pseudonyms because many Inakor and Asanakor people have adopted Christian names, some but not all of them when they were baptized. Using a Christian

name does not necessarily indicate that a person is Christian and I have followed the local practice in using Christian names for both Christians and non-Christians and also in giving Kwanga pseudonyms to both Christians and non-Christians.

20. Tuzin says of the neighboring Ilahita Arapesh that the male initiation system: "has the effect of maintaining authority in the hands of the old men, protecting them from serious challenges by the younger men" (Tuzin 1976: 287). Furthermore, the cult house artist is "an occupational category whose members routinely exercise *generalized* [italics in original] authority in the community" (Tuzin 1980: 194).

Chapter Two: The Kwanga

1. Forge (1965: 24) notes that the Nungwaiya people pushed the Arapesh to the north and the Kwanga to the west in the late 1920s or early 1930s.

2. These villages are Inakor, Asanakor, their southern neighbors, Yubanakor and Apangai, and, to the east, Sunahu and Kamanakor. The village of Apos approximately ten miles to the west of Inakor has an idiosyncratic dialect (Manabe 1982*a*).

3. These grades are: *Naku* (literally, sago, corresponding to the *Lefin* grade in Ilahita), *Ambwa Ke* (no equivalent in Ilahita), *Ambwa Mwe* (corresponding to the *Maolimu* grade in Ilahita), *Minja* (no equivalent in Ilahita), *Gwar* (corresponding to *Nggwal Bunafunei* in Ilahita) and, finally, *Mautakwa* (corresponding to *Nggwal Walipeine* in Ilahita).

Manabe (1982*a*: 48) reports a different sequence of cult grades for the eastern Kwanga village, Yubanakor: *Naku, Ambwa Ke, Ambwa, Kwari, Minja, Nakuhopo Minja.*

4. The Kwanga social structure is a simplified version of that found in Ilahita, which is not surprising since Kwanga villages have approximately one-third of Ilahita's population. Ilahita had a population of about 1,500 in the early 1970s and the population had exceeded 2,000 by 1984.

5. I have adopted this terminology from Tuzin (1976) who agrees that the Kwanga social structure is very similar to that of Ilahita (Tuzin, personal communication). But there are undoubtedly minor differences between the Kwanga and Ilahita groups so equivalence should not be assumed to be exact.

6. Schindlbeck (1984) notes that the 1978 cult initiation was part of an area-wide revival in the tambaran cult which had not been practiced for as much as thirty years in some villages in the area.

7. German colonial officials and Malaysians and Chinese seeking bird of paradise plumes penetrated as far as the Urat, Kombio, and Wam areas to the north of Inakor and Asanakor and brought with them steel implements and rifles (B. Allen 1976: chap. 3). Kwanga informants recalled an incident when

an enemy village recruited Wam people with rifles to aid in a fight with Inakor and two Inakor men were shot. This was their first experience with firearms.

8. The local magistrate often steps down because he is often related to some, if not all, of the participants.

9. Bryant Allen (1976: 198), who interviewed villagers and Australian officials on the introduction of cash crops, maintains that villagers had little understanding of cash-cropping. They viewed the planting, processing, and selling of rice as a ritual designed to achieve the lifestyle and material wealth of the white men and had unrealistically high expectations about the returns.

10. Many young married couples have not yet planted their own coffee gardens and rely on invitations from their parents to harvest beans from their gardens.

11. Memberships are basically shares in the company and members receive small annual dividends (usually under fifteen kina).

Chapter Three: Gossip, Innuendo, and Sorcery: Power without Responsibility

1. When someone dies in Inakor, for instance, the Asanakor people attend the first funeral discussion.

2. Sorcery is an indictable offense in Papua New Guinea, but due to the difficulties in finding evidence in sorcery cases, people are usually convicted on charges of possessing sorcery paraphernalia, and given jail sentences of six months to two years.

3. People believe that sorcerers often feel that they have been undercompensated for murders and will keep coming back and killing in the same village or family until a large payment satisfies them.

4. There were similar displays in all the burials I witnessed save those of very young children.

5. This meeting occurred early on in my stay in Inakor and I did not tape-record it. But most of the meeting was conducted in Neo-Melanesian for the benefit of Arawapi who was a Bumbita Arapesh and did not understand Kwanga. I took copious notes from which I have reconstructed these speeches.

6. Here he speaks of poison in the Western sense, not parcel sorcery. People reasoned that the two brothers could easily have eaten the same poisoned food and died on the same night whereas it was unlikely that a sorcerer or an illness would kill the two on the same night.

7. There were, in fact, five men in Asanakor who had been trained as sorcerers and they were each investigated.

8. I conducted this and other interviews in Neo-Melanesian and tape-recorded them.

9. Naomi's brothers would have had to appear in divorce court because

they had received brideprice when she married Jeremiah and had to voice their opinions on whether this money should be returned when the couple divorced.

10. The family will suspect that anyone who knows the identity of the murderer was involved in the murder or at least had foreknowledge of the attack and could have warned the victim.

11. It is a common belief that sorcerers always kill from both sides of a dispute. They may do so at the request of kinsmen of the first victim or may kill on their own volition and later ask the family of the first victim for payment for having avenged their kinsman's death.

12. There was an antisorcery campaign in conjunction with the Christian revival in spring and summer of 1984 and many of the sorcerers in the area went to jail at this time.

13. A compensation payment over sorcery both mollifies the murderer and also publicly identifies him, thus warning him that future action will bring reprisals.

14. Ronald had two wives, one Adam's daughter and the other Hapandi's daughter.

Chapter Four: Village Courts and the Art of Bluffing

1. In such cases, the child remains with her biological parents until marriage but her brideprice is given to the foster parents.

Chapter Five: Getting It All Out into the Open

1. Mediation sessions were usually handled by Ronald and the other village court officials but the village court system was under review at this time and so was inactive.

2. Fuku'asa apparently added the twenty kina of the second dream to the fifty kina of the first when he spoke of the talk of "seventy kina."

3. Pigs are supposed to be taken to the headman of the lineage that owns the bush in which they are caught.

4. Schwartz (1973) notes that this pervasive distrustfulness is common in Melanesian cultures and argues that it is part of a more general "paranoid ethos" that stems from unstable ecological conditions among other things.

5. Frankenberg (1957) describes village meetings in a small Welsh village, Pentrediwaith. Villagers are reluctant to make decisions on matters of communal concern, or even to suggest solutions, because any decision seems, almost inevitably, to arouse resentment and malicious gossip from members of

other families, and other religious and political groups. These people may even secretly sabotage ventures by doing such things as going out at night and tearing down advertising posters for the event. The ultimate failure of the venture is blamed on whoever made the key suggestion. Susan Hutson (1971: 44) also mentions that fear of malicious gossip and opposition create apathy in communal affairs in a small European village.

Chapter Six: Rivalry and Institutionalized Duplicity: The Sociology of Rumor

1. Interestingly *apwe umwe* is also called *mwa che*, which literally means "head child" and refers to the first child. This suggests some long-forgotten genealogical connection with the *kini che* (last child) subgroup and, indeed, the local people say that these two groups were once one.

2. The government encouraged young men to form work groups who would hire themselves out to do such things as cutting trees in gardens or making fences and would use the money earned for projects such as trade stores or buying a truck to hire out. This was part of a grassroots development scheme.

3. Kwanga women also participate in anumbo relations and the wives of two anumbo also call each other anumbo.

4. Normally each man will have only one anumbo. But a few men have two, and in a few cases two men share one anumbo.

5. In a few cases, large lineages are divided into two groups that are anumbo to each other. Some groups will have anumbo relations with members of two or three other groups.

6. This is somewhat different from the situation described by Tuzin (1976) and Leavitt (personal communication) for the Ilahita and Bumbita Arapesh, respectively, where large totemic clans are divided into two subclans that initiate each other's sons into the tambaran cult. As among the Kwanga, residential and gardening land of the two groups is contiguous and hunting bush is shared. The Ilahita and Bumbita, however, place a stronger emphasis on the idea that *gawas* (the Neo-Melanesian term) are brothers, as members of the same clan. Also in these two groups one initiation class is considered to be the older brother of the other.

7. This logic is no more than rhetorical, however, since uninitiated wives and children who have not consumed the animal leavings can safely eat meat caught in their own bush without fear of pollution.

8. Anumbo, however, have closer relations with each other due to proximity of residence and resources. The necessity to maintain a face of cooperation and support is not as great as with umweminga (though it is not entirely absent).

9. Here we see anumbo united in competition with umweminga.

10. Wangembor was given one domestic pig and two wild pigs and re-turned only the domestic pig. Wild and domestic pigs are not considered equivalent in exchanges because people realize that domestic pigs are most often purchased so involve considerable expenditure of money whereas wild pigs are free. Since returning a wild pig involves capturing one the timing of these exchanges is hard to control.

11. The term *hiba-rakambwe*, referring to the individual's set of classifica-tory and true siblings of both sexes (literally, a compound of *hibache* and *rakambwe*, that is, "younger sibling" and "older sibling") comes closest to de-scribing the kindred.

12. These obligations are reciprocal.

13. Theoretically, children are buried by their mother's brothers, father's sisters, and anumbo. But often the work is left to the anumbo and the kandere do not participate.

14. When the dead person has a considerable number of kandere, or when the kandere are particularly angry over the death, as for instance, in cases of obvious neglect, the family may have to present several pigs to different groups of kandere, often including distant kandere in other villages.

15. Almost all deaths are considered premature among the Kwanga. The idea that adult children neglect their aging parents is also virtually universal.

16. The burial payment also stops the kandere from using their mother's brother's resources, to which they had free access before he died. If there is no payment, the sisters' children can claim their dead kandere's resources. In one case, there was no funeral payment and, after several years, the kandere announced they were going to take over the dead man's resources unless his children made an immediate payment to stop them. That this was not an empty threat was shown when one of these kandere told me later that he would prefer not to receive the payment because he wanted the land. The threat was prob-ably more serious in this case because the dead men had no male heirs and his property was being used by his daughters and an adopted son who were viewed as having a weak claim on these resources.

17. This is part of a general approach to illness which emphasizes trying any possible cure including steaming various objects, taking Western medicine, and praying over the victim.

18. This is particularly true in village-wide exchanges when many people are making prestations at the same time. Brothers contribute to the efforts of their classificatory sisters first and help their true sisters only if they are in need.

19. This curse, appropriately, prevents her from making future prestations since she will be unable to provide a pig.

20. The logic behind these rules is not entirely alien to our own culture. We too recognize that blunt criticism and conveying unpleasant information does not endear a person to the one on the receiving end so that only someone with a certain amount of trust that the recipient is not going to retaliate, and a measure of concern about his or her welfare, would risk being the bearer of bad news.

21. For instance, initiates of some grades can construct sun shelters in their gardens whereas other grades cannot. Initiates of lower grades can only hang

the vines of four or five mounds of yams from one tree whereas initiates of higher grades can hang as many as they please from a tree.

22. There are many different varieties of short yams distinguished by such things as shape, presence or absence of root hairs on the surface, color, and taste.

23. My informants spoke only of death through sorcery but Tuzin (1976, 1980) and Leavitt (personal communication) gathered accounts of actual murders of those who found out cult secrets. When I asked my informants about this they were horrified and said that the Kwanga did not have this practice. This statement, however, must be taken with a grain of salt since outright killing may historically have been practiced and now be forgotten.

24. People are scrupulous about keeping the village clean of feces, which is thrown into rubbish heaps behind the houses.

Chapter Seven: The Power of Stories

1. By chance, Henry was also closely related to the baby's family and so took an active role in the discussion of the death. The baby's father was Henry's wife's classificatory brother and was also one of Henry's exchange partners.

2. The particular problems associated with evidence in cases of witchcraft or sorcery have been noted in other places as well. MacFarlane (1970) comments on the reliance on circumstantial evidence in sixteenth-century English witch trials. In many societies, people like the Kwanga distrust the results of divination and may, for instance, consult several diviners before finding a verdict they like (see, for instance, Chowning 1987: 165; Evans-Pritchard 1976; Harwood 1970; Hau'ofa 1981: 224; Knauft 1985; Middleton 1960; Young 1971).

3. Bennett and Feldman (1981) argue that people judge the validity of such stories by the two criteria of "did it happen that way" and "could it have happened that way" (1981: 33). The first addresses the empirical evidence. But the story constrains what evidence is relevant and what it means. The second addresses the plausibility of the story itself. This is judged, first, according to the story's completeness (in the case of a murder, are all the details of who did what when and how provided?); and, second, according to the extent to which the linkages in the story are consistent with prior experience (does X lead to Y in the person's experience as it does in the story?) (Bennett and Feldman 1981: 41). When a group of undergraduates were asked to judge whether several stories were true or false, for which they had no source of empirical verification, there was substantial agreement on the ratings, demonstrating that the characteristics of a story itself ("could it have happened that way") are important to assessing the truth of an account. Bennett and Feldman (1981: 89) argue that the criteria of "could it have happened that way" tends to become more important in situations for which the evidence is ambiguous or in which it is open to competing interpretations. In other words, when empirical evidence is incon-

clusive people tend to make their judgments based on the plausibility of the stories themselves.

4. This kind of belief seems to be quite widespread in Papua New Guinea. Kulick and Stroud (1990) and McKellin (1984) mention a similar distrustful attitude in other areas of the country.

Chapter Eight: Two Models of Government

1. People also believe that sorcerers, often at the bidding of initiated men, act as an impartial central authority, punishing wrongdoing and violations of tambaran laws which do not concern them personally. But such impersonal actions are not common and people are more worried about reprisals from those they have offended and their kin.

2. Frankenberg (1957) describes similar strategies in a Welsh village.

3. Tuzin (1976) stresses the importance of a large village for defense purposes among the neighboring Ilahita Arapesh.

4. Hogbin and Wedgewood (1953/54) coined the term "multicarpellary parish" to refer to a local group composed of more than one "carpel" or localized unilineal descent group.

Chapter Nine: Leadership, Authority, and "Egalitarianism"

1. He led one of the two coffee buying cooperatives, ran a trade store, and had large coffee and cocoa gardens.

2. For the larger groups, however, a single totem often masks structurally separate entities with their own resources and exchange obligations.

3. Initiates of the ambwa mwe tambaran are eligible to hear these secrets but the current holder may not impart this information until later.

4. Many lineages have origin myths stating that their first ancestor came out of a water hole or hole in the ground in the land belonging to that group.

5. In other instances, lineages that were originally one group view each other as "brothers" and retain a common origin myth. In Inakor, for instance, three lineages, Bwandunakor, Masmarko, and Umwanjimbi, are usually spoken of as separate lineages and have separate estates of gardening, residential, and hunting land and separate hunting magic. The senior man of Umwanjimbi, however, told me that these three groups are brothers and "came out of the ground together" (that is, have a common origin myth).

6. Anakwa remains a member of C even though she is female because she

had no brothers. She married an immigrant from another village and together they succeeded her father in C. This is a common practice.

7. Fission of groups caused by ambitious younger brothers is, of course, a well-known phenomenon in many areas. In the Sepik area this process does not involve one group leaving the village and claiming new territory. Rather, the new groups remain in the village and the original estate is divided. This is probably due to the fact that intervillage warfare in this area was endemic in the past and the local people realized the defensive advantages of larger, compact villages.

8. Tuzin says that 35 percent of Ilahita men are in different groups than their true brothers (1976: 236) and Kaberry (1971: 58) says that in the Abelam village of Kalabu, only 71.2 percent of adult men gave the name of their natal clan when asked their clan membership. These figures indicate that shifting of people among patrilineal descent groups is common in the region.

For the Kwanga, 67 percent of adult men were in their father's lineage but in many of these cases the father himself had been adopted into a group other than his natal lineage.

9. The shifting of sons to correct demographic imbalances is paralleled by a similar movement of daughters. Ideally, each family should have an equal number of sons and daughters to meet the demands of marriage through sister exchange and so families would "trade" sons and daughters. Again, this process usually does not involve the adoption of minors but only the transfer of rights to arrange the marriage of that child. At present, many families still continue to do this even though marriage through brideprice has almost completely replaced sister exchange. This avoids the problem of families with too many sons having to find large sums of money to pay for their sons' wives without receiving any compensation for daughters to make up for it.

10. Tuzin (1976: 237–240) also presents a case of a promising younger brother being shifted to a new lineage. Kaberry notes that ambitious individuals ally themselves with their mother's brother instead of their father (1941–1942: 257; 1971: 60).

11. Losche (1978) observed a meeting in which the senior men of the village met to assign people to different groups in order to even out group membership in preparation for performance of a tambaran initiation in an Abelam group.

12. When a man is initiated into the ambwa mwe tambaran he will receive the hunting magic for his bush from his initiator. When he, in turn, initiates this man's son, the magic will be returned. Pig magic, therefore, should always be in the hands of the group of men most recently initiated into the ambwa mwe tambaran. There is some indication, however, that the initiators in the ambwa mwe tambaran keep a portion of the pig magic, which increases the number of people who must cooperate to ensure a successful hunt.

13. When initiates first emerge from a period of seclusion in the cult house they are decorated and displayed to an audience of their own community members and people from other villages who decide which set of initiates is most impressive.

14. Although the people of Inakor value highly the position of being a true native of the village (that is, someone whose first ancestor was believed to have arisen in the village), in fact, few people can make this claim. Most are the descendents of people who immigrated to the village within historical memory. There are three major immigrant groups in the village. The most recent immigrants are the descendents of a group who lived in the now empty bush to the west of Inakor. They were chased out by the Wosera people to the south from the village of Nungwaiya and many took refuge in Inakor. A second group, *H*, came in mythical times from the Bumbita Arapesh area to the north. This group was chased out of its original land and after several relocations, settled just north of Inakor. According to a myth, the current members of *H* in Inakor are all thought to be descendents of one man. Finally, a third major immigrant group are the descendents of one man who arrived as a refugee to Inakor from a village to the west, Oweti.

Chapter Ten: Leaders as Bad Men and Victims

1. Knauft (1985) notes the close connection between autocratic attitudes and accusations of sorcery among the Gebusi.

2. These views gained some popularity as an explanation for illness. It was, in any case, a traditional view that exposure to magical items could make women and children sick. But the patient could be cured by reversing the effect and so few really believed contact with magical items could cause death. The practice of praying over sick people also gained several converts for the church as subsequent recoveries were felt to be dramatic proof of the power of God. But people argued that God would only strike Christians in this manner and had no power over non-Christians. Furthermore, no one seemed to believe that God could (or would) kill people, possibly because it had often been demonstrated in Christian healings that illness caused by God could be cured through prayer and repentance. The greater success of the Christians in claiming control of sickness than of death is perhaps due to the fact that successful curing is strong validation for new ideas about illness but it is much more difficult to present any such "proof" in matters of death.

Chapter Eleven: Conclusions

1. Of course, some words are viewed as particularly powerful because they are used in magical spells. Wagner (1972) suggests words in Daribi spells are believed to be powerful because they bring into conjunction, in the form of

metaphor, separate realms, thereby, in the local view, generating power. Favret-Saada (1980) also suggests that people (in that case in rural France) view the words used in magical spells as powerful.

2. Lindstrom (1988).

3. Sahlins's (1963) generalizations have sparked a number of debates about Melanesian leadership. Are hereditary bases of power really absent in all Melanesian societies (see Douglas 1979; Hau'ofa 1971; Standish 1980; A. Strathern 1971)? Are economic entrepreneurship and success in exchange really the most important ways of achieving leadership in Melanesia (see Chowning 1979; Godelier 1982; Keesing 1985; Lindstrom 1984; Modjeska 1982)? Did Sahlins underestimate the degree of hierarchy in at least some Melanesian societies? Did leaders in at least some areas have almost despotic power (Salisbury 1964; Standish 1980; Watson 1971)?

References

Allen, Bryant
    1976   Information Flow and Innovation Diffusion in the East Sepik District, Papua New Guinea. Ph.D. diss. Australian National University.

Allen, Michael
    1981   Innovation, Inversion and Revolution as Political Tactics in West Aoba. In *Vanuatu: Politics, Economics and Ritual in Island Melanesia*, ed. Michael Allen, pp. 105–134. London, New York, and San Francisco: Academic Press.

Allport, G. W., and L. J. Postman
    1947   *The Psychology of Rumor*. New York: Holt, Rinehart and Winston.

Arno, Andrew
    1980   Fijian Gossip as Adjudication: A Communication Model of Self Control. *Journal of Anthropological Research* 36: 343–360.

    1990   Disentangling Indirectly: The Joking Debate in Fijian Social Control. In *Disentangling: Conflict Discourse in Pacific Societies*, ed. Karen A. Watson-Gegeo and Geoffrey White, pp. 241–289. Stanford: Stanford University Press.

Atkinson, Jane M.
    1984   "Wrapped Words": Poetry and Politics among the Wana of Central Sulawesi. In *Dangerous Words: Language and Politics in the Pacific*, ed. Donald L. Brenneis and Fred R. Myers, pp. 33–68. New York and London: New York University Press.

    1989   *The Art and Politics of Wana Shamanship*. Berkeley, Los Angeles, London: University of California Press.

Bailey, F. G.
    1965   Decisions by Consensus in Councils and Committees. In *Political Systems and the Distribution of Power*, ed. Michael Banton, pp. 1–20. London and New York: Tavistock.

1971a   Gifts and Poison. In *Gifts and Poison: The Politics of Reputation*, ed. F. G. Bailey, pp. 1–25. Oxford: Basil Blackwell.

1971b   The Management of Reputations and the Process of Change. In *Gifts and Poison*, ed. F. G. Bailey, pp. 281–301. Oxford: Basil Blackwell.

1977   *Morality and Expediency: The Folklore of Academic Politics*. Oxford: Basil Blackwell.

1983   *The Tactical Uses of Passion: An Essay on Power, Reason and Reality*. Ithaca: Cornell University Press.

Bailey, F. G., ed.

1971c   *Gifts and Poison: The Politics of Reputation*. Oxford: Basil Blackwell.

Basso, Keith

1984   "Stalking With Stories": Names, Places and Moral Narratives Among the Western Apache. In *Text, Play, and Story: The Construction and Reconstruction of Self and Society, 1983 Proceedings of the American Ethnological Society*, ed. Edward M. Bruner, pp. 19–55. Washington: American Ethnologist.

Bateson, Gregory

1958   *Naven*. Stanford: Stanford University Press.

Bauman, Richard

1986   *Story, Performance, and Event: Contextual Studies of Oral Narrative*. Cambridge: Cambridge University Press.

Bauman, Richard, and Charles L. Briggs

1990   Poetics and Performance as Critical Perspectives on Language and Social Life. *Annual Review of Anthropology* 19: 59–88.

Bennett, W. Lance, and Martha Feldman

1981   *Reconstructing Reality in the Courtroom: Justice and Judgement in American Culture*. New Brunswick, N.J.: Rutgers University Press.

Bleek, Wolf

1976   Witchcraft, Gossip, and Death: A Social Drama. *Man* 11: 526–541.

Bloch, Maurice

1971   Decision Making in Councils Among the Merina of Madagascar. In *Councils in Action*, ed. Audrey Richards and Adam Kuper, pp. 29–62. Cambridge: Cambridge University Press.

1975   Introduction. In *Political Language and Oratory in Traditional Society*, ed. Maurice Bloch, pp. 1–28. London, New York, and San Francisco: Academic Press.

Bowden, Ross

1982   Lévi-Strauss in the Sepik: A Kwoma Myth of the Origin of Marriage. *Oceania* 52: 294–302.

1983a   *Yena: Art and Ceremony in a Sepik Society*. Oxford: Pitt Rivers Museum.

1983b   Kwoma Terminology and Marriage Alliance: The "Omaha" Problem Revisited. *Man* 18: 745–765.

1987   Sorcery in Kwoma Society. In *Sorcerer and Witch in Melanesia*, ed.

Michele Stephen, pp. 183–208. New Brunswick, N.J.: Rutgers University Press.

Bowen, John R.

1989   Poetic Duels and Political Change in the Gayo Highlands of Sumatra. *American Anthropologist* 91: 25–40.

1991   *Sumatran Politics and Poetics: Gayo History, 1900–1989.* New Haven: Yale University Press.

Brenneis, Donald L.

1978   The Matter of Talk: Political Performance in Bhatgaon. *Language in Society* 7: 159–170.

1984   Straight Talk and Sweet Talk: Political Discourse in an Occasionally Egalitarian Community. In *Dangerous Words*, ed. Donald L. Brenneis and Fred R. Myers, pp. 69–84. New York and London: New York University Press.

1986   Shared Territory: Audience, Indirection and Meaning. *Text* 6: 339–347.

1988   Language and Disputing. *Annual Review of Anthropology* 17: 221–237.

Brison, Karen

1988   Gossip, Innuendo and Sorcery: Village Politics Among the Kwanga, East Sepik Province, Papua New Guinea. Ph.D. diss. University of California, San Diego.

1989   All Talk and No Action?: Saying and Doing in Kwanga Meetings. *Ethnology* 28: 97–115.

1991   Community and Prosperity: Social Movements in a Papua New Guinea Village. *The Contemporary Pacific* 3: 325–356.

n.d.   Telling Stories about Sorcery in a Papua New Guinea Village. Unpublished manuscript.

Brown, Paula

1963   From Anarchy to Satrapy. *American Anthropologist* 65: 1–15.

Bruner, Edward M.

1984   Introduction: The Opening Up of Anthropology. In *Text, Play, and Story: The Construction and Reconstruction of Self and Society, 1983 Proceedings of the American Ethnological Society*, ed. Edward M. Bruner, pp. 1–18. Washington: American Ethnologist.

1986   Ethnography as Narrative. In *The Anthropology of Experience*, ed. Victor Turner and Edward M. Bruner, pp. 139–155. Urbana and Chicago: University of Illinois Press.

Burridge, Kenelm

1971   Tangu Political Relations. In *Politics in New Guinea*, ed. Ronald M. Berndt and Peter Lawrence, pp. 92–112. Nedlands: University of Western Australia Press.

1975   The Melanesian Manager. In *Studies in Social Anthropology: Essay in Memory of E.E. Evans-Pritchard*, ed. J. M. H. Beattie and R. G. Lienhardt, pp. 86–104. Oxford: The Clarendon Press.

Chowning, Ann

1974   Disputing in Two West New Britain Societies. In *Contention and*

Dispute, ed. A. L. Epstein, pp. 152–197. Canberra: Australian National University Press.

1979   Leadership in Melanesia. *Journal of Pacific History* 14: 66–84.

1987   Sorcery and Social Order in Kove. In *Sorcerer and Witch in Melanesia*, ed. Michele Stephen, pp. 149–182. New Brunswick, N.J.: Rutgers University Press.

Condon, Richard, and Richard Scaglion

1982   The Ecology of Human Birth Seasonality. *Human Ecology* 10: 495–511.

Counts, David, and Dorothy Counts

1974   The Kaliai Lupunga: Disputing in the Public Forum. In *Contention and Dispute: Aspects of Law and Social Control in Melanesia*, ed. A. L. Epstein, pp. 113–151. Canberra: Australian National University Press.

Darrouzet, Christopher P.

1985   *Sorcery, Salvation, and the Politics of Death: A Case Study of a Modernizing Culture and Consciousness*. Ph.D. diss. University of North Carolina at Chapel Hill.

Douglas, Bronwen

1979   Rank, Power, Authority: A Reassessment of Traditional Leadership in South Pacific Societies. *Journal of Pacific History* 14(1): 2–27.

Duranti, Alessandro

1986   The Audience as Co-Author: An Introduction. *Text* 6: 239–247.

Epstein, A. L.

1974*a*   Introduction. In *Contention and Dispute*, ed. A. L. Epstein, pp. 1–39. Canberra: Australian National University Press.

1974*b*   Moots On Matupit. In *Contention and Dispute*, ed. A. L. Epstein, pp. 93–112. Canberra: Australian National University Press.

Epstein, A. L., ed.

1974   *Contention and Dispute: Aspects of Law and Social Control in Melanesia*. Canberra: Australian National University Press.

Evans-Pritchard, E. E.

1976   *Witchcraft, Oracles, and Magic Among the Azande*. London and New York: Oxford University Press.

Eyre, Stephen

1988   Revival Christianity Among the Urat of Papua New Guinea: Some Motivational and Perceptual Antecedents. Ph.D. diss. University of California, San Diego.

Favret-Saada, Jeanne

1980   *Deadly Words: Witchcraft in the Bocage*. Cambridge: Cambridge University Press.

1989   Unbewitching as Therapy. *American Ethnologist* 16: 40–56.

Forge, Anthony

1965   Art and Environment in the Sepik. *Proceedings of the Royal Anthropological Institute* 1965: 23–31.

1967   The Abelam Artist. In *Social Organization. Essays Presented to*

Raymond Firth, ed. M. Freedman, pp. 65–84. London: Frank Cass.

1970a   Learning to See In New Guinea. In *Socialization: The Approach From Social Anthropology*, ed. Philip Mayer, pp. 269–291. London and New York: Tavistock.

1970b   Prestige, Influence, and Sorcery: A New Guinea Example. In *Witchcraft, Confession and Accusations*, ed. Mary Douglas, pp. 257–275. London and New York: Tavistock.

1972   The Golden Fleece. *Man* 7(4): 527–540.

1973   Style and Meaning in Sepik Art. In *Primitive Art and Society*, ed. Anthony Forge, pp. 169–192. London and New York: Oxford University Press.

Fortune, Reo

1939   Arapesh Warfare. *American Anthropologist* 41: 22–41.

1942   *Arapesh*. New York: J. J. Augustin.

Frankenberg, Ronald

1957   *A Village on the Border*. Manchester: Manchester University Press.

Gewertz, Deborah

1977   "On Whom Depends the Action of the Elements": Debating Among the Chambri People of Papua New Guinea. *Journal of the Polynesian Society* 86: 339–352.

Gluckman, Max

1963   Gossip and Scandal. *Current Anthropology* 4: 307–316.

Godelier, Maurice

1982   Social Hierarchies Among the Baruya of New Guinea. In *Inequality in the New Guinea Highlands*, ed. Andrew Strathern, pp. 3–34. Cambridge: Cambridge University Press.

1986   *The Making of Great Men: Male Domination and Power Among the New Guinea Baruya*. Cambridge: Cambridge University Press.

Goffman, Erving

1959   *The Presentation of Self in Everyday Life*. New York: Doubleday Anchor.

Goldman, Lawrence

1980   Speech Categories and the Study of Disputes: A New Guinea Example. *Oceania* 50: 209–227.

1983   *Talk Never Dies: The Language of Huli Disputes*. London and New York: Tavistock.

Goodwin, Marjorie

1982   Instigating: Storytelling as Social Process. *American Ethnologist* 9: 799–819.

Goody, Esther

1970   Legitimate and Illegitimate Aggression in a West African State. In *Witchcraft: Confession and Accusations*, ed. Mary Douglas, pp. 207–244. London and New York: Tavistock.

Gorlin, Paul

1974   Health, Wealth, and Agnation Among the Abelam. Ph.D. diss. Columbia University.

Gregor, Thomas
   1977   *Mehinaku: The Drama of Daily Life in a Brazilian Indian Village.*
           Chicago and London: University of Chicago Press.
Gulliver, Philip
   1979   *Disputes and Negotiations: A Cross Cultural Perspective.* London,
           New York, and San Francisco: Academic Press.
Harding, Susan
   1975   Women and Words in a Spanish Village. In *Toward an Anthropol-
           ogy of Women,* ed. Reyna Reiter, pp. 283–308. New York and
           London: Monthly Review Press.
Harrison, Simon
   1989   Magical and Material Polities in Melanesia. *Man* 24: 1–20.
   1990   *Stealing People's Names: History and Politics in a Sepik River Cosmolo-
           gy.* Cambridge: Cambridge University Press.
Harwood, Alan
   1970   *Witchcraft, Sorcery, and Social Categories Among the Safwa.* London
           and New York: Oxford University Press.
Hau'ofa, Epeli
   1971   Mekeo Chieftainship. *Journal of the Polynesian Society* 80: 152–
           169.
   1981   *Mekeo: Inequality and Ambivalence in a Village Society.* Canberra:
           Australian National University Press.
Havilland, John
   1977   *Gossip, Reputation and Knowledge in Zinacanton.* Chicago and Lon-
           don: University of Chicago Press.
Hayden, Robert M.
   1987   Turn-Taking, Overlap, and the Task at Hand: Ordering Speaking
           Turns in Legal Settings. *American Ethnologist* 14: 251–270.
Hogbin, H. Ian, and Camilla Wedgewood
   1953/54 Local Grouping in Melanesia. *Oceania* 33: 241–276, 34: 58–76.
Hutchins, Edwin
   1980   *Culture and Inference.* Cambridge: Harvard University Press.
Hutson, John
   1971   A Politician in Valloire. In *Gifts and Poison,* ed. F. G. Bailey, pp.
           69–96. Oxford: Basil Blackwell.
Hutson, Susan
   1971   Social Ranking in a French Alpine Community. In *Gifts and
           Poison,* ed. F. G. Bailey, pp. 41–68. Oxford: Basil Blackwell.
Irvine, Judith
   1979   Formality and Informality in Communicative Events. *American
           Anthropologist* 81: 773–790.
Just, Peter
   1986   Let the Evidence Fit the Crime: Evidence, Law, and "Sociological
           Truth" Among the Dou Donggo. *American Ethnologist* 13: 43–
           61.
Kaberry, Phyllis
   1940–   The Abelam Tribe, Sepik District, New Guinea: A Preliminary

1941   Report. *Oceania* 11: 233–258, 345–367.
1941–   Law and Political Organization in the Abelam Tribe, New Guinea.
1942   *Oceania* 12: 79–95, 209–225, 331–363.
1966   Political Organization Among the Northern Abelam. *Anthropological Forum* 1: 334–372.
1967   The Plasticity of New Guinea Kinship. In *Social Organization: Essays Presented to Raymond Firth*, ed. M. Freedman, pp. 105–123. London: Frank Cass.
1971   Political Organization Among the Northern Abelam. In *Politics in New Guinea*, ed. Ronald M. Berndt and Peter Lawrence, pp. 35–73. Nedlands: University of Western Australia Press.

Kahn, Miriam
1986   *Always Hungry, Never Greedy: Food and the Expression of Gender in a Melanesian Society*. Cambridge: Cambridge University Press.

Keenan, Elinor
1974   Norm-Makers, Norm-Breakers: Uses of Speech by Men and Women in a Malagasy Community. In *Explorations in the Ethnography of Speaking*, ed. Robert Bauman and Joel Scherzer, pp. 125–143. Cambridge: Cambridge University Press.
1975   A Sliding Sense of Obligatoriness: The Polystructure of Malagasy Oratory. In *Political Language and Oratory in Traditional Society*, ed. Maurice Bloch, pp. 93–112. London, New York, and San Francisco: Academic Press.

Keesing, Roger M.
1985   Killers, Big Men, and Priests on Malaita: Reflections on a Melanesian Troika System. *Ethnology* 24: 237–252.
1990   The Power of Talk. In *Disentangling: Conflict Discourse in Pacific Societies*, ed. Karen A. Watson-Gegeo and Geoffrey White, pp. 493–500. Stanford: Stanford University Press.

Knauft, Bruce
1985   *Good Company and Violence: Sorcery and Social Action in a Lowland New Guinea Society*. Berkeley, Los Angeles, and London: University of California Press.

Kracke, Waud
1978   *Force and Persuasion: Leadership in an Amazonian Society*. Chicago and London: University of Chicago Press.

Kuipers, Joel C.
1990   *Power Through Performance: The Creation of Textual Authority in Weyewa Ritual Speech*. Philadelphia: University of Pennsylvania Press.

Kulick, Don, and Christopher Stroud
1990   Christianity, Cargo and Ideas of Self: Patterns of Literacy in a Papua New Guinean Village. *Man* 25: 286–303.

Kuper, Adam
1971   The Kgalagari Lekgota. In *Councils in Action*, ed. Audrey Richards and Adam Kuper, pp. 80–99. Cambridge: Cambridge University Press.

Labov, William
1972   The Transformation of Experience in Narrative Syntax. In *Language in the Inner City*, ed. William Labov, pp. 354–396. Philadelphia: University of Pennsylvania Press.

Lawrence, Peter
1971   Introduction. In *Politics in New Guinea*, ed. Ronald M. Berndt and Peter Lawrence, pp. 1–34. Nedlands: University of Western Australia Press.

Laycock, D.
1965   *The Ndu Language Family (Sepik District, New Guinea)*. Series C, Number 1. Canberra: Linguistic Circle of Canberra.
1973   *Sepik Languages: Checklist and Preliminary Classification. Pacific Linguistics* Series B: 25.

Lea, David
1964   Abelam Land and Sustenance: Swidden Horticulture in an Area of High Population Density, Maprik, New Guinea. Ph.D. diss. Australian National University.

Leach, Jerry
1982   Socio-historical Conflict and the Kabisawali Movement in the Trobriand Islands. In *Micronationalist Movements in Papua New Guinea*, ed. R. J. May, pp. 249–289. Canberra: Department of Political and Social Change, Research School of Pacific Studies, Australian National University.

Leavitt, Stephen
1989   Cargo, Christ, and Nostalgia for the Dead: Themes of Intimacy and Abandonment in Bumbita Arapesh Social Experience. Ph.D. diss. University of California, San Diego.

Lederman, Rena
1984   Who Speaks Here?: Formality and the Politics of Gender in Mendi, Highlands Papua New Guinea. In *Dangerous Words*, ed. Donald L. Brenneis and Fred R. Myers, pp. 85–107. New York and London: New York University Press.

Leitch, Thomas W.
1986   *What Stories Are: Narrative Theory and Interpretation*. University Park and London: The Pennsylvania State University Press.

Lindstrom, Lamont
1984   Doctor, Lawyer, Wise Man, Priest: Big-Men and Knowledge in Melanesia. *Man* 19: 291–309.
1988   Big Men and the Conversational Marketplace on Tanna (Vanuatu). *Ethnos* 53: 159–189.
1990a   Straight Talk on Tanna. In *Disentangling: Conflict Discourse in Pacific Societies*, ed. Karen A. Watson-Gegeo and Geoffrey White, pp. 373–411. Stanford: Stanford University Press.
1990b   *Knowledge and Power in a South Pacific Society*. Washington: Smithsonian Institution.

Losche, Diane
1978   The Exchange of Men: The Abelam Balancing Act. Paper Deliv-

ered at the annual meeting of the American Anthropological Association, Los Angeles.

1982a   Male and Female in Abelam Society: Opposition and Complementarity. Ph.D. diss. Columbia University.

1982b   *The Abelam: A People of Papua New Guinea.* The Australian Museum.

Luhrmann, Tanya
1989   *Persuasions of the Witch's Craft.* Cambridge: Harvard University Press.

MacFarlane, Alan
1970   *Witchcraft in Tudor and Stuart England.* London and New York: Oxford University Press.

McKellin, William
1984   Putting Down Roots: Information in the Language of Managalase Exchange. In *Dangerous Words*, ed. Donald Brenneis and Fred Myers, pp. 108–128. New York and London: New York University Press.

1990   Allegory and Inference: Intentional Ambiguity in Managalase Negotiations. In *Disentangling: Conflict Discourse in Pacific Societies*, ed. Karen A. Watson-Gegeo and Geoffrey M. White, pp. 335–372. Stanford: Stanford University Press.

Malinowski, Bronaslav
1926   *Crime and Custom in a Savage Society.* London: Routledge and Kegan Paul.

Manabe, Takashi, and Kezue Manabe
1979a   Kwanga Grammar Essentials for Translation. Unpublished Summer Institute of Linguistics paper.

1979b   A Tentative Phonology of Kwanga. Unpublished Summer Institute of Linguistics paper.

1982a   Kwanga Anthropology Sketch: "Mami (A Type of Yam)" Reveals Dynamic Kwanga Social Structure. Unpublished Summer Institute of Linguistics paper.

1982b   *Kwanga Got Ri Mwangi.* Ukarampa, Papua New Guinea: Summer Institute of Linguistics.

Mansbridge, Jane
1980   *Beyond Adversary Democracy.* New York: Basic Books.

Marwick, Max
1965   *Sorcery in its Social Setting: A Study of the Northern Rhodesia Cewa.* Manchester: Manchester University Press.

Matthews, Holly
n.d.   The Directive Force of Morality Tales in a Mexican Community. Unpublished manuscript, East Carolina University.

Mead, Margaret
1938   *The Mountain Arapesh, I. An Importing Culture. Anthropological Papers of the American Museum of Natural History* 36(3).

1940   *The Mountain Arapesh. II. Supernaturalism. Anthropological Papers of the American Museum of Natural History* 37(3).

1947   *The Mountain Arapesh. III. Socio Economic Life. IV. Diary of Events in Alitoa. Anthropological Papers of the American Museum of Natural History* 40(3).

Merry, Sally Engle
1984   Rethinking Gossip and Scandal. In *Toward a General Theory of Social Control. Volume One: Fundamentals*, ed. Donald Black, pp. 271–302. London, New York and San Francisco: Academic Press.

Middleton, John
1960   *Lugbara Religion: Ritual and Authority Among an East African People*. London and New York: Oxford University Press.

Modjeska, Nicholas
1982   Production and Inequality: Perspectives From Central New Guinea. In *Inequality in New Guinea Highlands Society*, ed. Andrew Strathern, pp. 50–110. Cambridge: Cambridge University Press.

Murphy, William P.
1990   Creating the Appearance of Consensus in Mende Political Discourse. *American Anthropologist* 92: 21–41.

Myers, Fred R.
1986   Reflections on a Meeting: Structure, Language, and the Polity in a Small-Scale Society. *American Ethnologist* 13: 430–447.

Myers, Fred R., and Donald L. Brenneis
1984   Introduction: Language and Politics in the Pacific. In *Dangerous Words*, ed. Donald L. Brenneis and Fred R. Myers, pp. 1–30. New York and London: New York University Press.

Nader, Laura
1969   Styles of Court Procedure: To Make the Balance. In *Law in Culture and Society*, ed. Laura Nader, pp. 69–91. Chicago: Aldine.

Nuckolls, Charles
1991   Culture and Causal Thinking: Diagnosis and Prediction in a South Indian Fishing Village. *Ethos* 19: 3–51.

Obrist, Brigit
1987   Gegenstande aus dem Buschalltag von Tauhundor. In *Neuguinea. Nutzung und Deutung der Umwelt*, ed. Mark Munzel, pp. 263–288. Frankfurt am Main: Museum für Volkerkunde.
1990   The Study of Food in Its Cultural Context. In *Sepik Heritage: Tradition and Change in Papua New Guinea*, ed. Nancy Lutkehaus et al. Durham, North Carolina: Carolina Academic Press.

Paine, Robert
1967   What is Gossip About? An Alternative Hypothesis. *Man* 3: 305–308.
1970   Informal Communication and Information Management. *Canadian Review of Sociology and Anthropology* 7: 172–188.

Paine, Robert, ed.
1981   *Politically Speaking: Cross-Cultural Studies of Rhetoric*. Philadelphia: Institute for the Study of Human Issues.

Patterson, Mary
1974–   Sorcery and Witchcraft in Melanesia. *Oceania* 45: 132–160, 212–
1975   234.

Pinsker, Eve
1986   Point of Order, Point of Debate. Paper presented at the annual meetings of the American Anthropological Association, Chicago.

Pocock, J. G. A.
1984   Verbalizing a Political Act: Toward a Politics of Speech. In *Language and Politics*, ed. Michael J. Shapiro, pp. 25–43. New York and London: New York University Press.

Poole, Fitz John Porter
1986   Personal Control, Social Responsibility, and the Image of the Person and Self Among the Bimin-Kuskusmin of Papua New Guinea. *International Journal of Law and Psychiatry* 9: 295–319.

Price, Laurie
1987   Ecuadorian Illness Stories: Cultural Knowledge in Natural Discourse. In *Cultural Models in Language and Thought*, ed. Dorothy Holland and Naomi Quinn, pp. 313–337. Cambridge: Cambridge University Press.

Quinn, Naomi, and Dorothy Holland
1987   Culture and Cognition. In *Cultural Models in Language and Thought*, ed. Dorothy Holland and Naomi Quinn, pp. 3–42. Cambridge: Cambridge University Press.

Read, Kenneth
1959   Leadership and Consensus in a New Guinea Society. *American Anthropologist* 61: 425–436.

Reay, Marie
1959   *The Kuma: Freedom and Conformity in the New Guinea Highlands*. Melbourne: Melbourne University Press.

Richards, Audrey
1971   The Council System of the Bemba. In *Councils in Action*, ed. Audrey Richards and Adam Kuper, pp. 100–129. Cambridge: Cambridge University Press.

Richards, Audrey, and Adam Kuper
1971   *Councils in Action*. Cambridge: Cambridge University Press.

Riebe, Inge
1987   Kalam Witchcraft: a Historical Perspective. In *Sorcerer and Witch in Melanesia*, ed. Michele Stephen, pp. 211–248. New Brunswick, N.J.: Rutgers University Press.

Rodman, Margaret, and William Rodman
1983–   The Hundred Days of Sara Mata: Explaining Unnatural Death in
1984   Vanuatu. *Omega* 14: 135–144.

Rogers, Susan Carol
1975   Female Forms of Power and the Myth of Male Dominance: A Model of Male/Female Interaction in a Peasant Society. *American Ethnologist* 2: 727–756.

Rosaldo, Michelle
1973   I Have Nothing to Hide: The Language of Ilongot Oratory. *Language in Society* 2: 193–223.
1984   Words That Are Moving: The Social Meanings of Ilongot Verbal Arts. In *Dangerous Words*, ed. Donald L. Brenneis and Fred R.

Myers, pp. 131–160. New York and London: New York University Press.

Roscoe, Paul

1989   The Flight from the Fen: The Prehistoric Migration of the Boiken of the East Sepik Province of Papua New Guinea. *Oceania* 60(2): 139–154.

Rumsey, Alan

1985   *Oratory and the Politics of Metaphor in the New Guinea Highlands.* Sydney Studies in Society and Culture #3. Sydney: University of Sydney Press.

Sahlins, Marshall

1963   Poor Man, Rich Man, Big-Man, Chief: Political Types in Polynesia and Melanesia. *Comparative Studies in Sociology and History* 5: 285–303.

Salisbury, Richard

1964   Despotism and Australian Administration in the New Guinea Highlands. *American Anthropologist* 66: 225–239.

Scaglion, Richard

1976   Seasonal Patterns in Western Abelam Conflict Management Practices: The Ethnography of Law in the Maprik Sub-Province, East Sepik Province, Papua New Guinea. Ph.D. diss. University of Pittsburgh.

1978   Seasonal Births in a Western Abelam Village, Papua New Guinea. *Human Biology* 50: 313–323.

1979   Formal and Informal Operations of A Village Court in Maprik. *Melanesian Law Journal* 7: 116–129.

1981   Samukundi Abelam Conflict Management: Implications for Legal Planning in Papua New Guinea. *Oceania* 52: 28–38.

1983a   The Effects of Mediation Styles on Successful Dispute Resolution: The Abelam Case. *Windsor Yearbook of Access to Justice* 3: 256–269.

1983b   The "Coming" of Independence in Papua New Guinea: An Abelam View. *Journal of the Polynesian Society* 92: 463–486.

1985   Kiaps as Kings: Abelam Legal Change in Historical Perspective. In *History and Ethnohistory in Papua New Guinea*, ed. Deborah Gewertz and Edward Schieffelin, pp. 77–99. Sydney: University of Sydney.

1986   The Importance of Nighttime Observations in Time Allocation Studies. *American Ethnologist* 13: 537–545.

1987   Sexual Segregation and Ritual Pollution in Abelam Society. In *Self, Sex and Gender in Cross-Cultural Fieldwork*, ed. T. L. Whitehead and M. E. Conaway, pp. 151–163. Urbana and Chicago: University of Illinois Press.

Scaglion, Richard, and Richard Condon

1979   Abelam Yam Beliefs and Socio-Rhythmicity: A Study in Chrono-Anthropology. *Journal of Biosocial Science* 11: 17–25.

Schafer, Roy

1983   *The Analytic Attitude.* New York: Basic Books.

Schindlbeck, Markus
1981   Yamfest Der Kwanga (Nordost-Neuguinea). Paper presented at the congress of the Deutsche Gesellschaft für Volkerkunde, Munster.
1984   Tradition and Change in Kwanga Villages. Paper presented at Symposium on Sepik Research Today, Basel Switzerland.
1986   Dualism, a Motif of Thought in Sepik Societies. Paper Presented at Conference on Sepik Culture History: Variation, Innovation, and Synthesis, Mijas Spain.

Schwartz, Theodore
1962   *The Paliau Movement in the Admiralty Islands, 1946–54. Anthropological Papers of the Amercian Museum of Natural History* 49(2).
1973   Cult and Context: The Paranoid Ethos in Melanesia. *Ethos* 1: 153– 174.

Schwartzman, Helen B.
1987   The Significance of Meetings in an American Mental Health Center. *American Ethnologist* 14: 271–294.
1989   *The Meeting*. New York: Plenum.

Scott, James
1985   *Weapons of the Weak: Everyday Forms of Peasant Resistance*. New Haven: Yale University Press.

Spacks, Patricia Meyer
1985   *Gossip*. New York: Alfred A. Knopf.

Standish, William
1980   The "Big-Man" Model Reconsidered: Power and Stratification in Chimbu. IASER Discussion Paper Number 22.

Stephen, Michele
1987   Contrasting Images of Power. In *Sorcerer and Witch in Melanesia*, ed. Michele Stephen, pp. 249–304. New Brunswick, N.J.: Rutgers University Press.

Strathern, Andrew
1966   Despots and Directors in the New Guinea Highlands. *Man* 1: 356–367.
1971   *The Rope of Moka: Big-Men and Ceremonial Exchange in Mount Hagen, New Guinea*. Cambridge: Cambridge University Press.
1972   *One Father, One Blood*. Canberra: Australian National University Press.
1975   Veiled Speech in Mount Hagen. In *Political Language and Oratory in Traditional Society*, ed. Maurice Bloch, pp. 185–203. London, New York and San Francisco: Academic Press.
1984   *A Line of Power*. London and New York: Tavistock.

Strathern, Marilyn
1972   *Official and Unofficial Courts: Legal Assumptions and Expectations in a Highlands Community*. New Guinea Research Bulletin, 47. Port Moresby and Canberra: New Guinea Research Bulletin, Australian National University.
1974   Managing Information: The Problems of a Dispute Settler (Mount Hagen). In *Contention and Dispute*, ed. A. L. Epstein, pp. 271–316. Canberra: Australian National University Press.

Turner, Victor

1957   *Schism and Continuity in an African Society: A Study of Ndembu Village Life*. Manchester: Manchester University Press.

Turton, David

1975   The Relationship Between Oratory and the Exercise of Influence Among the Mursi. In *Political Language and Oratory in Traditional Society*, ed. Maurice Bloch, pp. 163–184. London, New York, and San Francisco: Academic Press.

Tuzin, Donald F.,

1972   Yam Symbolism in The Sepik: An Interpretive Account. *Southwestern Journal of Anthropology* 28: 230–254.

1974   Social Control and the Tambaran in the Sepik. In *Contention and Dispute*, ed. A. L. Epstein, pp. 317–344. Canberra: Australian National University Press.

1975   The Breath of a Ghost: Dreams and the Fear of the Dead. *Ethos* 3: 555–578.

1976   *The Ilahita Arapesh: Dimensions of Unity*. Berkeley, Los Angeles, London: University of California Press.

1977   Reflections of Being in Arapesh Water Symbolism. *Ethos* 5: 195–223.

1978a   Politics, Power, and Divine Artistry in Ilahita. *Anthropological Quarterly* 51: 60–67.

1978b   Sex and Meat-Eating in Ilahita: A Symbolic Study. *Canberra Anthropology* 1: 82–93.

1980   *The Voice of the Tambaran: Truth and Illusion in Ilahita Arapesh Religion*. Berkeley, Los Angeles, London: University of California Press.

1982   Ritual Violence Among the Ilahita Arapesh: The Dynamics of Moral and Religious Uncertainty. In *Rituals of Manhood: Male Initiation in Papua New Guinea*, ed. Gilbert Herdt. Berkeley, Los Angeles, London: University of California Press.

1983   Cannibalism and Arapesh Cosmology: A Wartime Incident With the Japanese. In *The Ethnography of Cannibalism*, ed. Paula Brown and Donald Tuzin. Washington D.C.: Society for Psychological Anthropology.

Van Velsen, J.

1964   *The Politics of Kinship: A Study of Social Manipulation Among the Lakeside Tonga of Malawi*. Manchester: Manchester University Press.

Wagner, Roy

1972   *Habu: The Innovation of Meaning in Daribi Religion*. Chicago and London: University of Chicago Press.

Watson, James

1971   Tairora: The Politics of Despotism in a Small Society. In *Politics in New Guinea*, ed. Ronald M. Berndt and Peter Lawrence, pp. 224–275. Nedlands: University of Western Australia Press.

Watson-Gegeo, Karen
   1986   The Study of Language Use in Oceania. *Annual Review of Anthropology* 15: 149–162.
Weatherford, J. McIver
   1981   *Tribes on the Hill*. New York: Rawson, Wade.
Weiner, Annette
   1984   From Words to Objects to Magic: "Hard Words" and the Boundaries of Social Interaction. In *Dangerous Words*, ed. Donald L. Brenneis and Fred R. Myers, pp. 161–191. New York and London: New York University Press.
White, Geoffrey
   1978   Ambiguity and Ambivalence in A'ara Personality Descriptors. *American Ethnologist* 5: 334–360.
   1985   "Bad Ways" and "Bad Talk": Interpretations of Interpersonal Conflict in a Melanesian Society. In *Directions in Cognitive Anthropology*, ed. Janet Dougherty, pp. 345–370. Urbana and Chicago: University of Illinois Press.
   1990   Emotion Talk and Social Inference: The Case of A'ara "Disentangling." In *Disentangling: Conflict Discourse in Pacific Societies*, ed. Karen A. Watson-Gegeo and Geoffrey White, pp. 53–121. Stanford: Stanford University Press.
White, Geoffrey, and Karen Watson-Gegeo
   1990   Disentangling Discourse. In *Disentangling: Conflict Discourse in Pacific Societies*, ed. Karen Watson-Gegeo and Geoffrey White, pp. 3–52. Stanford: Stanford University Press.
Whiting, John W. M.
   1941   *Becoming a Kwoma: Teaching and Learning in a New Guinea Tribe*. New Haven: Yale University Press.
Williamson, Margaret
   1975   Kwoma Society: Women and Disorder. Ph.D. diss. Oxford.
   1979   Who Does What to the Sago?: A Kwoma Variation of Sepik River Sex-Roles. *Oceania* 49: 210–220.
Young, Michael
   1971   *Fighting With Food: Leadership, Values and Social Control in a Massim Society*. Cambridge: Cambridge University Press.
   1974   Private Sanctions and Public Ideology: Some Aspects of Self-Help in Kalauna, Goodenough Island. In *Contention and Dispute*, ed. A. L. Epstein, pp. 40–66. Canberra: Australian National University Press.
   1983   *Magicians of Manumanua*. Berkeley, Los Angles, London: University of California Press.

Index

A'ara, Solomon Islands, 20, 95, 119, 248 n.9
Abelam: big-men among, 30, 70, 75, 200; community meetings among, 248 n.12; dispute settlement among, 46, 95, 118; fission of clans among, 196; migrations of (*see* Migration: of Abelam); recruitment to lineages among, 200, 257 nn. 8, 10, 11; studies of, 37; yam cult among, 38
Acephalous communities. *See* Egalitarian communities
Adoption: of females, 90, 252 n.1, 257 n.9; of males into lineages, 194, 196–200, 203–206, 257 n.9. *See also* Lineages: recruitment to
Adultery, 80, 83, 84, 88, 89, 100
Affines: institutionalized duplicity between, 79, 144–145; relations between parents and children's spouses, 80; relationship between brothers-in-law, 52, 53, 56, 57, 59; relationship between woman and husband's family, 87–88, 89; role in spreading rumor, 111, 122, 126
Allen, Bryant: on contact history of Dreikikir district, 40, 41, 251 n.7; on history of cash cropping in the Maprik and Dreikikir districts, 44–45, 251 n.9; on Urat, 37
Allen, Michael, 190

Allport, G., and L. Postman, 249 n.18
Ambiguity. *See* Innuendo; Veiled speech
Andrew: advised niece to postpone divorce, 87; held mediation session to look into adultery case, 83, 84; in case of Naifuku and Ambusuroho, 54, 58, 60
Anumbo. *See* Exchange partners: anumbo
Apangai Village, 35, 41, 44, 223, 227, 229
Apos Village, 35, 44, 101
Arapesh, 38. *See also* Bumbita Arapesh; Ilahita Arapesh; Mountain Arapesh
Arno, Andrew, 187
Asanakor: court cases in, 80, 83; cash cropping in (*see* Cash cropping); Christianity in (*see* Christianity: history of in Asanakor); Christian revival in (*see* Christian revival: history of in Asanakor); cooperatives in (*see* Cooperatives: history of in Inakor and Asanakor); inquests in, 50–66, 112–113, 227–229; location of, 34; marriage patterns in, 35; occupied by Japanese in World War II, 41; population of, 35; sorcerers of, 48, 56, 58, 251 n.7; Village Council System in, 43
Atkinson, Jane, 17, 23, 187, 249 n.14
Australian Colonial Administration, 40, 43, 130

200; restrictions on authority of, 202, 211; rights of, 30, 193–194, 252 n.3

Lineages, 58, 89, 140; description of, 35, 141, 193, 256 nn.2, 4; distrust between, 121; fission of, 194–196, 256 n.5; of the same moiety, 123; recruitment to, 203–206, 256–257 nn. 6, 8, 10, 11 (*see also* Adoption); rights over widows of, 99; role in escalating conflict, 187; tendency to support members, 60–61, 154

Losche, Diane, 37, 257 n.11

Luhrmann, Tanya, 172

Lus Development Corporation, 45–46

MacFarlane, Alan, 255 n.2

McKellin, William, 17, 21, 155, 249 n.14, 256 n.4

Magic, for hunting and gardening: learned in tambaran cult, 40, 71, 161, 257 n.12; opposed by Christians, 25, 112, 223; shared by anumbo, 127, 191

Magicians, hunting, 191, 200, 210

Magicians, rain, 6, 203

Magistrates. *See* Village Court System

Malinowski, Bronislaw, 2, 30, 219

Manabe, Takashi, 37, 38, 250 nn. 2, 3

Mansbridge, Jane, 12, 234, 239

Manus Province, 181

Maprik, 44, 73

Maprik District, 34. *See also* Cash cropping: history of in Maprik and Dreikikir districts

Marriage: relationship between co-wives, 90, 97; relationship between spouses, 52–53, 80, 83, 88, 89, 100

Marriage patterns, 34–35, 125, 127–128, 257 n.9

Marwick, Max, 155

Matthews, Holly, 21

Mead, Margaret, 34

Meetings: address fear of covert attack, 102, 107–108, 109, 116–117; among the Gahuku-Gama, 22; among the Gebusi, 24; in Chambri, 16; dominated by initiated men, 191–192; duplicitous behavior in, 101–102, 108, 179, 180, 182–183, 184; form of, 95; as a forum for impression management, 88–93, 153, 208; his-

tory and description of among the Kwanga, 46; and interpretation of misfortune, 23–24, 26, 249 n.14; local beliefs about efficacy of publicizing conflict in, 95–96, 115–116, 117, 186; in Mendi, 19; as outlet for aggression, 236; in Pacific societies, 248 n.12; problems in negotiating consensus in, 100–102; to address rumor, 1, 5–9, 10, 11, 94, 96, 102, 103–109, 154, 156, 239, 247 n.1; to redefine problematic events, 19–20, 96, 168, 243; social impact of, 2, 3, 15–21, 24–26, 241, 247–248 n.8; turn-taking rules in, 16. *See also* Egalitarian communities: meetings in; Inakor: Monday community meetings in; Inquests

Meetings, funeral. *See* Inquests

Mekeo, 118, 155, 207, 234

Melpa, 182, 212, 216–219, 221, 237

Merry, Sally, 2, 11, 120, 215, 240

Middleton, John, 24, 249 n.16, 255 n.2

Migration: of Abelam, 37; of Abelam, Kwanga, and Arapesh in 1920s, 250 n.1; of Kwanga language speakers, 35, 37, 258 n.14; of Nukuma language family, 37

Millenarianism, 42. *See also* Cargo cults; Christian revival

Missionaries, 9

Modjeska, Nicholas, 244, 259 n.3

Moieties: description of, 40, 122–124; and inquests, 49; institutionalized duplicity between, 121, 138, 139; magicians of, 191; rivalry between, 6–7, 114, 122, 124, 128–139, 149; role in escalating conflict, 187; tendency to support members, 85, 154

Morobe Province, 40

Mother's brother. *See* Cross-nepotic kin

Mountain Arapesh, 34

Multicarpellary parishes, 187, 256 n.4

Murphy, William, 27

Musendai Village, 35

Myers, Fred, 22, 248 n.12. *See also* Myers, Fred, and Donald Brenneis

Myers, Fred, and Donald Brenneis: on political language in egalitarian communities, 20, 22, 247–248 n.8, 248 n.13, on political language in the

Widows, remarriage of, 92, 96–100
Wiru, 217
World War II, 41
Wosera. *See* Abelam

Yams, 38. *See also* Subsistence gardening
Young, Michael: on ambivalence about power on Goodenough Island, 183, 207, 209, 212–214, 218, 220, 221; on attitudes toward gossip on Goodenough Island, 1, 118–119, 216, 239, 247 n.1; on fear of covert aggression on Goodenough Island, 118, 234; on Goodenough Island leaders, 30, 188, 220, 221, 259 n.3; on inconclusive nature of divination, 255 n.2; on interpretation of natural misfortune on Goodenough Island, 248 n.12, 249 n.15; on self-directed aggression, 235
Youth groups, 253 n.2
Yubanakor Community School, 41
Yubanakor Village, 8, 35, 38, 41, 44

Designer: U.C. Press Staff
Compositor: Asco Trade Typesetting Ltd., Hong Kong
Text: 10/13 Galliard
Display: Galliard
Printer: Bookcrafters
Binder: Bookcrafters